Aesthetic Ideology

Theory and History of Literature
Edited by Wlad Godzich and Jochen Schulte-Sasse

For other books in the series, see p. 197

Aesthetic Ideology

Paul de Man

Edited with an Introduction
by Andrzej Warminski

Theory and History of Literature, Volume 65

University of Minnesota Press
Minneapolis / London

Copyright 1996 by the Regents of the University of Minnesota

Published by the University of Minnesota Press
111 Third Avenue South, Suite 290, Minneapolis, MN 55401-2520
Printed in the United States of America on acid-free paper

Library of Congress Cataloging-in-Publication Data

De Man, Paul.
    Aesthetic ideology / Paul de Man ; edited with an introduction by
Andrzej Warminski.
        p.   cm. — (Theory and history of literature ; v. 65)
    Includes bibliographical references and index.
    ISBN 0-8166-2203-5
    ISBN 0-8166-2204-3 (pbk.)
    1. Criticism. I. Warminski, Andrzej. II. Title. III. Series.
PN81.D378   1997
801'.95—dc20   96-16240

The University of Minnesota is an
equal-opportunity educator and employer.

Contents

Introduction
Allegories of Reference
Andrzej Warminski

*la fonction référentielle est un
piège, mais inévitable*[1]

Aesthetic Ideology

The texts collected in the present volume were written, or delivered as lectures on the basis of notes, during the last years of de Man's life, between 1977 and 1983. With the possible exception of the earliest text[2]—"The Concept of Irony" (1977)—all of these essays and lectures were produced in the context of a project that we might call, for shorthand purposes, a critique or, better, a "critical-linguistic analysis," of "aesthetic ideology."[3] This project is clearly the animating force of *all* the essays de Man produced in the early 1980s—and not just those explicitly concentrating on philosophical aesthetics to be included in the book

---

1. Last entry in de Man's notebook for the last class he gave in a seminar on the topic "Théorie rhétorique au 18ème et 20ème siècle" (fall 1983).

2. I say "possible" here because "The Concept of Irony," which is on Fichte and Schlegel, nevertheless covers part of the subject matter de Man planned for the seventh chapter of his projected book *Aesthetics, Rhetoric, Ideology*: "Aestheticism: Schiller and Friedrich Schlegel's Misreading of Kant and Fichte." See note 4.

3. The phrase "critical-linguistic analysis" is de Man's in his 1983 interview with Stefano Rosso, reprinted in Paul de Man, *The Resistance to Theory* (Minneapolis: University of Minnesota Press, 1986).

project he called *Aesthetics, Rhetoric, Ideology*,[4] but also the essays on literary critics and theorists like Riffaterre, Jauss, and Benjamin that made up a second of de Man's book projects—part of which appeared posthumously as *The Resistance to Theory* (1986)—as well as the two late essays (on Baudelaire and Kleist) expressly written for the collection *The Rhetoric of Romanticism* (1984). Although the general project is recognizable throughout these texts, it takes different forms in the context of the three particular book projects.

The essays on Riffaterre and Jauss, for example, demonstrate how both the critic whose point of departure is based on "formalist" presuppositions and the critic whose point of departure is based on "hermeneutic" presuppositions depend on the category of the "aesthetic," indeed, on a certain "aesthetization," to negotiate the passage between the formal linguistic structures and the meaning of the literary texts they interpret. This "aesthetization" turns Riffaterre into something of "a classical metaphysician, a Platonic swan disguised in the appearance of a technician of teaching" (*Resistance*, p. 40), and it allows Jauss to arrive at a "condensation of literary history and structural analysis" (*Resistance*, p. 64)—as though,

---

4. Although de Man certainly used the phrase "aesthetic ideology" on occasion, the title he provided for the projected book in a typed Table of Contents (sent with a letter 11 August 1983 to Lindsay Waters, then an editor at the University of Minnesota Press) was *Aesthetics, Rhetoric, Ideology*. The Table of Contents reads as follows:

Aesthetics, Rhetoric, Ideology

1. Epistemology of Metaphor*
2. Pascal's Allegory of Persuasion*
3. Diderot's Battle of the Faculties°
4. Phenomenality and Materiality in Kant*
5. Sign and Symbol in Hegel's *Aesthetics*
6. Hegel on the Sublime*
7. Aestheticism: Schiller and Friedrich Schlegel's Misreading of Kant and Fichte°
8. Critique of Religion and Political Ideology in Kierkegaard and Marx°
9. Rhetoric/Ideology (theoretical conclusion)

Completion expected by the summer of 1985.
* completed
° in progress

It may be worth noting that the present volume is very nearly complete—except for chapters 3 (the essay on Diderot), 8 (the essay on Kierkegaard and Marx), and 9 (the theoretical conclusion on Rhetoric/Ideology)—since we can surmise a great deal about the missing chapter 7 from the transcribed lectures on "Kant and Schiller" and "The Concept of Irony." That de Man's "theoretical conclusion" to the book was going to focus on the question of Rhetoric/Ideology is significant and supports our insistence on the importance of the word "rhetoric" in the title of the projected book. In his "Foreword, The Tiger on the Paper Mat" in *The Resistance to Theory*, Wlad Godzich is vague about how the projected book "came to be entitled *The Aesthetic Ideology*" (p. xi). Further references to *The Resistance to Theory* will be given in the body of the text as *Resistance* followed by a page number.

for both, "the hermeneutics of reading" could indeed be made compatible with "the poetics of literary form" (*Resistance*, p. 31). But since this compatibility depends on the stability of the category of the aesthetic, it becomes questionable once this category is shown to be as problematic as it has in fact always been for literary texts like those of Baudelaire, for "theoreticians" of the literary and of allegory like Benjamin, and for truly critical philosophers like Kant and Hegel. In the case of Riffaterre, the uncritical confidence in the stability of the category of the aesthetic comes at the price of a certain "evasion"—"a figural evasion which, in this case, takes the subtly effective form of evading the figural" (*Resistance*, p. 51); and in Jauss it is thanks to a certain "omission"—characteristic of which is "Jauss's lack of interest, bordering on outright dismissal, in any considerations derived from what has, somewhat misleadingly, come to be known as the 'play' of the signifier, semantic effects produced on the level of the letter rather than of the word or sentence and which therefore escape from the network of hermeneutic questions and answers" (*Resistance*, p. 65). And whether by "evasion" or "omission," the recourse of each to the stability of the category of the aesthetic ends up turning away from that which de Man calls the "materiality" of the text and which, in the case of both the Riffaterre and the Jauss essays, is given the name "inscription." It is inscription, the "literalism of the letter," that renders Baudelaire's (and Benjamin's) allegory "material or materialistic" and "cuts it off sharply from symbolic and aesthetic syntheses" (*Resistance*, p. 68), that renders the song of the sphinx in Baudelaire's "Spleen II" "not the sublimation but the forgetting, by inscription, of terror, the dismemberment of the aesthetic whole into the unpredictable play of the literary letter" (*Resistance*, p. 70).

We could say, then, that the essays on Riffaterre and Jauss demonstrate how their projects rest upon an unwarranted confidence in the stability of the category of the aesthetic and how this uncritical confidence itself depends on an evasion or omission of factors and functions of language that resist being phenomenalized and that therefore disable any sublation or sublimation of texts to the status of "aesthetic objects" that would afford a cognition proper to them. But if these essays go a long way toward demonstrating the *in*stability of the category of the aesthetic—with the help of Benjamin and Nietzsche, and, in *The Rhetoric of Romanticism*, "literary" texts like Kleist's *Marionettentheater* and Baudelaire's "Correspondances"—the essays and lectures collected in the present volume (in particular the essays on Kant's *Critique of Judgment* and Hegel's *Aesthetics*) examine the nature of this instability in texts whose project is not an uncritical acceptance or use of the aesthetic for pedagogical or ideological purposes but rather a critique of the aesthetic as a philosophical category. For both Kant and Hegel, the investment in the aesthetic as a category capable of withstanding "critique" (in the full Kantian sense) is considerable, for the possibility of their respective systems' being able to close themselves off (i.e., *as* systems) depends on it: in Kant, as a principle of articulation between theoretical and practical reason; in Hegel, as the moment of transition between objective spirit and absolute spirit. One does not need to be all that familiar with the divisions of Kant's and Hegel's systems or their terminology to recognize that such articulation and such transition are crucial. For without an account of reflective aesthetic judgment—its grounding as a transcendental principle—in Kant's third *Critique,* not only does the very possibility of the critical philosophy itself get put into question but also the possibility of a bridge between the concepts of freedom and the concepts of nature and necessity, or, as Kant puts it, the possibility of "the transition from our way of thinking in terms of principles of nature to our way of thinking in terms of principles of freedom."[5] To put it in stark and downright brutal terms, what this means is that the project of Kant's third *Critique* and its transcendental grounding of aesthetic judgment has to succeed if there is to be—as "there *must* after all be," says Kant, "it *must* be possible" (my emphasis)—"a basis *uniting [Grund der Einheit]* the supersensible that underlies nature and that the concept of freedom contains practically";[6] in other words, if morality is not to turn into a ghost.[7] And Hegel's absolute spirit *(Geist)* and its drive beyond representation *(Vorstellung)* on its long journey back home from the moment of "objective spirit"—that is, the realm of politics and law—to dwell in the prose of philosophical thought's thinking itself absolutely would also turn into a mere ghost if it were not for its *having passed through* the moment of the aesthetic, its phenomenal appearance in art, "the sensory appearance of the Idea." In other words, it is not a great love of art and beauty that prompts Kant and Hegel to include a consideration of the aesthetic in their systems but rather philosophically self-interested reasons. As de Man put it in one of his last seminars, with disarming directness and brutal good humor: "Therefore the investment in the aesthetic is considerable—the whole ability of philosophical discourse to develop as such depends entirely on its ability to develop an adequate aesthetics. This is why both Kant and Hegel, who had little interest in the arts, had to put it in, to make possible the link between real events and philosophical discourse."[8]

What de Man's work on Kant and Hegel shows, however, is that rather than being able to develop "an adequate aesthetics"—that is, adequate for the role prescribed it by their respective systems—both Kant's third *Critique* and Hegel's

5. Immanuel Kant, *Critique of Judgment,* trans. Werner S. Pluhar (Indianapolis/Cambridge: Hackett Publishing Company, 1987), p. 15.

6. Ibid.

7. We should add, however, that there are ghosts and there are ghosts. What we would call "material ghosts" would have to be distinguished from the "idealist ghosts" we are talking about here. For some "material ghosts," see my "Facing Language: Wordsworth's First Poetic Spirits," *Diacritics* 17:4 (winter 1987): 18–31; and "Spectre Shapes: 'The Body of Descartes?'" *Qui parle* 6:1 (fall–winter 1992): 93–112.

8. Paul de Man, "Aesthetic Theory from Kant to Hegel" (fall 1982), compiled from the notes of Roger Blood, Cathy Caruth, and Suzanne Roos.

Aesthetics wind up instead "undoing . . . the aesthetic as a valid category" ("Phenomenality and Materiality in Kant," included in this volume). Exactly how and why this happens and has to happen—and hence is in fact a real event, truly historical, for de Man—we can leave aside for the moment. Suffice it to say that both Kant and Hegel cannot complete and close off their systems because they cannot ground their own philosophical discourses on principles internal to these systems. In the very attempt to ground or validate the aesthetic, both must have recourse to factors and functions of language that *dis*articulate the aesthetic and its linking or mediating role. Kant's sublime is one example. Instead of being a "transcendental principle," the mathematical sublime turns out to be a "linguistic principle"—in fact, a familiar metaphorico-metonymical tropological system that cannot close itself off and that in turn issues in Kant's dynamic sublime, whose linguistic "model" would be that of language as performative. Hence there would be "a deep, perhaps fatal, break or discontinuity" at the center of the third *Critique,* for "it depends on a linguistic structure (language as a performative as well as a cognitive system) that is not itself accessible to the power of transcendental philosophy" ("Phenomenality and Materiality"). But the aporia or disjunction between cognitive and performative familiar to readers of *Allegories of Reading* and its fatal break undergoes a new development in de Man's reading of Kant on the sublime (a development in fact characteristic of the texts in this volume and of de Man's other work in the 1980s). For this "disruption" or "disarticulation" becomes apparent, or at least legible, in the text of the third *Critique* at the end of the analytic of the sublime in a general remark (section 29) where it occurs as a purely "material vision"—"devoid of any reflexive or intellectual complication . . . devoid of any semantic depth and reducible to the formal mathematization or geometrization of pure optics" ("Phenomenality and Materiality")—whose equivalent in the order of language would once again be "the prosaic materiality of the letter" ("Phenomenality and Materiality").

Hegel's *Aesthetics* contains—or, better, *occurs as*—a similar disruption or disarticulation. Officially "dedicated to the preservation and the monumentalization of classical art, it also contains all the elements which make such a preservation impossible from the start" ("Sign and Symbol in Hegel's *Aesthetics*," included in this volume). These "elements" include the fact that the paradigm for art in the *Aesthetics*—once read—"is thought rather than perception, the sign rather than the symbol, writing rather than painting or music" ("Sign and Symbol"), and hence also mechanical memory by rote, memorization (*Gedächtnis*), rather than a memory (*Erinnerung*) that would work by the internalization and recollection of images. Hence the *Aesthetics* "turns out to be a double and possibly duplicitous text." Since the only activity of the mind to occur as "the sensory appearance of the Idea"—Hegel's "definition" of the beautiful—is a rather *un*aesthetic, if not downright ugly, mechanical memory by rote (which always entails *some* notation or inscription), such a memory is "a truth of which the aesthetic is the defensive, ideological, and censored translation" ("Sign and Symbol"). This reading of the "duplicity" of Hegel's *Aesthetics* allows de Man to reconcile the two main statements of the text—"Art is the sensory appearance of the Idea"/"Art is for us a thing of the past"—for they turn out to be in fact the same statement: "Art is 'of the past' in a radical sense, in that, like memorization, it leaves the interiorization of experience forever behind. It is of the past to the extent that it materially inscribes, and thus forever forgets, its ideal content. The reconciliation of the two main theses of the *Aesthetics* occurs at the expense of the aesthetic as a stable philosophical category" ("Sign and Symbol"). In other words, as in the case of that which Riffaterre "evaded" and Jauss "omitted," the "bottom line" of the factors and functions of language that disarticulate the aesthetic in both Kant and Hegel turns out to be material inscription, "the prosaic materiality of the letter," which "no degree of obfuscation or ideology can transform . . . into the phenomenal cognition of aesthetic judgment" ("Phenomenality and Materiality").

Since this account of de Man's "critical-linguistic" analysis of Kant and Hegel on the category of the aesthetic may sound very much like what is commonly called "deconstruction" or "deconstructive reading"—and it is indeed that, but in a sense far more radical and far more precise than those who still use the "d-word" are ready for—some precautions may be in order, lest we think that this is familiar, all too familiar, and that we have read, digested, and understood all of this before and can therefore relegate it to the past (and a shady, if not downright abject, past at that).[9] First of all, it would be a mistake to think that what happens to the aesthetic, as a philosophical category, in the texts of Kant and Hegel—in short, its disarticulation—happens on account of some kind of weakness, lapse, or lack of rigor, and as though the critical-linguistic or "deconstructive" reader had tools at his or her disposal to see better and know more. On the contrary, as is legible in every one of de Man's essays, what happens in, and *as*, the texts of Kant and Hegel happens on account of the critical power of their thought, indeed, on account of their very "excess of rigor," as de Man puts it in the Pascal essay. And this means, for starters, that, however double or duplicitous these texts may be, they are in fact *not* to be confused with documents of "aesthetic ideology" on which we could exert the power of our demystifying "critique" from some external vantage point. Rather than ending up in "aesthetic ideology," these truly critical texts instead leave us with a "materialism" whose radicality most later critical thinking (whether of the left or the right) has not been able to face. Indeed, because this *dis*ruption or *dis*articulation of the aesthetic is something that happens—a "real event," as it were—it is what renders these texts truly historical and ensures that they have a history, or, better, *are* history and have a future. What does *not* happen, is *not* historical, and does *not* have a future is the ideologization of these

---

9. On de Man's "abjection," see Tom Cohen, "Diary of a Deconstructor Manqué: Reflections on post 'Post-Mortem de Man,'" *Minnesota Review* 41/42 (March 1995): 157–74.

(historical, material) text-events in the recuperative nonhistory of their reception in the nineteenth and twentieth centuries—an ideologization for which Schiller's (mis)appropriation of Kant is paradigmatic and that coincides with the way "we" still think about and teach literature, that is, as an aesthetic function. "We are all Schillerians," de Man quipped on one lecture occasion, "no one is Kantian anymore." (In the lecture "Kant and Schiller," de Man offers other instantiations of this paradigm—wherein the truly critical thrust of a thought is blunted in its reception—and its inverse, wherein a successor "de-Schillerizes" or "re-Kantizes" an ideologizing predecessor: with "Nietzsche/Heidegger" being possibly one example of the former and "Schopenhauer/Nietzsche" or "Heidegger/Derrida" examples of the latter.) Schiller's ideologization of Kant amounts to his turning the philosophical category of the aesthetic—which, as a category, is something susceptible to "critique" but which is not something one can be for or against—into a value, and a value on which he can found not only an aesthetic anthropology but also an "aesthetic state." The irony of this (mis)appropriation of Kant and its properly ideological moment comes in a certain (predictable) reversal: namely, Schiller's utter lack of philosophical interest in Kant's critical project and his empiricization, anthropologization, psychologization, indeed, humanization, of the Kantian sublime ends up in sheer idealism, the separation of the mind from the body, and a conception of an "aesthetic state" all too cozy for the likes of some later aesthetico-politicians, for example, Joseph Goebbels. The irony is that the inhumanly "formalist" philosopher Kant winds up with materialism, whereas the thought of the humanist psychologizing anthropologizer Schiller issues in an utter, and frightening, idealism. It is worth stressing this reversal, its irony, and the difference between the "bottom line" of Kant's and Hegel's critical projects—that is, material inscription, a radical materialism—and Schiller's ideologizing aesthetization because they reach to the heart of de Man's project in *Aesthetics, Rhetoric, Ideology* and distinguish it from what is often taken as mere "ideology-critique" or "critique of ideology."

If what de Man calls "ideology" were just some kind of mystified "naturalization" of the linguistic and conventional, then its "critique" would indeed be little more than a demystification from a more reliable, because "critical," vantage point. In such a case we could confine our "ideology-critical" activity to what would amount to repeated demystifications of Schiller: demonstrating again and again how he had misunderstood the project of critical philosophy and its transcendental principles by empiricizing and thereby ideologizing Kant. Although always a pedagogically useful (and sometimes entertaining) exercise—it is clear this is what de Man means it as in "Kant and Schiller"—such an activity would, at best, be little more than an insistence upon relatively traditional "philosophical" rigor and would not even begin to account (allegorically or otherwise) for the radicality of Kant's (or Hegel's) "materialism." This is in fact how de Man's "definition" of ideology in "The Resistance to Theory"—"What we call ideology is precisely the confusion of linguistic with natural reality, of reference with phenomenalism" (*Resistance*, p. 11)—has been (mis)read and dismissed by critics on both the left and the right. For instance, in his *Ideology* (as well as in his *The Ideology of the Aesthetic*), Terry Eagleton characterizes de Man's thought as an "essentially tragic philosophy" for which

> mind and world, language and being, are eternally discrepant; and ideology is the gesture which seeks to conflate these quite separate orders, hunting nostalgically for a pure presence of the thing within the word, and so imbuing meaning with all the sensuous positivity of material being. Ideology strives to bridge verbal concepts and sensory intuitions; but the force of truly critical (or "deconstructive") thought is to demonstrate how the insidiously figural, rhetorical nature of discourse will always intervene to break up this felicitous marriage. "What we call ideology," de Man observes in *The Resistance to Theory*, "is precisely the confusion of linguistic with natural reality, of reference with phenomenalism."[10]

Again, if this is all de Man meant by, or rather all that "we call," ideology, Eagleton would be right to continue as he does by dismissing it as a blatant attempt to have "one particular paradigm of ideological consciousness . . . do service for the whole array of ideological forms and devices" and by identifying de Man's thought with such a one: "There are styles of ideological discourse other than the 'organicist'—the thought of Paul de Man, for example, whose gloomy insistence that mind and world can never harmoniously meet is among other things a coded refusal of the 'utopianism' of emancipatory politics."[11] But to identify "what we call ideology" and "the confusion of linguistic and natural reality, of reference with phenomenalism" so hastily with "organicism" or the "spurious naturalization of language" (Eagleton's wording) is in fact overhasty and mistaken as a critique of de Man. It is overhasty because it presumes to know ahead of time what it is we mean, what it is we are referring to, when we speak here of "language," "linguistic," and "reference" (as distinguished from but confusable with "natural" and "phenomenalism"), when it is precisely the referential, not to say rhetorical, status of these terms that makes all the difference to de Man's account of ideology and deposits it well beyond Eagleton's (it is true typical) mischaracterization of de Man and "truly critical (or 'deconstructive') thought." That Eagleton has to misrepresent "the insidiously figural, rhetorical nature of discourse" and its function in critical as well as ideological thought is an indication—as is his (again typical) literalization of de Man's tone as "tragic" and "gloomy"—of where to look for the "aberrancy" of his (mis)reading. As always in the case of de Man, it has to do with rhetoric, the rhetorical dimension of lan-

---

10. Terry Eagleton, *Ideology* (London: Verso, 1991), p. 200.
11. Ibid., pp. 200–201.

guage, and its relation to reference and the referential function of language.[12] In other words, if we want to understand anything about de Man's project in his last essays, we need to begin to read the term "rhetoric" in his title *Aesthetics, Rhetoric, Ideology*, for it is indeed "rhetoric" that makes all the difference and that distinguishes de Man's project from that of a mere "critique of aesthetic ideology."

De Man's account of the "doubleness" or "duplicity" of Kant's and Hegel's texts on the aesthetic and their (self-)disarticulating critical power—and our attributing this disarticulation to "factors and functions of language" that resist phenomenalization—already provides us with a hint of how to read rhetoric "between" aesthetics and ideology. For, as should be clear even from our preliminary sketch, whatever it is that de Man's readings of Kant and Hegel do, and whatever it is that *happens* (historically, materially) in (and *as*) their texts, it is not a matter of an external demystifying critique ("deconstructive" or otherwise) of a mystified viewpoint from the vantage point of superior knowledge and insight. As de Man's texts make abundantly clear, what we are left with "after" the reading of Kant's or Hegel's disarticulation of the aesthetic is certainly neither an integrated critical or philosophical system (or "science")—since its ability to close itself off and ground it own critical discourse depended on the stability of the aesthetic— nor, equally certainly, are we left with mere ideology. One of de Man's summaries of Kant on the sublime says it best:

> The critical power of a transcendental philosophy undoes the very project of such a philosophy leaving us, certainly not with ideology—for transcendental and ideological (metaphysical) principles are part of the same system—but with a materialism that Kant's posterity has not yet begun to face up to. This happens not out of a lack of philosophical energy or rational power, but as a result of the very strength and consistency of this power."
> ("Phenomenality and Materiality")

It is because transcendental (or "critical") and ideological thought and principles are interdependent, part of the same system, that any attempt at a mere demystification of the latter is in danger of collapsing "ideology into mere error and critical thought into idealism" ("Phenomenality and Materiality"). In other words, such a demystification and its collapse cannot account for the *production* of ideology, its necessity—as a necessary "formation of the superstructure," to put it in Althusserian terms—precisely the historical, *material* conditions of its production. And late Althusser—the (self-allegorizing) Althusser of the *Autocritique* who "confesses" his "theoreticist error" of having taken "ideology" in *The German*

---

12. I have made some preliminary steps toward clarifying the relation of reference, rhetoric, and ideology in "Ending Up/Taking Back (with Two Postscripts on Paul de Man's Historical Materialism)," in Cathy Caruth and Deborah Esch, eds., *Critical Encounters: Reference and Responsibility* (New Brunswick, N.J.: Rutgers University Press, 1995), pp. 11–41. See also my detailed discussion in "Ideology, Rhetoric, Aesthetics," forthcoming in my *Material Inscriptions*.

Ideology as "error"!—is the right citation here.[13] For de Man, as for Althusser, we are never so much "in" ideology as when we think ourselves to be "outside" it:[14] for instance, when, like Terry Eagleton, we think that a presumably cheerful insistence on the possibility or the *promesse* that mind and world *can* harmoniously meet (versus de Man's "gloomy" insistence on the opposite) would necessarily be tantamount to an acceptance (versus de Man's coded "refusal") of "the 'utopianism' of emancipatory politics"—and not the "politics" of the kind of totalitarian "aesthetic state" that is all too familiar in the twentieth century and that would make Schiller shudder. But if even a "critical" ("transcendental" or otherwise) thought cannot step "out" of ideology—or "by-pass or repress ideology" ("Phenomenality and Materiality")—without losing its critical thrust and risking being repossessed by what it forecloses because it is "part of the same system" as the ideology it would "critique," then how is what de Man's readings do, end up in, or leave us with *different* from such "merely" critical activity? Clearly enough, to the extent that they purport to "leave us with" a radical "materiality" or "materialism," they *have to be* "different," and they have to have some way of accounting for "the same system" of which critical and ideological thought and discourse are a part. And such "accounting" would indeed have to be an account of the *production* of the system, its putting into place on the basis of conditions of production that would be historical and material. This is where, again, the question of rhetoric—and its role in the confusion of "reference with phenomenalism"— comes in and is indispensable for an understanding of the specificity of what de Man has to say and teach about ideology.

For, when de Man speaks here of critical and ideological thought's being "part of the same system," there is no doubt that this "system" is, for him, always a tropological system, a system of tropological transformations and substitutions. In the case of critical and ideological principles and discourses, for example, this tropological system would want to include within itself—that is, reduce to its own principles of transformation and substitution—both the (purportedly) self-defining and self-validating semiosis of a critical discourse and what amounts to the symbolic phenomenal figuration of an ideological discourse. Kant's characterization of the difference between and relation of what he calls "transcendental" and "metaphysical" principles—which de Man does not hesitate to identify with "critical" and "ideological," respectively—would be one, global, example of such a "system" (and the one that de Man is referring to). And the articulation of number and space or extension that Kant's attempt to ground the mathematical sublime as a transcendental principle requires—and that can "take place" only as a

---

13. Louis Althusser, *Essays in Self-Criticism,* trans. Grahame Lock (London: New Left Books, 1976), p. 119.

14. The reference here is, of course, to Louis Althusser, "Ideology and Ideological State Apparatuses," in *Lenin and Philosophy* (London: New Left Books, 1971), pp. 127–86.

"linguistic principle" (i.e., as a tropological system that is "purely formal," *cannot* ground itself, and cannot be closed off)—would be another, more "local," example. But global and local examples aside, the point should be clear: given such a "tropological system," it cannot ever be sufficient to unmask or to demystify it because all such "critique" manages to do is to substitute one trope for another— even if it is the substitution of a "trope of the literal" (i.e., "real," "true," "demystified," "critical," etc.) for, as it were, a "trope of the figural," or, if one likes, in the more traditional, but insufficiently understood, terms of *The German Ideology*'s critique, a "true" or "critical" consciousness for a "false consciousness"—and thereby to remain very much *within* (and hence to *confirm*) the tropological system it would want to criticize. What is needed, therefore, is a different activity, one that could begin to account for the putting into place of the tropological system itself, its inaugural grounding or founding on the basis of principles that, wherever they may come from, cannot come from within the tropological system itself and cannot be reduced to *its* principles of transformation, substitution, or exchange. This is where our "factors and functions of language" finally return— those factors and functions of language that resist the phenomenalization made possible (and necessary) by tropes and their system but that nevertheless lie at the bottom of all tropological systems as their material condition of possibility. But as their *material*, *non*phenomenal, and *non*phenomenalizable conditions of possibility, these factors and functions—and they have several names in de Man, (e.g., the "positional power" of language, "material inscription," "the play of the letter")—are also necessarily always their conditions of *im*possibility; they leave marks and traces "within" (or "without"?) these tropological systems, marks and traces that may not be accessible to the knowing, consciousness, or science of "critical critics" but that nevertheless remain legible in the texts of these systems: in their inability to close themselves off, for instance, which always produces an excess (or lack) of tropology, a residue or remainder of trope and figure irreducible to them. Like the truth, this excess or lack outs and has to out; and, like Hölderlin's "the true" (*das Wahre*), it is what happens, what takes place, an event—like the *text* of Kant's sublime, for instance, or, we might add, like the *text* of de Man's readings of Kant and Hegel.

Reference and Rhetoric

That the "materiality of actual history"[15] gets produced, *happens*, as the residue or excess of tropology is just another way of saying what de Man himself says about his apparently new "interest" or "turn to" questions of ideology, history, and politics in these essays. Asked in 1983 about the frequent recurrence of the terms "ide-

---

15. The phrase is from de Man's "Anthropomorphism and Trope in the Lyric," in *The Rhetoric of Romanticism* (New York: Columbia University Press, 1984), p. 262.

ology" and "politics" in his recent work, de Man replies: (1) that he was never away from these problems ("they were always uppermost in my mind"); (2) that he has always maintained "that one could approach the problems of ideology and by extension the problems of politics only on the basis of critical-linguistic analysis, which had to be done in its own terms" ("An Interview with Paul de Man," *Resistance*, p. 121). He characterizes the "critical-linguistic analysis" that has been, for him, preparatory for the work contained in the present volume as an attempt to achieve a certain control "over technical problems of language, specifically problems of rhetoric, of the relation between tropes and performatives, of saturation of tropology as a field that in certain forms of language goes beyond that field" (ibid.). And, now that he has achieved a certain control over these problems—de Man is clearly referring to *Allegories of Reading* and his (still largely *un*read or grievously *mis*read) work on Rousseau, where he was "able to progress from purely linguistic analysis to questions which are really already of a political and ideological nature"—he finds that he can "do it [i.e., deal with questions of ideology and politics] a little more openly, though in a very different way than what generally passes as 'critique of ideology.'" In other words, de Man's "progress" or progression from apparently purely linguistic questions to talking more openly about ideology and politics itself takes place on the basis of a critical-linguistic analysis of rhetoric—tropological systems, their inability to close themselves off, and their production of "forms of language" that "go beyond" their domain—and, as such, itself takes place as the residue or excess of tropology. In short, rather than just a "logical" (and historicizable) development, this progression is in fact a material event in its own right, the product of a critical-linguistic analysis, a *reading*, of rhetoric rather than a critique, or self-critique, of a former "ideological" or "theoreticist" (or pre-"epistemological break") self.[16] That it is in fact the *impossibility* of reducing texts to rhetoric, to tropes, to tropological models of language, and that therefore a simply "rhetorical reading" is in fact *never* a sufficient activity, may come as a surprise to (non)readers of de Man who think that what he does is to reduce everything to rhetoric and tropes and that his rhetorical readings only demonstrate again and again "how the insidiously figural, rhetorical nature of discourse will always intervene to break up [the] felicitous marriage"[17] of mind and world, language and being, and so on. For instance, in the present context we could as easily say that it is in fact *rhetoric* that makes the "marriage" of mind and world, language and being, possible because such a meeting of mind and world is possible *only* thanks to a phenomenalizing (and hence aesthetico-ideologizing) trope! Tropes accomplish the phenomenalization of reference that "we call" ideology,

---

16. To say this is by no means to criticize Althusser—only those who took him literally on "the epistemological break" and ideology versus science, something Althusser himself never did, even in "early" work like *For Marx*. Another essay, a critical-linguistic analysis, is necessary to demonstrate this.

17. Eagleton, *Ideology*, p. 200.

but, of course, because it is indeed *tropes* that do this, such phenomenalized reference cannot help but be "aberrant," to use one of de Man's favorite terms for it, and produce "ideological aberrations." In any event, if we want to understand the role of rhetoric and tropes in de Man's "critical-linguistic analysis," we need to clarify its relation to one of those "factors and functions" of language: namely, reference, the referential function, what one could call the *irreducibility* of reference in de Man. For reference is deeply involved, to put it still vaguely, not only in de Man's "definition" of ideology—the confusion "of reference with phenomenalism"—but also in the double impossibility that runs like a leitmotif through all of de Man's work: the impossibility of constructing an epistemologically reliable tropological model of language and text and, the other side of the coin, the impossibility of constructing an epistemologically reliable purely semiotic (or grammatical) model of language and text. Although a number of the Rousseau essays in *Allegories of Reading* offer much help on the question of reference and the referential function, perhaps the most explanatory and suggestive discussion comes in "The Resistance to Theory," its infamous "definition" of ideology, and the immediate context of this passage. The essay is most suggestive in part because its general, programmatic statement allows it to explain most succinctly both the project de Man is coming from (call it *Allegories of Reading*) and the one he is moving toward (the essays in *Aesthetics, Rhetoric, Ideology*).

In order to appreciate the considerable import of de Man's "definition" (or, better, *denomination*—"we call") of ideology as the confusion "of reference with phenomenalism" and the role of the rhetorical dimension of language in this definition, it is necessary to read what "follows" from it: "What we call ideology is precisely the confusion of linguistic with natural reality, of reference with phenomenalism. It follows that, more than any other mode of inquiry, including economics, the linguistics of literariness is a powerful and indispensable tool in the unmasking of ideological aberrations, as well as a determining factor in accounting for their occurrence" (*Resistance*, p. 11). The claim being made here for "the linguistics of literariness" may certainly appear exorbitant to some, or, at the very least, surprising, given de Man's trenchant critiques of semiology and what goes by the name of "structuralism" in literary study. And yet it is the linguistics of literariness that is said to be "a powerful and indispensable tool" not only in the unmasking or demystifying of ideological aberrations *but also* in "accounting for their occurrence"—that is, precisely the double operation that would qualify this activity as the "critical-linguistic analysis" that not only demystifies ideology but also accounts for its necessity, that is, its *production* and the (historical, material) conditions of its production. It certainly seems strange that de Man should attribute such power to the linguistics of literariness. Nevertheless, the claims make perfect sense once we try to understand the relation between reference and the linguistics of literariness in context, and they turn out to be rather less exorbitant once we read their own "referential," not to say rhetorical, status. The relations among "the linguistics of literariness," "reference," and the possibility of a confusion "of reference with phenomenalism" are very clearly and carefully determined in "The Resistance to Theory." By "linguistics of literariness" de Man means primarily the application of Saussurian linguistics to literary texts. Indeed, according to "The Resistance to Theory," the advent of literary theory as such "occurs with the introduction of linguistic terminology in the metalanguage about literature," and "contemporary literary theory comes into its own in such events as the application of Saussurian linguistics to literary texts" (*Resistance*, p. 8). The difference that the advent, occurrence, or event of "literary theory" proper makes has very specifically to do with its different conception of "reference as a function of language and not necessarily as an intuition." De Man's "intuition" here should be read in German (as *Anschauung*), as the following sentences confirm: "Intuition implies perception, consciousness, experience, and leads at once into the world of logic and of understanding with all its correlatives, among which aesthetics occupies a prominent place. The assumption that there can be a science of language which is not necessarily a logic leads to the development of a terminology which is not necessarily aesthetic" (*Resistance*, p. 8). In other words, what the "nonphenomenal linguistics" of Saussure and its application in literary study ("the linguistics of literariness") suspend is not the referential function of language—that is *always* there, irreducibly, whenever we talk about anything called "language"—but rather its ability to give us, or, better, to designate, the *referent* reliably, predictably, and epistemologically consistently enough to allow us to mistake what is a product of a function of language for an object of consciousness, its "faculties" (intuition, perception), and the logic, the phenomeno-logic, that follows in its train. It is no surprise, then, that such a nonphenomenal "linguistics of literariness" should be "a powerful and indispensable tool in the unmasking of ideological aberrations" if ideology, or rather what we call ideology, is precisely the confusion "of reference with phenomenalism"—that is, taking reference *as an intuition* and not as a function of language. As de Man points out in "Roland Barthes and the Limits of Structuralism" (1972), semiology's demystifying power is genuine and undeniable:

> One can see why any ideology would always have a vested interest in theories of language advocating correspondence between sign and meaning, since they depend on the illusion of this correspondence for their effectiveness. On the other hand, theories of language that put into question the subservience, resemblance, or potential identity between sign and meaning are always subversive, even if they remain strictly confined to linguistic phenomena. (*Romanticism*, p. 170)[18]

---

18. All quotations from "Roland Barthes and the Limits of Structuralism" are from Paul de Man, *Romanticism and Contemporary Criticism*, ed. E. S. Burt, Kevin Newmark, and Andrzej Warminski (Baltimore: Johns Hopkins University Press, 1993), and will be given as *Romanticism*, followed by the page number.

What de Man calls the "correspondence between sign and meaning" in this essay is quite clearly what ten years later is called the confusion of reference with phenomenalism or, still more precisely, "the phenomenalization of the sign" in "Hegel on the Sublime."[19]

But however legitimate and convincing its claim to being a powerful tool in the unmasking of ideological aberrations, literary semiology's (the linguistics of literariness) being also "a determining factor in accounting for their occurrence" is a more complicated and overdetermined "claim." The complications begin to unfold if we try to figure out what this determining factor's "accounting for" amounts to. On a first level, the meaning seems relatively straightforward: the linguistics of literariness can "account for" the occurrence of referential aberrations in the sense of being able "to render a reckoning" of them, to explain them and their mechanisms. Based as it is on a *non*phenomenal linguistic model, the linguistics of literariness could certainly be expected to be able to unmask any undue phenomenalization of language's referential function and to reveal the mechanics of an ideology's workings. Nevertheless, the linguistics of literariness "accounts for" ideological aberrations in still another sense if it is a "determin*ing* factor" in accounting for their occurrence. In other words, and with only a slight shift of emphasis, the linguistics of literariness also "accounts for" ideological aberrations in the sense of being "the explanation or cause of," as the dictionary puts it—of being a determining factor that itself "causes" or produces the ideological aberrations. This sense may seem a bit odd in the context of what seems to be unmitigated "praise" of the "linguistics of literariness," but it is in fact a necessary sense, as predictable and inevitable as ideology itself. This becomes clear if we recall the immediate context of our ideology-paragraph in "The Resistance to Theory." For what de Man has just stated and demonstrated in the preceding paragraphs is that the nonphenomenal linguistics of literariness *itself* succumbs to the temptation or the seduction of phenomenalism when it confuses "literariness" for "another word for, or another mode of, aesthetic response" (*Resistance*, p. 9), to the point of a "Cratylism" of the sign that "assumes a convergence of the phenomenal aspects of language, as sound, with its signifying function as referent" (*Resistance*, p. 9). This self-ideologizing rephenomenalization of the sign is inevitable, and even a nonphenomenal "linguistics of literariness" is subject to it: "It is inevitable that semiology or similarly oriented methods be considered formalistic, in the sense of

---

19. See "Hegel on the Sublime": "The phenomenality of the linguistic sign can, by an infinite variety of devices or turns, be aligned with the phenomenality, as knowledge (meaning) or sensory experience, of the signified toward which it is directed. It is the phenomenalization of the sign that constitutes signification, regardless of whether it occurs by way of conventional or by way of natural means. The term phenomenality here implies not more and not less than that the process of signification, in and by itself, can be known, just as the laws of nature as well as those of convention can be made accessible to some form of knowledge."

being aesthetically rather than semantically valorized, but the inevitability of such an interpretation does not make it less aberrant. Literature involves the voiding, rather than the affirmation, of aesthetic categories" (*Resistance*, p. 10). De Man's use of the word "aberrant" to describe this (mis)interpretation brings us back, "refers" us, as it were, to the ideology-paragraph and our "ideological aberrations." Quite clearly, as de Man has just pointed out, the linguistics of literariness itself undergoes a rephenomenalization of reference: in short, even the discourse of literary semiology, for all its demystifying power, has ideology (and aesthetic ideology at that) built into it, as it were, internal to it as a necessary and inevitable moment. And de Man's using Barthes—the Barthes of "Proust et les noms"—as the example of such self-ideologization recalls an analogous move ten years earlier in "Roland Barthes and the Limits of Structuralism." There de Man had demonstrated that (the early) Barthes's own demystifying discourse suffers a self-mystification on the level of method when, carried away by the headiness of the power that bracketing the referential function of literature grants it, it aspires to "scientific" status—as though all the "mess and muddle of signification," its "referential, representational effectiveness," and "referential suggestiveness" did not need to be "accounted for" because it could be "dismissed as contingency or ideology and not taken seriously as a semantic interference within the semiological structure . . . the reasons for the recurrent aberration [being] not linguistic but ideological" (*Romanticism*, pp. 171-73). But the irreducibility of reference, of the referential function, as "internal" to *any* discourse, no matter how demystifying its power and how "scientific" its aspirations, comes back inevitably:

> That literature can be ideologically manipulated is obvious but does not suffice to prove that this distortion is not a particular aspect of a larger pattern of error. Sooner or later, any literary study must face the problem of the truth value of its own interpretations, no longer with the naive conviction of a priority of content over form, but as a consequence of the much more unsettling experience of being unable to cleanse its own discourse of aberrantly referential implications. The traditional concept of reading used by Barthes and based on the model of an encoding/decoding process is inoperative if the master code remains out of reach of the operator, who then becomes unable to understand his own discourse. A science unable to read itself can no longer be called a science. The possibility of a scientific semiology is challenged by a problem that can no longer be accounted for in purely semiological terms. (*Romanticism*, p. 174)

I quote de Man's summary (1972) of Barthes's predicament at length for several reasons. First of all, it confirms our suspicions about the linguistics of literariness being a determin*ing* factor in "accounting for" the occurrence of ideological aberrations. The linguistics of literariness may be able to demystify ideological aberrations and it may be able to explain them, but because it cannot do so without

its own discourse's being subject to the very factors that determine the inevitability of ideological aberrations, it also cannot help but *re*-produce those aberrations
in its own discourse. Barthes's inability to cleanse[20] his own "scientific" discourse
of "referentially aberrant implications" means that "ideological aberration" is not
something that comes from "outside" language but rather is very much "internal"
to it, to its irreducible referential function and its inevitable aberrancy. If we ask
what it is "about" reference, "about" the referential function, that makes it inevitable and yet inevitably aberrant—what it is that makes a rephenomenalization
of reference, and hence ideology, inevitable even for the most "nonphenomenal"
of linguistics—we already get an answer in de Man's characterization of Barthes's
predicament as the inability to read his own discourse (because unable to "account
for" its own referential aberrations). "A science unable to read itself" can indeed
no longer be called a science, and instead would have to be called an *allegory*
of science. And here it would be quite clearly an allegory, an "account," of its inability to read the story, the "account," of its (quite legitimate) demystifying
"science." And since the targets of its demystifying, unmasking, operation are
the unwarranted phenomenalizations of reference performed by tropes, by the
rhetorical dimension of language, it is of course rhetoric, tropes, the rhetorical
dimension of any and every demystifying discourse that turn it into an allegory of
the impossibility of reading—and very precisely, as page 205 of *Allegories of
Reading* puts it, an allegory of the unreadability of "the prior narration," that is,
the narrative of "a trope and its deconstruction." However tortuously, we have
arrived at a *third* sense of "accounting," of how it is that the linguistics of literariness can be a determining factor in accounting for ideological aberrations: that is,
it can be such only as an "account," a story, a narrative, an allegory of (the impossibility of) reading and never a "science" or a critical discourse transparent to itself that could "account for" ideology by "balancing the books" of credit and debit
without remainder.

That accounting for ideological aberrations should turn into an allegory of (the
impossibility of) reading is certainly no surprise for readers of *Allegories of
Reading*, but what needs to be stressed here is that the inevitable aberrancy of the
referential function, its inevitable phenomenalization and ideologization in and by
tropes, the rhetorical dimension of language, is something that is very much "part
of" reference, very much a "moment" of the referential function. This is most
compactly legible in a few pages of de Man's *Social Contract* essay ("Promises
[Social Contract]") in *Allegories of Reading*. Reference, according to this essay,
"is the application of an undetermined, general potential for meaning to a specific
unit" (*Allegories*, p. 268). This undetermined, general potential for meaning is

---

20. See de Man on "some preventative semiological hygiene" in "Semiology and Rhetoric," in
Allegories of Reading (New Haven: Yale University Press, 1979), p. 6. Further references to *Allegories
of Reading* will be given as *Allegories,* followed by the page number.

grammar, "the system of relationships that generates the text and that functions independently of its referential meaning" (*Allegories*, p. 268), and "just as no text is conceivable without grammar, no grammar is conceivable without the suspension of referential meaning" (*Allegories*, pp. 268–69). But even though "the logic of grammar generates texts only in the absence of referential meaning" (*Allegories*, p. 269), the very "application" or *determination* of grammar's undetermined, general, and nonreferential potential for meaning "to a specific unit"— that is, reference, the referential function necessary for the "generation" of a text—means that "every text generates a referent that subverts the grammatical principles to which it owed its constitution" (*Allegories*, p. 269). In other words, there is a "fundamental incompatibility between grammar and meaning" (*Allegories*, p. 269), and this "divergence between grammar and referential meaning is what we call the figural dimension of language" (*Allegories*, p. 270). De Man's account here could not be clearer or more precise: texts get generated by the *determination* of reference, which determining, however, necessarily diverges from and indeed "subverts" the text's *un*determined, general, *non*referential potential for meaning, the grammar without which the text could not "come into being" in the first place. And the necessity of this divergence or subversion is "what we call" the figural dimension of language, that is, rhetoric. In short, rhetoric, the rhetorical dimension of language, is a necessary moment *of* reference, of the text-producing referential function, "itself." As the "moment" of reference that necessarily and inevitably produces aberrant reference, the rhetorical dimension of language is also what makes "text" into "something" that we cannot "define" but can only "call":

> We call *text* any entity that can be considered from such a double perspective: as a generative, open-ended, non-referential grammatical system and as a figural system closed off by a transcendental signification that subverts the grammatical code to which the text owes its existence. The "definition" of the text also states the impossibility of its existence and prefigures the allegorical narratives of this impossibility. (*Allegories*, p. 270)

What goes for "text" in this passage holds equally well for "what we call ideology" in "The Resistance to Theory," and it is the reason why the linguistics of literariness being a "determining factor" in accounting for ideological aberrations can also be only an allegorical "account" *of* the impossibility of defining or determining ideology—except in and as a text to be read in turn, in an other allegory, an allegory of . . . an other . . . of. The potential stutter here is not just play with the "meaning" of allegory—*allos* + *agorein*, other speaking, speaking of the other— but rather also a necessary "conclusion" to be drawn from everything we have been saying. Namely—in the case of *what we call* ideology, *what we call* the figural dimension of language, *what we call* text, and, we might add, *what we call* language—if we ask what these allegories are allegories *of*, the most "direct" answer would have to be that they are allegories *of* reference, which amounts to the same thing as saying that they are all "allegories of *of*," since "of" is the very bearer of the referential function, the "carrying-back" function, "itself." Our stuttering repetition "allegories of *of*," then, would suggest still a fourth (and "last") meaning for the "accounting" that the linguistics of literariness as a determining factor can purportedly perform: the mechanical counting, recounting, numbering, enumeration of ideological aberrations, one by one, one after the other, in order. Such purely "grammatical" (as in *gramma*) juxtaposition or notation is, indeed, finally the only *material* (and *because* material, historical) "accounting" for ideological aberrations possible (and it is also the reason why it is better at accounting for ideological aberrations than the dicourse of economics, which, in brief, has to literalize and reify the "economic base" and whose "demystifications" cannot help but amount to mere substitutions of one trope for another, one "consciousness" for another, to put it in the terms of *The German Ideology*—in short, even *economics* is never economic enough when dealing with the economy of phenomenalism and reference that we call ideology!).[21] If this is so, then it is no wonder that, as de Man puts it in the Barthes essay, "The mind cannot remain at rest in a mere repertorization of its own recurrent aberrations; it is bound to systematize its own negative self-insights into categories that have at least the appearance of passion and difference" (*Romanticism*, p. 175). There is much to be read in this sentence, but we would underline only the fact that the mind is *bound* to do this—it has no choice, it is necessary and inevitable, for it is the irreducible referential function, its inevitable phenomenalization in tropes, and the production of referential aberrations, that is, ideology. It happens and has to happen whenever we denominate something, anything—call it "ideology," "the figural dimension of language," "text," or even "allegory" ("we can call such narratives . . . *allegories*" [*Allegories*, p. 205])—and attempt to account for it in a narrative: "A narrative endlessly tells the story of its own denominational aberration and it can only repeat this aberration on various levels of rhetorical complexity" ("Self [Pygmalion]," *Allegories*, p. 162).

Excess of Rigor

If it indeed reaches dead ends and breaking points, it does so by excess of rigor rather than for lack of it.
—"Pascal's Allegory of Persuasion"

The characterization of de Man's "accounting" as a stuttering repertorization, repetition, enumeration, or *numbering* of referential (i.e., ideological) aberrations

---

21. I have explained this in excruciating detail and at excessive length in my ex-Introduction to *Aesthetic Ideology*, "Ideology, Rhetoric, Aesthetics" (forthcoming).

takes us back to the project of *Aesthetics, Rhetoric, Ideology* and its specificity in relation to de Man's previous work. Our attempt to explain, or at least to account for, the "relation" of reference and rhetoric in de Man's "definition" of ideology (as the confusion of reference with phenomenalism) and its ending up in "allegories of reference" would certainly link this project to *Allegories of Reading*. Nevertheless, there is a definite and determinable specificity to the "allegories of reference" that make up the present volume, which distinguishes it from the critical-linguistic analyses in *Allegories of Reading*. One way to formulate this distinctive feature is by returning once again to "The Resistance to Theory" and its characterization of "the most familiar and general of all linguistic models, the classical *trivium*, which considers the sciences of language as consisting of grammar, rhetoric, and logic (or dialectics)" in its relation to "the *quadrivium*, which covers the non-verbal sciences of number (arithmetic), of space (geometry), of motion (astronomy), and of time (music)" (*Resistance*, p. 13). To put it directly though a bit proleptically: whereas the project of *Allegories of Reading* comes from the side of the trivium—the sciences of language—that of *Aesthetics, Rhetoric, Ideology* comes from the side of the quadrivium—the nonverbal, mathematical sciences. This requires some explanation. Insofar as the analyses in *Allegories of Reading* are concerned with the way that rhetoric, the rhetorical dimension of language, always comes to interfere "between" grammar and logic, thereby making impossible any easy, unbroken passage between the formal structures and the (universalizability of the) meaning of texts, these analyses would be demonstrations of the instability of the linguistic model of the trivium (*as* a model of language). Whether out to show how the rhetorical dimension always interferes with attempts to set up grammatical models of language or how grammar (in various forms) interferes with attempts to set up closed tropo-*logical* models of language—for instance, most programmatically, in "Semiology and Rhetoric"[22]—or how the performative function (or "performative rhetoric," as de Man calls it on occasion) does not easily coexist with reliable epistemological claims to truth, the essays in *Allegories of Reading* can, for the most part, be said to take the trivium as their domain. The fact that they concentrate on "literary" texts so much of the time and that even the "theoretical" texts they treat are mostly "hybrid" or "semi-literary" texts—rather than texts of systematic philosophy like treatises of logic or epistemology—would be consistent with this observation. The texts contained in *Aesthetics, Rhetoric, Ideology*, on the other hand, are, we would say, quite clearly coming from the other side of the *artes liberales*, and not for thematic reasons only—that is, not just because nearly all of them are "about" texts that take a determinate place in philosophical systems. The texts in this volume come from the side of the quadrivium in the more particular sense that their discussions of the

---

22. See my "Ending Up/Taking Back (with Two Postscripts on Paul de Man's Historical Materialism)."

category of the aesthetic are all concerned with the relation of the aesthetic to epistemology.[23] Indeed, as has already been suggested, aesthetics, the category of the aesthetic, is a rigorous philosophical discourse's way of attempting to ground its own discourse on principles internal to its system and thereby to close it off *as a system*: that is, as a logic. Philosophical aesthetics is in fact the attempt to verify that a science of language does indeed have to be a logic (something that "literary theory," with its "nonphenomenal linguistics," necessarily puts into question). Logic, as de Man summarizes in "The Resistance to Theory," would provide the "link" between the trivium and the quadrivium:

> In the history of philosophy, this link is traditionally, as well as substantially, accomplished by way of logic, the area where the rigor of the linguistic discourse about itself matches up with the rigor of the mathematical discourse about the world. Seventeenth-century epistemology, for instance, at the moment when the relationship between philosophy and mathematics is particularly close, holds up the language of what it calls geometry (*mos geometricus*), and which in fact includes the homogeneous concatenation between space, time and number, as the sole model of coherence and economy. Reasoning *more geometrico* is said to be "almost the only mode of reasoning that is infallible, because it is the only one to adhere to the true method, whereas all other ones are by natural necessity in a degree of confusion of which only geometrical minds can be aware." This is a clear instance of the interconnection between a science of the phenomenal world and a science of language conceived as definitional logic, the pre-condition for a correct axiomatic-deductive, synthetic reasoning. The possibility of

---

23. Cf. the opening of de Man's 1982 seminar "Aesthetic Theory from Kant to Hegel":

"This course is part of a cycle on aesthetic theory around Hegel. Precursor courses include: 'Hegel's Aesthetics' and 'Hegel and English Romanticism.'

"We're concerned with the aesthetic as a philosophical category—a category in the Aristotelian sense. As a category, it is not something that one can be for or against; it is not open to valorization.

"And, with the relationship of the category of the aesthetic to questions of epistemology in the existing general philosophical tradition.

"And, to the elements of critical philosophy, which involves a testing of a variety of categories against an epistemological truth and falsehood.

"Critical philosophy here is thus the testing of the categories in terms of questions of epistemology. . . .

"What we have here is an explicit philosophical theme: the relation of the category of the aesthetic to epistemology. The implicit question is the relation of the category of the aesthetic to the theory of language.

"'Language' here means consideration of sign, symbol, trope, rhetoric, grammar, etc.

"Therefore, the relation of the category of the aesthetic to the theory of language is implicit but *ungedacht*: the place of the theory of language is unarticulated—it's inscribed in other concerns.

"Our object, then, will be a critique of the *Kritik* in terms of linguistic categories. Our interest will be in how Kant uses grammar and trope and see (because I'm giving the course) if there's a tension between the explicit formulation and the usage of tropes, or a tension between the explicit theses and the implicit assumptions about language."

thus circulating freely between logic and mathematics has its own complex and problematic history as well as its contemporary equivalences with a different logic and a different mathematics. What matters for our present argument is that this articulation of the sciences of language with the mathematical sciences represents a particularly compelling version of a continuity between a theory of language, as logic, and the knowledge of the phenomenal world to which mathematics gives access. In such a system, the place of aesthetics is preordained and by no means alien, provided the priority of logic, in the model of the *trivium*, is not being questioned. (*Resistance*, p. 13)

De Man's offering seventeenth-century epistemology as an example of how logic would accomplish the "link" between the trivium and the quadrivium— since it is "the area where the rigor of the linguistic discourse about itself matches up with the rigor of the mathematical discourse about the world"—and his quotation of Pascal's "De l'esprit géométrique" help to explain what is at stake in epistemo-logic. For what the discourse of epistemology would want is to be able to construct a logical model to ground and verify *itself* as rigorously as the definitional self-verifying logic of the mathematical sciences. This is how the rigor of the linguistic discourse about itself could "match up" with the rigor of the mathematical discourse about the world. If in the seventeenth century the "geometric method" is held up as a model for epistemological discourse, it is because this method's own discourse as definitional logic would be precisely *non*referential, or, better, *self*-referential enough *not* to leave a remainder of reference or the "referential aberrations" we have been worrying about. (It should come as no surprise even to delirious formalists that if "literary" discourse is taken to be self- or autoreferential, then mathematical discourse would be the most "literary" language of all!) In other words, the discourse of epistemology would claim to be able to cleanse itself of aberrant reference—that is, ultimately, the rhetorical dimension of language—by basing itself on the "linguistic" (i.e., logical) model of the mathematical sciences. It is no wonder, then, that in such a system the "place of aesthetics"—or, we would add, an "aesthetic moment," a moment of aesthetization—is preordained, for the aesthetic is, as we know, the place where a rigorous logic would bypass or repress or displace or transform the irreducible referential function of language, its inevitable phenomenalization in trope, and its production of referential, ideological aberrations. Nevertheless, as we have said, these philosophical discourses cannot do this without in fact *de*stabilizing the category of the aesthetic—since they can "ground" their tropological systems only by resorting to factors and functions of language that resist phenomenalization— and ending up in a radical materialism irreducible to the phenomenal cognition of aesthetic judgment. To be added at this point is the fact that de Man understands and formulates the project of the sought-after articulation of aesthetics and epistemology and its "failure" or *dis*articulation very much in the terms of the problematics of seventeenth-century epistemology (which, of course, is not surprising, since both Kant [especially] and Hegel take it upon themselves to resolve the problems they have inherited from seventeenth-century thought). De Man's account of Kant's mathematical sublime as an attempt to articulate number with extension—which turns out to "work" only as a tropological system that cannot close itself off and necessarily produces the "dynamic sublime" of a performative "model" of language—would be one obvious example; but even his reading of Hegel's sublime takes place against the background of the principles and problems of the quadrivium. This is also the case of the opening essay of this volume—"The Epistemology of Metaphor"—with its treatment of the "theme" of "rhetoric and epistemology" in Locke, Condillac, and Kant. But the text most explicitly concerned with the question of an epistemological discourse's being able to model itself on the discourse of mathematics is the first half of the second essay: "Pascal's Allegory of Persuasion." This essay could serve as something of a "key" to the project and the other texts in the volume. Not only does it act as a bridge between the "themes" of "rhetoric and epistemology," and "rhetoric and aesthetics,"[24] but it also provides an "early" (1979) instance of the text's producing what de Man will shortly call "materiality." In doing so, it may also be the best example of what we have called "allegories of reference"—from the side of the quadrivium.

"Pascal's Allegory of Persuasion" plays itself out in the space between its opening words ("Attempts to *define* allegory keep reencountering a set of predictable problems . . .") and its very last words (". . . is what we *call* allegory" [my emphasis]). It in fact turns out that the predictable problems in attempts to define allegory are such that they make any "definition" impossible and leave us instead with allegory's being that which we can only "call." That these predictable problems are, one, allegory's "referential status," and, two, "a recurrent ambivalence in [allegory's] aesthetic valorization" very precisely deposits the essay's problematic within the space of our concerns: *between* "rhetoric and epistemology" *and* "rhetoric and aesthetics." Let's take up the first "theme" first, for, as we already

---

24. "Rhetoric and Aesthetics" was the title of de Man's Messenger lecture series delivered at Cornell in February and March of 1983. The titles of the lectures were announced as:

    I. Anthropomorphism and Trope in Baudelaire
    II. Kleist's *Über das Marionettentheater*
    III. Hegel on the Sublime
    IV. Kant on the Sublime
    V. Kant and Schiller
    VI. Conclusions

"Kant on the Sublime" was entitled "Phenomenality and Materiality in Kant" by the time de Man wrote it. "Conclusions" was the lecture on Benjamin's "The Task of the Translator," now included in *The Resistance to Theory*.

know, it will take us back to the second all too predictably—in numerical order, as it were, one by one. "What is it," de Man asks, "in a rigorous epistemology, that makes it impossible to decide whether its exposition is a proof or an allegory?" That the rigorous epistemology's *exposition* should be what makes it impossible to decide it as proof or as allegory already provides us with an indication of where the problem lies: it of course "has to do" with the epistemology's own discourse—indeed, with the referential (and thus rhetorical) status of its own language of definition and proof. The "rigorous epistemology" in question is Pascal's in the first part of a text entitled *Réflexions sur la géométrie en général; De l'esprit géométrique et de l'art de persuader*, translated as "The Mind of the Geometrician" in de Man's English version. "De l'esprit géométrique" begins its exposition in clear and classical terms: with the distinction between nominal and real definitions, *définitions de nom* and *définitions de chose*. The advantage of the geometric method, according to Pascal, is that it recognizes only nominal definitions, "giving a name only to those things which have been clearly designated in perfectly known terms." Nominal definition would be a simple process of denomination, "a kind of stenography," as de Man puts it, "a free and flexible code used for reasons of economy to avoid cumbersome repetitions, and which in no way influences the thing itself in its substance or in its properties." If "we call every number which is divisible by two without a remainder an even number," this is a nominal, geometrical definition, says Pascal, "because, after having clearly designated a thing—for example, every number divisible by two without a remainder—we give this thing a name from which we exclude any other meaning it may have, in order to apply to it only the meaning of the thing indicated."[25] In other words, with nominal definitions we know what it is we are talking about at all times because it amounts to a simple process of naming whose designation is clear and unambiguous. Should there be any doubt about what "even number" designates, we can always reiterate its definition. In short, the system of nominal definitions would be a closed semiotic system, *non*referential in the sense that its signs do not carry us back to anything outside its system of arbitrary, conventional linkings between *chose* and *nom,* or, better, self- or autoreferential in the sense that its terms or units, names, always take back to other units or names constituted not by some essence or substance but only by their clear, determined, and determinable relation (of *désignation*) to other terms internal to the system. What could be clearer? Real definitions (*définitions de chose*), on the other hand, are really not definitions at all but rather axioms, propositions in need of being proven, because they make claims about the existence and the nature of *things* outside of, other than, the sign system of the definitions themselves. Rather than being non- or autoreferential, real definitions are clearly referential, they take us "out" or

---

25. Blaise Pascal, "The Mind of the Geometrician," in *Great Shorter Works of Pascal,* trans. Emilie Caillet (Philadelphia: Westminster Press, 1948), p. 190.

back to something other than the relations among signs in that they try to say something about the nature of the *chose* signified by the sign. (Hence they can be contradicted, they are not "free," they may occasion confusions, etc.) The geometrician, then, in order to know what he is talking about, must be able to keep nominal definitions and real definitions apart. Can he really do so?

As we might anticipate, the answer is: "Not for very long." As soon as the distinction between nominal and real definitions is instituted—or "enunciated," as de Man puts it—it runs into problems on account of Pascal's having to introduce what he calls "primitive terms" into his epistemological discourse. These terms are so basic and so elementary that they cannot be defined, indeed, need not and should not be defined, because they are clear as day, perfectly intelligible by natural light; and they "include the basic topoi of geometrical discourse, such as motion, number, and extension." In geometric discourse, primitive terms are "coextensive" with nominal definitions because their designation, according to Pascal, would be as clear and as unarguable as that of nominal definitions. Nevertheless, the truly Pascalian complication in the "definition" of primitive terms arises because Pascal does not take the dogmatist's route. In the case of primitive terms, he insists, it is not that all men have the same idea of the nature or essence of the thing designated, but rather only the *relation* between the name and the thing: upon hearing the word "time," for example, "all turn (or direct) the mind toward the same object [*tous portent la pensée vers le même objet*]." They may disagree about what time is or about the "nature" of time, but each time they hear or say "time," their thought, the mind, is carried toward the same object. Pascal's having to use a figure (the mind of all being *carried* toward the same spot) provides de Man with the first turning point of his reading, for, quite clearly, the primitive term is *not* a sign constituted by its relation to other signs—not like a nominal definition—but rather a trope:

> Here the word does not function as a sign or a name, as was the case in the
> nominal definition, but as a vector, a directional motion that is manifest
> only as a turn, since the target toward which it turns remains unknown. In
> other words, the sign has become a trope, a substitutive relationship that
> has to posit a meaning whose existence cannot be verified, but that confers
> upon the sign an unavoidable signifying function. The indeterminacy of
> this function is carried by the figural expression "porter la pensée," a figure
> that cannot be accounted for in phenomenal terms. ("Pascal's Allegory")

That the sign here is "a vector" or a "directional motion" that can manifest itself only as a turn or a trope means, in short, that the determination of its referential, carrying-back, function necessarily and inevitably takes place as a trope, and a phenomenalizing trope at that. In other words, it has acquired, or has "conferred" upon it, a "signifying function," as de Man says, which function has to be understood very precisely in terms of the Saussurian distinction between the "signification" and the "value" of a given utterance. (Signification always takes back to the context, the referential context, of an utterance, and is like the exchange of a dollar for a quantity of bread, whereas value is purely intrasemiotic, and is like exchanging a dollar for four quarters or 4.9 francs. As always in the case of Saussure, the distinction goes back to the founding *langue/parole* distinction.) De Man's conclusion is inescapable: "in the language of geometry, nominal definition and primitive terms are coextensive, but the semantic function of the primitive terms is structured like a trope. As such, it acquires a signifying function that it controls neither in its existence nor in its direction" ("Pascal's Allegory"). If it cannot control the signifying function introduced into it by primitive terms, geometric discourse turns into a referentially aberrant discourse. The consequences are considerable. Since primitive terms were supposed to be coextensive with the system of nominal definitions, that system is parasitized, contaminated, from the start by *real* definitions and the potentially aberrant reference of their phenomenalizing tropes. And there would be a further consequence for the system of nominal definition, for the inaugural definition *of* nominal definition itself: namely, that it can take place only by, as, a *real definition*. This should be no surprise since, after all, the very institution of the distinction between nominal and real definition necessarily takes place by the definition of a *relation* between a purportedly closed semiotic system of nominal definitions and an indeterminate world of natures and essences "outside" it that would be the object of real definitions. As the reading of primitive terms demonstrates, this relation cannot be controlled, the borderline between nominal and real definition is itself divided, perforated, for the very means by which we draw the border is itself a real definition (or a "primitive term") that introduces aberrant reference (on the back of an aberrant trope) into the system of nominal definitions. The upshot is that the system of nominal definitions, as a system of signs, cannot account for itself *as* a system, that is, as closed off, because it cannot render itself homogeneous as a sign system. It is contaminated from the start, from the very first definition of nominal definition, by tropes, the signifying function, and the real definition.[26]

This does not mean, of course, that the "system" of Pascal's epistemological discourse and its "geometric method" falls apart or collapses under the pressure of a "self-deconstruction." On the contrary, one could go so far as to say that it is the very rigor of its critical discourse (and the rigor of de Man's account of it)—with its refusal of dogmatic solutions like those of Arnauld and Nicole in *La Logique de Port-Royal*[27]—that is responsible for Pascal's text's *occurring*, its tak-

---

26. Again, the *act* of suspending the referential function is itself referential and leaves traces within the system so constituted.

27. See Louis Marin's *La Critique du discours* (Paris: Éditions de Minuit, 1975) on the relation between Pascal's epistemology and that of the *Logique*. De Man clearly profited a great deal from his reading of Marin's chapter 8—and went further.

ing place as a historical, material event. Its "excess of rigor" means rather that the referential/rhetorical status of Pascal's epistemological discourse is other than, different from, what literalists call philosophy or philosophical discourse—more like allegory than like proof. In the case of "The Mind of the Geometrician," the initial complication of definitional logic inevitably leaves traces and a residue "within" the geometric discourse of Pascal's epistemology—a (material) residue of (aberrant) reference, one might call it, that renders the text an allegory. One place this residue is legible is in Pascal's refutation of the Chevalier de Méré, who would put into question the principle of double infinity (infinite smallness and infinite bigness) that subtends Pascal's cosmos and grounds the "necessary and reciprocal link" among the intraworldly dimensions of motion, number, space, and time. What Méré does, in brief, is to use "the principle of homogeneity between space and number, which is also the ground of Pascal's cosmology, to put the principle of infinitesimal smallness into question" ("Pascal's Allegory"). If it is possible to make up numbers out of units that are themselves devoid of number (i.e., the *one*), then it is possible in the order of space to conceive of an extension made up of parts that are themselves devoid of extension, "thus implying that space can be made up of a finite quantity of indivisible parts, rather than of an infinity of infinitely divisible ones." Pascal's work is cut out for him: on the one hand, he has to dissociate the laws of number from the laws of geometry "by showing that what applies to the indivisible unit of number, the *one*, does not apply to the indivisible unit of space"; but, on the other hand, he has also to suspend the separation between number and space while maintaining it "because the underlying homology of space and number, the ground of the system, should never be fundamentally in question," for theological reasons. Pascal accomplishes the former easily enough by demonstrating that the *one*, despite being (nominally) a nonnumber, "a nominal definition of nonnumber," is nevertheless also homogeneous to the system of number since it is of the same "species" (*genre*) as number. In which case the relation between the *one* and the number system would *not* be like that of the relation between the "indivisible" of extension and space, since the "indivisible" would be *heterogeneous* to space as extension. A "unit" of extension that cannot be divided must be heterogeneous to the order of extension, whereas the one, in being both a number and a nonnumber, is (dialectically) homogeneous to the order of number. Pascal's demonstration works well enough, but it does so because it reintroduces "the ambivalence of definitional language," in which the nominally indivisible number (the one) is distinguished from the *really* indivisible space, "a demonstration that Pascal can accomplish easily, but only because the key words of the demonstration—indivisible, spatial extension (*étendue*), species (*genre*), and definition—function as real, and not as nominal, definitions." This ambivalence returns—and with incalculable effects—in Pascal's second demonstration, in which he in turn must *heal* the break he has introduced between number and space by coming up with an "element" *in* the order of number that would nevertheless be *heterogeneous to* the order of number just as the indivisible is heterogeneous to the order of space as extension. This element is the zero, which, unlike the one, is "radically not a number, absolutely heterogeneous to the order of number." With its equivalences in the order of time and motion—instant and stasis—the zero would reestablish the necessary and reciprocal link among the four intraworldly dimensions: "At the end of the passage, the homogeneity of the universe is recovered, and the principle of infinitesimal symmetry is well established." But the price of this reconciliation is heavy: "the coherence of the system is now seen to be entirely dependent on the introduction of an element—the zero and its equivalences in time and motion—that is itself entirely heterogeneous with regard to the system and is nowhere a part of it." The zero, it turns out, is another moment of signification, of the signifying function or the real definition, without which "a theory of language as sign or as name (nominal definition)" cannot come into existence. It is worth quoting de Man's difficult conclusion on the zero at length:

> The notion of language as sign is dependent on, and derived from, a different notion in which language functions as rudderless signification and transforms what it denominates into the linguistic equivalence of the arithmetical zero. It is as sign that language is capable of engendering the principles of infinity, of genus, species and homogeneity, which allow for synecdochal totalizations, but none of these tropes could come about without the systematic effacement of the zero and its reconversion into a name. There can be no *one* without zero, but the zero always appears in the guise of a *one*, of a (some)thing. The name is the trope of the zero. The zero is always *called* a one, when the zero is actually nameless, "innommable."

The difficulty of this passage and de Man's summary of the effects of the zero is due in part to the fact that his own reading, in its very "excess of rigor," has itself introduced something of a "signifying function" into its own discourse, which threatens to carry it away, or rather back, to a most mechanical, repetitive, stuttering, indeed material, numbering and spacing. For, despite de Man's own apparent suggestion—at least at the beginning of the passage—that we should understand the disruption introduced by the zero as the same as, or at least as similar to, the disruption of the system of nominal definition by primitive terms, there is much more going on here—as the tropological agitation of the passage would already suggest. If "at the end of the most systematic exposition of the theory of the two infinites . . . we find *once again* the ambivalence of the theory of definitional language, which we encountered at the start" (my emphasis), the repetition of our finding "once again" at the end what we encountered at the start has to be understood as a repetition with a difference—indeed, as an allegorical recounting (and reencountering—cf. the predictable problems that attempts to define allegory "keep reencountering" at the start of the essay!) in which the "once" of "once again" should be read like the "once" of "Once upon a time . . . ," as though what we find "once again" and *keep* reencountering were the allegorical start of "Once upon a time . . ." time and time again. What is it, then, that we encounter once again in the reading of the zero and its disruption of the possibility of grounded knowledge? Whatever it is, it is *not* the one and not *like* the one, and explaining the zero's difference from, or, better, *heterogeneity* in relation to, the one may help us to account for the genuine difficulty of de Man's "ending" (and ending *once again* "at the start"). The one, we should remember, was in fact *both* a sign (or a name) *and* a trope: that is, as a mere name given to "the entity that does not possess the properties of number, a nominal definition of nonnumber," the one is clearly a sign; but, as an entity that "partakes of number" and is homogeneous to the system of number, the one is a synecdochal trope that allows for the "synec-dochal totalization of infinitude." In other words, Pascal's dissociating number and space and rendering them heterogeneous in relation to one another by demonstrating that the one is *not* like the indivisible of extension rests upon his homogenization of the one to the number system. And this homogeneity, we would stress, is that of a closed semio-tropological system in which the "line" between sign and trope can be crossed thanks to the dialectical resources of determinate negation, the "non-" of a nonnumber that is nevertheless of the same species as number (a "non-" that was no doubt *already* the result of a "systematic effacement of the zero" which is *not* a nothing, *not* a negation . . .).

The zero, however, is first of all neither a sign nor a trope. Although de Man's saying that the zero introduces a "signifying function" into the order of number and his referring to "the zero of signification" may sound as though we should understand it on the model of primitive terms and their vectorlike "directional motion," we should note that the signifying function of the zero is in fact what de Man calls "rudderless signification." In other words, this may be a signifying function all right, but it is a signifying function deprived of precisely its directionality: as "rudderless," its directional motion is not just indeterminate but nonexistent. In short, if the zero is a trope, it is a still more "primitive" trope than that of primitive terms: at best, it is a trope for trope "itself," or rather for the potentially always aberrant reference that tropes produce. That the zero is also *not* a sign is even more evident, since it is "by definition" (nominal or real? or either?) that which is heterogeneous to the number system in the same way that the indivisible is heterogeneous to space. The zero, one could say, is a bit of space or extension introduced into the system of number considered as a sign system; but, on the other hand, it is also a bit of "pure sign" introduced into the number system considered as synecdochal trope because the zero does not represent or "stand for" something or anything that could be numbered or counted (like the "one more" house in Pascal's demonstration that by itself is *not* a city, "yet a city is made up of houses that are of the same species as the city, since one can always add a house to a city and it remains a city" ["Pascal's Allegory"]). If the zero disrupts Pascal's geometric epistemological discourse and the knowledge of the "marvels" of nature (that its principles of the double infinity and the homogeneity of the universe give access to), it disrupts its claim to being a totalized semio-tropological system. It *signifies* too much (and too little) to be a sign; it *designates* too much (and too little) to be a trope.

This would be at least *some* of the meaning contained in de Man's ambiguous phrase "the zero of signification"; that is, the trouble with the "signifying function" *of* the zero is not that it signifies (and hence is a trope for) something or nothing—for as soon as it is made to do so, it is always some name, some *one*, *some thing*, that it would signify—but rather that it is "really" a "zero *of* signification." It signifies only signification "itself"; in this case, only the impossible attempt to have the number system, as a closed, homogeneous, semio-tropological system, "signify" reliably that which would be outside it, space, extension, the perceivable phenomenal world. In short, again, the "indivisible" may signify something mysterious and impossible to grasp in space, but the zero signifies nothing but that which is undefinable either nominally or really in number. Hence it disjoins, disrupts, interrupts the homogeneity between number as sign (nominal definition) and number as trope (real definition), in the case of the one between the one as nominally nonnumber and the one as synecdochally homogeneous to number. This is where de Man's saying later that the zero (like irony) is "a term that is not susceptible to nominal or real definition" may be of some help. The zero is not susceptible to nominal definition—this would be clear enough, for what does it name, what is it a sign of? It is a "sign" of the other than number, "something" outside the number system, that cannot be accounted for *in terms of number*. But it is also not susceptible to real definition, for in order for it to be a real definition, the zero would have to be a claim about the nature and properties of something outside the number system; it would have to be a *trope* for something, whereas it is rather a trope for *nothing*—but not the nothing *of* space so much as the "nothing" *of* number, the infinitude *un*totalizable for the closed sign/synecdochal trope system that would totalize infinity. One can give a name to infinity, but this name will not be definable *in terms of other names*; and one can signify infinity by means of a trope, but this trope cannot help but be drawn back in, reinscribed into, the sign/trope system that can signify only "the *limit* of the infinitely small, the almost zero that is the one," as de Man puts it. If the zero is neither a sign nor a trope—and both (a sign in the number system as synecdochal trope; a trope in the number system as nominal definition)—but rather a cipher, or a counter, or a marker, that makes the crossing of the "line" between sign and trope (designation and signification) possible (and *im*possible—*except* by recourse to the zero), then what is it? Clearly enough, precisely that: a cipher, counter, marker, or placeholder, a mere device or technique of writing, notation, inscription, a presemiological and prefigural "element" of "language" that makes language as sign and language as trope (im)possible—*une cheville syntaxique*, as Derrida writes, "a syntactical plug," or, better, "a syntactical dowell."[28] If the zero introduces a bit of "space" into number, as we put it folksily, it is a rather peculiar spatiality—not that of space as extension, but rather the spatiality, the spacing, of writing, inscription, the utter exteriority and otherness to designation and signification of inscribed letters. So: it is the zero as material inscription, the zero as *thing*, rather than as sign or as trope, that is the material (and hence historical) condition of the knowledge based on the principles of the infinitesimal and the homogeneous.

In the case of the zero, we have not just the signifying function (trope) interfering within a system of signs, but rather "something" that is neither sign nor trope and (heterogeneously) both at once disrupting a semio-tropo-logical system. The best name (or trope?) for this something is once again material inscription, a bit of materiality in (and of) Pascal's text that cannot but be reproduced (once again) in de Man's account of it. Indeed, we would go so far as to say that de Man's reading of the zero is the place or the moment in his text where his analysis gets pushed beyond its own presuppositions and anticipations to produce something that happens, an event. As it turns out, it is the historical, material event at the "origin" of the texts in this volume—itself a material inscription, whose stutter of sheerly mechanical enumeration is somewhat legible in the sentence that says what it is "we are actually saying" here: "To say then, as we are actually saying, that allegory (as sequential narration) is the trope of irony (as the one is the trope of zero) is to say something that is true enough but not intelligible, which also implies that it cannot be put to work as a device of textual analysis" ("Pascal's Allegory").

That de Man's saying what he wants to say here should interrupt itself with something of a parabasis that calls attention to the *act* of saying—in the phrase "as we are actually saying"—is most appropriate in the context of his own "sequential narration." For he has just been discussing the rhetorical terms that "come close to designating" a disruption like that of the zero—that is, anacoluthon and parabasis—as long as one remembers that the zero's disruption is not topical, that it cannot be located in a single point, and that therefore "the anacoluthon is omnipresent, or, in temporal terms and in Friedrich Schlegel's deliberately unintelligible formulation, the parabasis is permanent." If what "we are actually saying" in de Man's sentence is "not intelligible"—just as unintelligible as Schlegel's "definition" of irony (which, like the zero, is not susceptible to either nominal or real definition) as a "permanent parabasis," the constant possibility of a disruption of narrative intelligibility at every "point" of the narrative line—it is not least of all on account of a certain indeterminacy, a certain aberrancy, of reference here. For the parabasis of "as we are actually saying" refers, takes back, not only to the

---

28. This is a phrase that occurs in the context of Derrida's "definition" of the undecidable. See Jacques Derrida's "La double séance," in *La Dissémination* (Paris: Éditions du Seuil, 1972), p. 250. It is translated by Barbara Johnson as "syntactical plug" in *Dissemination* (Chicago: University of Chicago Press, 1981), p. 221.

unintelligible "something" that follows ("that allegory . . . is the trope of irony [as the one is the trope of zero]"), but also inevitably to the mere act of saying "itself"—"To say . . . , as we are actually saying." And this reference back to the act of saying ends up saying more (or less?) than something as idiomatic and as innocuous as "To say, then, that . . . ," and introduces a certain unaccountable aberrancy because the mere marker or placeholder that calls attention to the act of speaking is already written in the sentence's "then": "To say *then*, as we are actually saying. . . ." If we ignore the apparent mispunctuation for the moment—the poor Belgian should, after all, have written "To say, then, . . ."—this amounts to saying something already quite peculiar: a stutter like "To say, then, then . . . ," which only gets extended (permanently?) if we notice that the "actually" may also carry such a merely marking or placeholding function. There seems to be no end to the self-replicating power of saying mere saying, whatever it is one wants to say, whenever one says something or whenever one says anything at all. The missing comma after "To say" only enforces the madness of this mechanical repetition, for it insists quite clearly and grammatically that what we are actually saying when we say "To say then, as we are actually saying" is in fact only "then"—in which case what we are "actually" saying *now* (as in *actuellement*), in the present, is in fact only a certain weird pastness of saying "itself" ("To say then, then, then, then . . ."), as though all we could say were a certain disjunction between saying and itself, between saying (then) and saying that . . . we are saying (then). And the fact that whenever we say all we can say ("then") we *cannot* tell whether we are saying "then" as a temporal (or causal) indicator or as a mere placeholder that calls attention to the act of saying only accelerates the maddening vertiginousness of our predicament. But however overdetermined and potentially vertiginous the stutter of what we are actually saying may be, it is clear enough what its bottom line amounts to: the narrativization of a stutter, as it were, an allegory of reference that is necessarily also always an "ironic allegory" and "the systematic undoing, in other words, of understanding" (*Allegories*, p. 301). Perhaps most maddening, however, is the fact that our saying all we can say (when we say saying) is not *just* unintelligible (deliberately or otherwise), but also "true enough"—not "true" or "the truth" but only "true enough," as if to say "true, in a sense" or "true, as it were" or "true, figuratively speaking." To ask "How true is 'true enough'?" is, of course, the wrong question, but it is one we are bound to ask over and over, and always once again. It is, in any event, an ironic, allegorical "Truth" that, "far from closing off the tropological system . . . enforces the repetition of its aberration" (*Allegories*, p. 301). As such, such a Truth, or, better, "the true (enough)," is indeed what happens materially, historically—an event. No wonder that its reading will be resisted and deferred for now and for then.[29]

---

29. On irony as "permanent parabasis" and on Friedrich Schlegel's "authentic language" as the language of "error, madness, and simpleminded stupidity," see "The Concept of Irony" in this volume.

Detailed information about the provenance of the texts in this volume is provided in unnumbered footnotes on the first page of each text. The status of the three texts that de Man did not publish himself—"Kant's Materialism" (a Modern Language Association convention talk), "Kant and Schiller," and "The Concept of Irony" (lectures transcribed from audiotapes)—is of course different from the others, and this is why they (along with the previously published "Reply to Raymond Geuss") appear after the essays de Man planned to include in his projected book. (See note 4 of my Introduction for information about de Man's original project for the volume, its Table of Contents, and his [provisional?] title.) I have purposely left the two lectures transcribed from audiotapes in relatively rough, "spoken" form in part because there is no reason to pretend that they were "written" by de Man; they are, in any case, quite legible, and what they lose in "writerliness," they more than make up in the flow and rhythm of de Man's oral delivery (not to mention their humor).

Many people helped in the production of this book. I want to thank Patricia de Man for much generous and good-humored assistance with de Man's papers; Tom Keenan for transcribing and editing "The Concept of Irony"; William Jewett and Thomas Pepper for transcribing "Kant and Schiller"; Deborah White, David McClemont, Georgia Albert, Christopher Diffee, and Madeline Jaroch for editorial and proofreading assistance; Christopher Fynsk, Rick Lightbody, and Marilyn Migiel for tapes; Barbara Spackman for computer help; Tom Cohen and J. Hillis Miller for timely encouragement; Wlad Godzich, Lindsay Waters, Elizabeth Stomberg, and, especially, Biodun Iginla for sublime patience—and, in Biodun's case, for knowing how to draw a deadline. Thanks also to Ellen Burt and Kevin Newmark for friendship and intellectual support; and to Barbara and Chico for not losing faith. I am also grateful to David Thorstad for his careful and intelligent copyediting.

The Epistemology of Metaphor

Metaphors, tropes, and figural language in general have been a perennial problem and, at times, a recognized source of embarrassment for philosophical discourse and, by extension, for all discursive uses of language including historiography and literary analysis. It appears that philosophy either has to give up its own constitutive claim to rigor in order to come to terms with the figurality of its language or that it has to free itself from figuration altogether. And if the latter is considered impossible, philosophy could at least learn to control figuration by keeping it, so to speak, in its place, by delimiting the boundaries of its influence and thus restricting the epistemological damage that it may cause. This attempt stands behind recurrent efforts to map out the distinctions between philosophical, scientific, theological, and poetic discourse and informs such institutional questions as the departmental structure of schools and universities. It also pertains to the received ideas about differences between various schools of philosophical thought, about philosophical periods and traditions, as well as about the possibility of writing a history of philosophy or of literature. Thus, it is customary to assume that the common sense of empirical British philosophy owes much of its superiority over certain continental metaphysical excesses to its ability to circumscribe, as its own style and decorum demonstrate, the potentially disruptive power of rhetoric. "The Skywriters," says a contemporary literary critic (with tongue in cheek) in a recent polemical article, "march under the banner of Hegel and Continental Philosophy,

"The Epistemology of Metaphor" was published in a "Special Issue on Metaphor" of *Critical Inquiry* 5:1 (autumn 1978): 13–30. All notes are de Man's, slightly modified.

while the Common Sense school [of literary criticism] is content with no philosophy, unless it be that of Locke and a homespun organicism."[1]

The mention of Locke in this context certainly does not come unexpectedly since Locke's attitude toward language, and especially toward the rhetorical dimensions of language, can be considered as exemplary or, at any rate, typical of an enlightened rhetorical self-discipline. At times it seems as if Locke would have liked nothing better than to be allowed to forget about language altogether, difficult as this may be in an essay having to do with understanding. Why would one have to concern oneself with language since the priority of experience over language is so obvious? "I must confess then," writes Locke in the *Essay Concerning Human Understanding*, "that, when I first began this discourse of the understanding, and a good while after, I had not the least thought that any consideration of words was at all necessary to it."[2] But, scrupulous and superb writer that he is, by the time he reaches book 3 of his treatise, he can no longer ignore the question:

> But when, having passed over the original and composition of our *ideas*, I began to examine the extent and certainty of our knowledge, I found it had so near a connexion with words that, unless their force and manner of signification were first well observed, there could be very little said clearly and pertinently concerning knowledge, which, being conversant about truth, had constantly to do with propositions. And though it terminated in things, yet it was, for the most part, so much by the intervention of words that they seemed scarce separable from our general knowledge. At least they interpose themselves so much between our understandings and the truth which it would contemplate and apprehend that, like the *medium* through which visible objects pass, their obscurity and disorder does not seldom cast a mist before our eyes and impose upon our understandings. [Bk. 3, chap. 9, pp. 87–88]

Neither is there any doubt about what it is in language that thus renders it nebulous and obfuscating: it is, in a very general sense, the figurative power of language. This power includes the possibility of using language seductively and misleadingly in discourses of persuasion as well as in such intertextual tropes as allusion, in which a complex play of substitutions and repetitions takes place between texts. The following passage is famous but always deserves extensive quotation:

> Since wit and fancy finds easier entertainment in the world than dry truth and real knowledge, *figurative speeches* and allusion in language will

---

1. Geoffrey Hartman, "The Recognition Scene of Criticism," *Critical Inquiry* 4 (winter 1977): 409; now in Hartman's *Criticism in the Wilderness* (New Haven: Yale University Press, 1980).

2. John Locke, *An Essay Concerning Human Understanding*, ed. John W. Yolton, 2 vols. (London and New York: Dutton, 1961), 2:bk. 2, chap.9, p. 87. All further references will appear in the text.

hardly be admitted as *an* imperfection or *abuse* of it. I confess, in discourses where we seek rather pleasure and delight than information and improvement, such ornaments as are borrowed from them can scarce pass for faults. But yet, if we would speak of things as they are, we must allow that all the art of rhetoric, besides order and clearness, all the artificial and figurative application of words eloquence hath invented, are for nothing else but to insinuate wrong *ideas*, move the passions, and thereby mislead the judgment, and so indeed are perfect cheat; and therefore however laudable or allowable oratory may render them in harangues and popular addresses, they are certainly, in all discourses that pretend to inform or instruct, wholly to be avoided and, where truth and knowledge are concerned, cannot but be thought a great fault either of the language or person that makes use of them. What and how various they are will be superfluous here to take notice, the books of rhetoric which abound in the world will instruct those who want to be informed; only I cannot but observe how little the preservation and improvement of truth and knowledge is the care and concern of mankind, since the arts of fallacy are endowed and preferred. It is evident how much men love to deceive and be deceived, since rhetoric, that powerful instrument of error and deceit, has its established professors, is publicly taught, and has always been had in great reputation; and I doubt not but it will be thought great boldness, if not brutality, in me to have said thus much against it. *Eloquence*, like the fair sex, has too prevailing beauties in it to suffer itself ever to be spoken against. And it is in vain to find fault with those arts of deceiving wherein men find pleasure to be deceived. [Bk. 3, chap. 10, pp. 105–6]

Nothing could be more eloquent than this denunciation of eloquence. It is clear that rhetoric is something one can decorously indulge in as long as one knows where it belongs. Like a woman, which it resembles ("like the fair sex"), it is a fine thing as long as it is kept in its proper place. Out of place, among the serious affairs of men ("if we would speak of things as they are"), it is a disruptive scandal—like the appearance of a real woman in a gentlemen's club where it would only be tolerated as a picture, preferably naked (like the image of Truth), framed and hung on the wall. There is little epistemological risk in a flowery, witty passage about wit like this one, except perhaps that it may be taken too seriously by dull-witted subsequent readers. But when, on the next page, Locke speaks of language as a "conduit" that may "corrupt the fountains of knowledge which are in things themselves" and, even worse, "break or stop the pipes whereby it is distributed to public use," then this language, not of poetic "pipes and timbrels" but of a plumber's handyman, raises, by its all too graphic concreteness, questions of propriety. Such far-reaching assumptions are then made about the structure of the mind that one may wonder whether the metaphors illustrate a cognition or if the cognition is not perhaps shaped by the metaphors. And indeed, when Locke then develops his own theory of words and language, what he constructs turns out to be in fact a theory of tropes. Of course, he would be the last man in the world to realize and to acknowledge this. One has to read him, to some extent, against or regardless of his own explicit statements; one especially has to disregard the commonplaces about his philosophy that circulate as reliable currency in the intellectual histories of the Enlightenment. One has to pretend to read him ahistorically, the first and necessary condition if there is to be any expectation of ever arriving at a somewhat reliable history. That is to say, he has to be read not in terms of explicit statements (especially explicit statements about statements) but in terms of the rhetorical motions of his own text, which cannot be simply reduced to intentions or to identifiable facts.

Unlike such later instances as Warburton, Vico, or, of course, Herder, Locke's theory of language is remarkably free of what is now referred to as "cratylic" delusions. The arbitrariness of the sign as signifier is clearly established by him, and his notion of language is frankly semantic rather than semiotic, a theory of signification as a substitution of words for "ideas" (in a specific and pragmatic sense of the term) and not of the linguistic sign as an autonomous structure. "Sounds have no natural connexion with our *ideas*, but have all their signification from the arbitrary imposition of men. . . ." Consequently, Locke's reflection on the use and abuse of words will not start from the words themselves, be it as material or as grammatical entities, but from their meaning. His taxonomy of words will therefore not occur, for example, in terms of parts of speech but will espouse his own previously formulated theory of ideas as subdivided in simple ideas, substances, and mixed modes,[3] best paraphrased in this order since the first two, unlike the third, pertain to entities that exist in nature.

On the level of simple ideas, there seem to be no semantic or epistemological problems since the nominal and the real essence of the species designated by the word coincide; since the idea is simple and undivided, there can in principle be no room for play or ambivalence between the word and the entity, or between property and essence. Yet this lack of differential play immediately leads to a far-reaching consequence: "The *names of simple* ideas *are not capable of any definitions* . . ." (bk. 3, chap. 4, p. 26). Indeed not, since definition involves distinction and is therefore no longer simple. Simple ideas are, therefore, in Locke's system, simpleminded; they are not the objects of understanding. The implication is clear but comes as something of a shock, for what would be more important to understand than simple ideas, the cornerstones of our experience?

In fact, we discourse a great deal about simple ideas. Locke's first example is in the term "motion," and he is well aware of the extent to which metaphysical

---

3. An apparent exception to this principle would be bk. 3, chap. 7, where Locke pleads for the necessity of studying particles of speech as well as nouns. But the assimilation of particles to "some action or insinuation of the mind" of which they are "tracks" reintegrates them at once into the theory of ideas (p. 73).

speculation, in the scholastic as well as in the more strictly Cartesian tradition, centers on the problem of the definition of motion. But nothing in this abundant literature could be elevated to the level of a definition that would answer the question: What is motion? "Nor have the modern philosophers, who have endeavoured to throw off the *jargon* of the Schools and speak intelligibly, much better succeeded in defining simple *ideas*, whether by explaining their causes or any otherwise. The *atomists*, who define motion to be a *passage from one place to another*, what do they more than put one synonymous word for another? For what is *passage* other than *motion*? And if they were asked what passage was, how would they better define it than by *motion*? For is it not at least as proper and significant to say *passage is a motion from one place to another* as to say *motion is a passage*, etc. This is to translate and not to define . . ." (bk. 3, chap. 4, p. 28). Locke's own "passage" is bound to continue this perpetual motion that never moves beyond tautology: motion is a passage and passage is a translation; translation, once again, means motion, piles motion upon motion. It is no mere play of words that "translate" is translated in German as *übersetzen,* which itself translates the Greek *meta phorein* or metaphor. Metaphor gives itself the totality which it then claims to define, but it is in fact the tautology of its own position. The discourse of simple ideas is figural discourse or translation and, as such, creates the fallacious illusion of definition.

Locke's second example of a word for a simple idea is "light." He takes pains to explain that the word "light" does not refer to the perception of light and that to understand the causal process by which light is produced and perceived is not at all the same as to understand light. In fact, to understand light is to be able to make this very distinction between the actual cause and the idea (or experience) of a perception, between aperception and perception. When we can do this, says Locke, then the *idea* is that which is *properly* light, and we come as close as we can come to the proper meaning of "light." To understand light as idea is to understand light properly. But the word "idea" (*eide*), of course, itself means light, and to say that to understand light is to perceive the idea of light is to say that understanding is to see the light of light and is therefore itself light. The sentence: to understand the idea of light would then have to be translated as to light the light of light (*das Licht des Lichtes lichten*), and if this begins to sound like Heidegger's translations from the Pre-Socratics, it is not by chance. Etymons have a tendency to turn into the repetitive stutter of tautology. Just as the word "passage" translates but fails to define motion, "idea" translates but does not define light and, what is worse, "understand" translates but does not define understanding. The first idea, the simple idea, is that of light in motion or figure, but the figure is not a *simple* idea but a delusion of light, of understanding, or of definition. This complication of the simple will run through the entire argument, which is itself the motion of this complication (of motion).

Things indeed get more complex as one moves from simple ideas to substances.

They can be considered in two perspectives: either as a collection of properties or as an essence which supports these properties as their ground. The example for the first model of a substance is "gold," not unrelated, in some of its properties, to the solar light in motion. The structure of substances considered as a collection of properties upsets the convergence of nominal and real essences that made the utterer of simple ideas into something of a stuttering idiot but, at least from an epistemological point of view, a happy one. For one thing, properties are not just the idea of motion, they actually move and travel. One will find gold in the most unexpected places—for instance, in the tail of a peacock. "I think all agree to make [gold] stand for a body of a certain yellow shining colour; which being the *idea* to which children have annexed that name, the shining yellow part of a peacock's tail is properly to them gold" (bk. 3, chap. 9, p. 85). The closer the description comes to that of metaphor, the more dependent Locke becomes on the use of the word "properly." Like the blind man who cannot understand the idea of light, the child who cannot tell the figural from the proper keeps recurring throughout eighteenth-century epistemology as a barely disguised figure of our universal predicament. For not only are tropes, as their name implies, always on the move— more like quicksilver than like flowers or butterflies, which one can at least hope to pin down and insert in a neat taxonomy—but they can disappear altogether, or at least appear to disappear. Gold not only has a color and a texture, but it is also soluble. "For by what right is it that fusibility comes to be a part of the essence signified by the word *gold*, and solubility but a property of it? . . . That which I mean is this: that these being all but properties, depending on its real constitution, and nothing but powers either active or passive in reference to other bodies, no one has authority to determine the signification of the word *gold* (as referred to such a body existing in nature) . . ." (bk. 3, chap. 9, pp. 85–86). Properties, it seems, do not properly totalize, or, rather, they totalize in a haphazard and unreliable way. It is indeed not a question of ontology, of things as they are, but of authority, of things as they are decreed to be. And this authority cannot be vested in any authoritative body, for the free usage of ordinary language is carried, like the child, by wild figuration which will make a mockery of the most authoritarian academy. We have no way of defining, of policing, the boundaries that separate the name of one entity from the name of another; tropes are not just travelers, they tend to be smugglers and probably smugglers of stolen goods at that. What makes matters even worse is that there is no way of finding out whether they do so with criminal intent or not.

Perhaps the difficulty stems from a misconceived notion of the paradigm "substance." Instead of being considered as a collection, as a summation of properties, the accent should perhaps fall on the link that binds the properties together. Substances can be considered as the support, the ground of the properties (*hypokeimenon*). Here Locke's example will be "man"; the question to be accounted for then becomes: What essence is the proper of man? The question in fact amounts to whether the proper, which is a linguistic notion, and the essence, which exists independently of linguistic mediation, can coincide. As the creature endowed with conceptual language, "man" is indeed the entity, the place where this convergence is said to take place. The epistemological stakes are therefore higher in the case of the example "man" than in the case of "gold." But so are the difficulties, for, in answer to the question "What essence is the proper of man?" the tradition confronts us with two perhaps incompatible answers. Man can be defined in terms of his outward appearance (as in Plato: *animal implume bipes latis unguibus*) but also in terms of his inner soul or being. "For though the sound *man*, in its own nature, be as apt to signify a complex *idea* made up of animality and rationality, united in the same subject, as to signify any other combination: yet, used as a mark to stand for a sort of creatures we count of our own kind, perhaps the outward shape is as necessary to be taken into our complex *idea*, signified by the word *man*, as any other we find in it . . . for it is the shape, as the leading quality, that seems more to determine that species than a faculty of reasoning, which appears not at first and in some never" (bk. 3, chap. 11, p. 115). The problem is that of a necessary link between the two elements in a binary polarity, between "inside" and "outside," that is to say, by all accounts, that of metaphor as the figure of complementarity and correspondence. One now sees that this figure is not only ornamental and aesthetic but powerfully coercive since it generates, for example, the ethical pressure of such questions as "to kill or not to kill." "And if this be not allowed to be so," says Locke, "I do not know how they can be excused from murder who kill monstrous births (as we call them) because of an unordinary shape, without knowing whether they have a rational soul or no, which can be no more discerned in a well-formed than ill-shaped infant as soon as born" (bk. 3, chap. 11, p. 115). The passage is, of course, primarily a mock argument, a hyperbolical example to unsettle the unquestioned assumption of definitional thought. Yet it has its own logic, which will have to run its course. For how could anyone "allow" something to be if it is not necessarily the case that it is? For it is not necessarily the case that the inner and the outer man are the same man, that is to say, are "man" at all. The predicament (to kill or not to kill the monstrous birth) appears here in the guise of a purely logical argument. But not much further along in the *Essay*, what is "only" an argument in book 3 becomes an ethically charged issue in book 4, chapter 4, which is entitled "Of the Reality of Knowledge."[4] The problem there under discussion is what to do with the "changeling"; the simple-minded child so called because it would be natural for anyone to assume that this child has been substituted by mistake for his real offspring. The substitutive text of tropes now has extended to reality.

---

4. Examples used in logical arguments have a distressing way of lingering on with a life of their own. I suppose no reader of J. L. Austin's paper "On Excuses" has ever been quite able to forget the "case" of the inmate in an insane asylum parboiled to death by a careless guard.

The well-shaped *changeling* is a man, has a rational soul, though it appear not: this is past doubt, say you. Make the ears a little longer and more pointed, and the nose a little flatter than ordinary, and then you begin to boggle; make the face yet narrower, flatter, and longer, and then you are at a stand; add still more and more of the likeness of a brute to it, and let the head be perfectly that of some other animal, then presently it is a *monster*, and it is demonstration with you that it hath no rational soul and must be destroyed. Where now (I ask) shall be the just measure, which the utmost bounds of that shape that carries with it a rational soul? For since there have been human *foetuses* produced, half-beast and half-man, and others three parts one and one part the other, and so it is possible they may be in all the variety of approaches to the one or the other shape and may have several degrees of mixture of the likeness of a man or a brute, I would gladly know what are those precise lineaments which, according to this hypothesis, are or are not capable of a rational soul to be joined to them. What sort of outside is the certain sign that there is or is not such an inhabitant within? [Bk. 4, chap. 4, p. 175]

If we then are invited by Locke, in conclusion, to "quit the common notion of species and essences," this would reduce us to the mindless stammer of simple ideas and make us into a philosophical "changeling," with the unpleasant consequences that have just been conjectured. As we move from the mere contiguity between words and things in the case of simple ideas to the metaphorical correspondence of properties and essences in substances, the ethical tension has considerably increased.

Only this tension could account for the curious choice of examples selected by Locke when he moves on to the uses and possible abuses of language in mixed modes. His main examples are manslaughter, incest, parricide, and adultery—when any nonreferential entity such as mermaid or unicorn would have done just as well.[5] The full list of examples—"motion," "light," "gold," "man," "manslaughter," "parricide," "adultery," "incest"—sounds more like a Greek tragedy than the enlightened moderation one tends to associate with the author of *On Government*. Once the reflection on the figurality of language is started, there is no telling where it may lead. Yet there is no way *not* to raise the question if there is to be any understanding. The use and abuse of language cannot be separated from each other.

"Abuse" of language is, of course, itself the name of a trope: catachresis. This is indeed how Locke describes mixed modes. They are capable of inventing the

---

5. In the general treatment of mixed modes, Locke lists "adultery" and "incest" (p. 34). In the subsequent discussion of the abuses of language, he returns to the problem of mixed modes and gives as examples manslaughter, murder, and parricide, as well as the legal term often associated with manslaughter, "chance medley." Mermaids and unicorns are mentioned in another context in bk. 3, chap. 3, p. 25.

most fantastic entities by dint of the positional power inherent in language. They can dismember the texture of reality and reassemble it in the most capricious of ways, pairing man with woman or human being with beast in the most unnatural shapes. Something monstrous lurks in the most innocent of catachreses: when one speaks of the legs of the table or the face of the mountain, catachresis is already turning into prosopopeia, and one begins to perceive a world of potential ghosts and monsters. By elaborating his theory of language as a motion from simple ideas to mixed modes, Locke has deployed the entire fan-shape or (to remain within light imagery) the entire spectrum or rainbow of tropological totalization, the anamorphosis of tropes which has to run its full course whenever one engages, however reluctantly or tentatively, the question of language as figure. In Locke, it began in the arbitrary, metonymic contiguity of word-sounds to their meanings, in which the word is a mere token in the service of the natural entity, and it concludes with the catachresis of mixed modes in which the word can be said to produce of and by itself the entity it signifies and that has no equivalence in nature. Locke condemns catachresis severely: "he that hath *ideas* of substances disagreeing with the real existence of things, so far wants the materials of true knowledge in his understanding, and hath instead thereof *chimeras*. . . . He that thinks the name *centaur* stands for some real being, imposes on himself and mistakes words for things" (bk. 3, chap. 10, p. 104). But the condemnation, by Locke's own argument, now takes all language for its target, for at no point in the course of the demonstration can the empirical entity be sheltered from tropological defiguration. The ensuing situation is intolerable and makes the soothing conclusion of book 3, entitled "Of the Remedies of the Foregoing Imperfections and Abuses [of Language]," into one of the least convincing sections of the *Essay*. One turns to the tradition engendered by Locke's work in the hope of finding some assistance out of the predicament.

Condillac's *Essai sur l'origine des connaissances humaines* constantly advertises, perhaps even exaggerates, its dependence on Locke's *Essay*. It contains at least two sections that explicitly deal with the question of language; in fact, its systematic commitment to a theory of mind that is in fact a theory of the sign makes it difficult to isolate any part of the treatise that is not modeled on a linguistic structure. Two sections, however, openly and explicitly deal with language: the chapter on the origins of language, "Du langage et de la méthode," which makes up the second part of the *Essai*, and another section, "Des abstractions" (pt. 1, sec. 5). From Rousseau to Michel Foucault, the former section (which elaborates the notion of "langage d'action") has received much attention. But the chapter on abstract terms also deals with language in a more inclusive way than its title would seem to indicate. It can be shown, though this is not my present purpose, that the subsequent chapters on "langage d'action" are a special case of the more inclusive model and history set up in this section. Read in conjunction with

Locke's "On Words," it allows for a wider perspective on the tropological structure of discourse.

At first sight, the brief chapter seems to deal with only one rather specialized use of language, that of conceptual abstractions. But "abstractions" are defined from the start in a way that considerably expands the semantic field covered by the term. They come into being, says Condillac, "by ceasing to think [*en cessant de penser*] of the properties by which things are distinguished in order to think only of those in which they agree [or correspond: the French word is *conviennent*] with each other."[6] The structure of the process is once more precisely that of metaphor in its classical definition. Some hundred and thirty years later, Nietzsche will make the very same argument to show that a word such as "leaf" (*Blatt*) is formed by "making what is different equal [*Gleichsetzen des Nichtgleichen*]" and by "arbitrarily dropping individual differences [*beliebiges Fallenlassen der individuellen Verschiedenheiten*]."[7] And a few years after Condillac, Rousseau will make the same argument in his analysis of denomination in the second *Discourse*.[8] It is entirely legitimate to conclude that when Condillac uses the term "abstraction," it can be "translated" as metaphor or, if one agrees with the point that was made with reference to Locke about the self-totalizing transformation of all tropes, as trope. As soon as one is willing to be made aware of their epistemological implications, concepts are tropes and tropes concepts.

Condillac spells out these implications in what reads like the plot of a somewhat odd story. He implicitly acknowledges the generalized meaning of the term "abstraction" by insisting that no discourse would be conceivable that does not make use of abstractions: "[abstractions] are certainly absolutely necessary [*elles sont sans doute absolument nécessaires*]" (sec. 2, p. 174). On the other hand, he cautions at once against the threat their seductive power constitutes for rational discourse: just as certainly as they are indispensable, they are necessarily defective or even corruptive—"however corruptive [*vicieux*] this contradiction may be, it is nevertheless necessary" (sec. 6, p. 176). Worse still, abstractions are capable of infinite proliferation. They are like weeds, or like a cancer; once you have begun using a single one, they will crop up everywhere. They are said to be "marvelously fecund" (sec. 7, p. 177), but there is something of Rappaccini's garden about them, something sinister about those vigorous plants that no gardener can do without nor keep in check. Even after their ambivalent nature has been ana

6. Condillac, *Essai sur l'origine des connaissances humaines* (1746), ed. Charles Porset (Paris: Galilée, 1973), bk. 1, sec. 2, p. 194. All further references will be from bk. 1, chap. 5 and will appear in the text; here and elsewhere, my translation.

7. Friedrich Nietzsche, "Über Wahrheit und Lüge im außermoralischen Sinne" in *Werke*, ed. Karl Schlechta, 3 vols. (Munich: Hanser, 1969), 3:313.

8. Jean-Jacques Rousseau, *Deuxième Discours (Sur l'origine et les fondements de l'inégalité)*, ed. Jean Starobinski, in *Œuvres complètes*, 5 vols. (Paris: Gallimard, 1964), 3:148.

lyzed on an advanced level of critical understanding, there is very little hope they can be mastered: "I don't know if, after all that I have said, it will at last be possible to forego all these 'realized' abstractions: many reasons make me fear the opposite is true" (sec. 12, p. 179).[9] The story is like the plot of a Gothic novel in which someone compulsively manufactures a monster on which he then becomes totally dependent and does not have the power to kill. Condillac (who, after all, went down in the anecdotal history of philosophy as the inventor of a mechanical statue able to smell roses) bears a close resemblance to Ann Radcliffe or Mary Shelley.

From the recognition of language as trope, one is led to the telling of a tale, to the narrative sequence I have just described. The temporal deployment of an initial complication, of a structural knot, indicates the close, though not necessarily complementary, relationship between trope and narrative, between knot and plot. If the referent of a narrative is indeed the tropological structure of its discourse, then the narrative will be the attempt to account for this fact. This is what happens in the most difficult, but also the most rewarding, section of Condillac's text.

Paragraph 6 starts out with a description of first or simple ideas in a manner reminiscent of Locke; the main stress is on *ideas* rather than on *first*, for Condillac stresses the conceptual aspect of all ideas, regardless of order. He contrasts a reality, which is presumably that of things in themselves, with what he calls, somewhat tautologically, "a true reality [*une vraie réalité*]." This true reality is not located in things but in the subject, which is also the mind as *our* mind ("notre esprit"). It is the result of an operation the mind performs upon entities, an aperception ("apercevoir en nous") and not a perception. The language which describes this operation in Condillac's text is consistently, and more so than in Locke's, a language of mastery of the subject over entities: things become "truly real" only by being appropriated and seized upon with all the etymological strength implied in *Begriff*, the German word for concept. To understand is to seize (*begreifen*) and not to let go of what one has thus taken hold of. Condillac says that impressions will be considered by the mind only if they are "locked up [*renfermées*]" in it. And as one moves from the personal subject "nous" to the grammatical subject of all the sentences ("notre esprit"), it becomes clear that this action of the mind is also the action of the subject.

Why does the subject have to behave in such a potentially violent and authoritarian way? The answer is clear: this is the only way in which it can constitute its own existence, its own ground. Entities, in themselves, are neither distinct nor defined; no one could say where one entity ends and where another begins. They are mere flux, "modifications." By considering itself as the place where this flux

---

9. The French word *réaliser* is used in a precise technical sense. The abstractions are mistaken for "real" objects in the same way Locke speaks of the danger of mistaking words for things. The reason for this error becomes clear later in the text.

occurs, the mind stabilizes itself as the ground of the flux, the *lieu de passage* through which all reality has to pass: ". . . these 'modifications' change and follow each other incessantly in [our mind's] being, which then appears to itself as a ground [*un certain fond*] that remains forever the same" (sec. 6, p. 176). The terminology is a mixture of Locke and Descartes (or Malebranche). The subject seen as a compulsive stabilization that cannot be separated from an unsettling action upon reality performed by this very subject is a version of a Cartesian cogito— except that the function performed in Descartes's second and third "Meditation" by hyperbolic doubt becomes here, in the tradition of Locke, a function of empirical perception. Hyperbolic doubt, a mental act in Descartes, now extends to the entire field of empirical experience.

The self-constitutive act of the subject has, in Condillac (as in Descartes), a much more openly reflexive status than in Locke. The verb most frequently associated with the subject "mind" is "to reflect [*réfléchir*]": "since our mind is too limited to *reflect* . . ."; "the mind cannot *reflect* on nothing. . . ." To reflect is an analytical act that distinguishes differences and articulates reality; these articulations are called abstractions, and they would have to include any conceivable act of denomination or predication. This is also the point at which an act of ontological legerdemain enters the system: the subject (or mind) depends on something which is not itself, here called "modifications" ("certain sensations of light, color, etc., or certain operations of the soul . . ."), in order to be at all, but these modifications are themselves as devoid of being as the mind—cut off from its differentiating action, they are nothing. As the other of the mind, they are devoid of being, but by recognizing them as similar to itself in this negative attribute, the mind sees them, as in a specular reflection, as being both itself and not itself at the same time. The mind "is" to the extent that it "is like" its other in its inability to be. The attribute of being is dependent on the assertion of a similarity which is illusory, since it operates at a stage that precedes the constitution of entities. "How will these experiences, taken abstractly, or separately, from the entity [the mind] to which they belong and to which they correspond only to the extent that they are locked up in it, how will these experiences become the object of the mind? Because the mind persists in considering them as if they were entities in themselves. . . . The mind contradicts itself. On the one hand, it considers these experiences without any relation to its own being, and then they are nothing at all; on the other hand, because nothingness cannot be comprehended, it considers them as if they were something, and persists in giving them the same reality with which it at first perceived them, although this reality can no longer correspond to them." Being and identity are the result of a resemblance which is not in things but posited by an act of the mind which, as such, can only be verbal. And since to be verbal, in this context, means to allow substitutions based on illusory resemblances (the determining illusion being that of a shared negativity), then mind, or subject, is the central metaphor, the metaphor of metaphors. The power of tropes, which Locke sensed in a diffuse way, is here condensed in the key metaphor of the subject as mind. What was a general and implicit theory of tropes in Locke becomes in Condillac a more specific theory of metaphor. Locke's third-person narrative about things in the world becomes here the autobiographical discourse of the subject. Different as the two narratives may be, they are still the allegory of the same tropological aporia. It now also becomes more directly threatening since we, as subjects, are explicitly inscribed within the narrative. One feels more than ever compelled to turn elsewhere for assistance and, staying in the same philosophical tradition, Kant would seem to be the obvious place.

Kant rarely discusses the question of tropes and rhetoric directly but comes closest in a passage from the *Critique of Judgment* that deals with the distinction between schemata and symbolic language. He starts out from the term "hypotyposis," which, used, as he does, in a very inclusive way, designates what, after Peirce, one might call the iconic element in a representation. Hypotyposis makes present to the senses something which is not within their reach, not just because it does not happen to be there but because it consists, in whole or in part, of elements too abstract for sensory representation. The figure most closely akin to hypotyposis is that of prosopopeia; in its most restricted sense, prosopopeia makes accessible to the senses, in this case the ear, a voice which is out of earshot because it is no longer alive. In its most inclusive and also its etymological sense, it designates the very process of figuration as giving face to what is devoid of it.

In section 59 of the *Critique of Judgment* ("Of the Beautiful as a Symbol of Public Morality"), Kant is primarily concerned with the distinction between schematic and symbolic hypotyposes. He begins by objecting to the improper use of the term "symbolic" for what we still call today *symbolic* logic. Mathematical symbols used in algorithms are in fact semiotic indices. They should not be called symbols because "they contain nothing that belongs to the representation [*Anschauung*] of the object." There is no relationship whatever between their iconic properties and those of the object, if it has any. Things are different in the case of a genuine hypotyposis. A relationship exists but it can differ in kind. In the case of schemata, which are objects of the mind (*Verstand*), the corresponding aperception is a priori, as would be the case, presumably, for a triangle or any other geometrical shape. In the case of symbols, which are objects of reason (*Vernunft*) comparable to Condillac's abstractions, no sensory representation would be appropriate (*angemessen*, i.e., sharing a common ratio), but such a similarity is "understood" to exist by analogy (*unterlegt*, which could be translated by saying that an "underlying" similarity is created between the symbol and the thing symbolized). Kant then illustrates at some length the distinction between an actual and an analogical resemblance. In an analogy, the sensory properties of the *analogon* are not the same as those of the original, but they function according to a similar formal principle. For example, an enlightened state will be symbolized by an organic body in which part and whole relate in a free and harmonious way, whereas a tyranny will be properly symbolized by a machine such as a treadmill. Everyone understands that the state *is* not a body or a machine but that it functions like one, and that this function is conveyed more economically by the symbol than by lengthy abstract explanations. We seem at last to have come closer to controlling the tropes. This has become possible because there seem to be, for Kant, tropes that are epistemologically reliable. The denominative noun "triangle," in geometry, is a trope, a hypotyposis which allows for the representation of an abstraction by a substitutive figure, yet the representation is fully rational and *angemessen*. By showing that one can move from the symbolic order, which is indeed imprecise and therefore exists in the restrictive mode of the *only* (the word *bloß* recurs four times in the passage), to the rational precision of the schemata, while remaining within the general tropological field defined by the hypotyposis, the epistemological threat that disturbed Locke and Condillac seems to have been laid to rest. The solution is dependent, however, on a decisive either/or distinction between symbolic and schematic language. Representation is either schematic or symbolic ("entweder Schemate oder Symbole"), and the critical mind can decisively distinguish between both.

At this point in the argument, Kant interrupts his exposition for a digression on the all-too-often-overlooked prevalence of figures in philosophical discourse, an important question which "would deserve a more exhaustive examination." But this is not the time nor the place for such an examination—which he, in fact, never undertook in a systematic way. The terminology of philosophers is full of metaphors. Kant cites several examples, all of them having to do with grounding and standing: "ground [*Grund*]," "to depend [*abhängen*]," "to follow from [*fließen*]" and, with a reference to Locke, "substance." All these hypotyposes are symbolic and not schematic, which means that they are not reliable from an epistemological point of view. They are "a mere translation [*Übertragung*] from a reflexion upon a represented object into an entirely different concept, to which *perhaps* no representation could ever correspond [*dem* vielleicht *nie eine Anschauung direkt korrespondieren kann*]" (emphasis mine). The appearance of the word "perhaps" in this sentence, even though it sounds like a casual side remark, is most surprising. It has been the point of the entire argument that we know for certain whether a representation directly corresponds to a given concept or not. But the "perhaps" raises the question of how such a decision can be made, whether it is in the nature of things or whether it is merely assumed (*unterlegt*). Is the distinction between schemata and symbol itself a priori or is it merely "understood" in the hope of having it perform the definitional work that cannot be performed directly? From the moment this decision can be said, even in passing, to be "perhaps" possible, the theory of a schematic hypotyposis loses much of its power of conviction. Things happen, in the text, as if Kant had not at first been aware of the metaphorical status of his own term *unterlegen* when he used it in support of a crucial distinction between two modes of support. The considerations about the possible danger of uncontrolled metaphors, focused on the cognate figures of support, ground, and so forth, reawaken the hidden uncertainty about the rigor of a distinction that does not hold if the language in which it is stated reintroduces the elements of indetermination it sets out to eliminate. For it is not obvious that the iconic representation that can be used to illustrate a rational concept is indeed a figure. In the second *Discourse,* Rousseau confronts a similar question[10] but concludes that the particular representation that any general concept necessarily engenders is a psychological epiphenomenon related to memory and to the imagination and not a conceptual trope that belongs to the realm of language and knowledge. What Kant calls a schematic hypotyposis would, then, not be a cognition at all but a mere mnemotechnic device, the equivalent of the mathematical sign in the area of the psychology of perception rather than of language. In that case, the sentence, which emphasizes that the decision as to whether a representation can be adequate to its object is of the order of the "perhaps," is more rigorous than the either/or distinction, despite, or rather because, of its vagueness. If the distinction between a priori and symbolic judgments can only be stated by means of metaphors that are themselves symbolic, then Locke's and Condillac's difficulties have not been overcome. Not only our knowledge of God, to which the passage under examination returns at the end, but the knowledge of knowledge is then bound to remain symbolic. He who takes it for schematic and gives it the attributes of predictability and transcendental authority that pertain to the objective reality of entities unmediated by language is guilty of reification (the opposite figure of prosopopeia); and he who thinks that the symbolic can be considered a stable property of language, that language, in other words, is purely symbolic and nothing else, is guilty of aestheticism—"whereby nothing is seen as it is, not in practice either."

In all three instances, we started out from a relatively self-assured attempt to control tropes by merely acknowledging their existence and circumscribing their impact. Locke thought that all we needed to banish rhetoric from the councils of the philosophers was an ethical determination of high seriousness coupled with an alert eye for interlopers. Condillac limits the discussion to the sphere of abstractions, a part of language that appeals neither to poets nor to empirical philosophers; he seems to claim that all will be well if we abstain from taking these cumbersome terms for realities. Kant seems to think that the entire question lacks urgency and that tidy critical housekeeping can rehabilitate rhetoric and make it epistemologically respectable. But, in each case, it turns out to be impossible to maintain a clear line of distinction between rhetoric, abstraction, symbol, and all other forms of language. In each case, the resulting undecidability is due to the

---

10. Rousseau, *Deuxième Discours,* p. 150.

asymmetry of the binary model that opposes the figural to the proper meaning of the figure. The ensuing anxiety surfaces obliquely in the case of Locke and Condillac; it would take a much longer demonstration to indicate that Kant's critical philosophy is disturbed by similar hesitations, but the somewhat surprising theological allusion at the end of our passage may be a symptom. The manifest effacement of such anxiety-traces in the texts is much less important, however, than the contradictory structures of the texts themselves, as it is brought out by a reading willing to take their own rhetoric into consideration.

As Kant just taught us, when things run the risk of becoming too difficult, it is better to postpone the far-reaching consequences of an observation for a later occasion. My main point stresses the futility of trying to repress the rhetorical structure of texts in the name of uncritically preconceived text models such as transcendental teleologies or, at the other end of the spectrum, mere codes. The existence of literary codes is not in question, only their claim to represent a general and exhaustive textual model. Literary codes are subcodes of a system, rhetoric, that is not itself a code. For rhetoric cannot be isolated from its epistemological function, however negative this function may be. It is absurd to ask whether a code is true or false, but impossible to bracket this question when tropes are involved—and this always seems to be the case. Whenever the question is repressed, tropological patterns reenter the system in the guise of such formal categories as polarity, recurrence, normative economy, or in such grammatical tropes as negation and interrogation. They are always again totalizing systems that try to ignore the disfiguring power of figuration. It does not take a good semiotician long to discover that he is in fact a rhetorician in disguise.

The implications of these parallel arguments for literary history and for literary aesthetics are equally controversial. A historian caught in received models of periodization may find it absurd to read texts that belong to the Enlightenment as if one were reading Nietzsche's "Über Wahrheit und Lüge im außermoralischen Sinne" or Jacques Derrida's "La mythologie blanche." But if we assume, just for the sake of argument, that these same historians would concede that Locke, Condillac, and Kant can be read as we have here read them, then they would have to conclude that our own literary modernity has reestablished contact with a "true" Enlightenment that remained hidden from us by a nineteenth-century romantic and realist epistemology that asserted a reliable rhetoric of the subject or of representation. A continuous line could then be said to extend from Locke to Rousseau to Kant and to Nietzsche, a line from which Fichte and Hegel, among others, would very definitely be excluded. But are we so certain that we know how to read Fichte and Hegel in the properly rhetorical manner? Since we assume that it is possible to coordinate Locke and Nietzsche by claiming that their similarly ambivalent attitudes toward rhetoric have been systematically overlooked, there is no reason to assume a priori that a similar argument could not be made with regard to Fichte or Hegel. It would have to be a very different argument, of course, especially in the case of Hegel, but it is not inconceivable that it can be made. And if one accepts, again merely for the sake of argument, that syntagmatic narratives are part of the same system as paradigmatic tropes (though not necessarily complementary), then the possibility arises that temporal articulations, such as narratives or histories, are a correlative of rhetoric and not the reverse. One would then have to conceive of a rhetoric of history prior to attempting a history of rhetoric or of literature or of literary criticism. Rhetoric, however, is not in itself a historical but an epistemological discipline. This may well account for the fact that patterns of historical periodization are at the same time so productive as heuristic devices yet so demonstratively aberrant. They are one way of access, among others, to the tropological structure of literary texts and, as such, they necessarily undermine their own authority.

Finally, our argument suggests that the relationship and the distinction between literature and philosophy cannot be made in terms of a distinction between aesthetic and epistemological categories. All philosophy is condemned, to the extent that it is dependent on figuration, to be literary and, as the depository of this very problem, all literature is to some extent philosophical. The apparent symmetry of these statements is not as reassuring as it sounds since what seems to bring literature and philosophy together is, as in Condillac's argument about mind and object, a shared lack of identity or specificity.

Contrary to common belief, literature is not the place where the unstable epistemology of metaphor is suspended by aesthetic pleasure, although this attempt is a constitutive moment of its system. It is rather the place where the possible convergence of rigor and pleasure is shown to be a delusion. The consequences of this lead to the difficult question whether the entire semantic, semiological, and performative field of language can be said to be covered by tropological models, a question which can only be raised after the proliferating and disruptive power of figural language has been fully recognized.

Pascal's Allegory of Persuasion

Attempts to define allegory keep reencountering a set of predictable problems, of which the summary can serve as a preliminary characterization of the mode. Allegory is sequential and narrative, yet the topic of its narration is not necessarily temporal at all, thus raising the question of the referential status of a text whose semantic function, though strongly in evidence, is not primarily determined by mimetic moments; more than ordinary modes of fiction, allegory is at the furthest possible remove from historiography. The "realism" that appeals to us in the details of medieval art is a calligraphy rather than a mimesis, a technical device to ensure that the emblems will be correctly identified and decoded, not an appeal to the pagan pleasures of imitation. For it is part of allegory that, despite its obliqueness and innate obscurity, the resistance to understanding emanates from the difficulty or censorship inherent in the statement and not from the devices of enunciation: Hegel rightly distinguishes between allegory and enigma in terms of allegory's "aim for the most complete clarity, so that the external means it uses must be as transparent as possible with regard to the meaning it is to make apparent."[1] The difficulty of allegory is rather that this emphatic clarity of representation does not stand in the service of something that can be represented.

"Pascal's Allegory of Persuasion" was published in Stephen J. Greenblatt, ed., *Allegory and Representation, Selected Papers from the English Institute, 1979–80* (Baltimore: Johns Hopkins University Press, 1981), pp. 1–25. All notes (except 18) are de Man's, slightly modified.

1. G. W. F. Hegel, *Vorlesungen über die Ästhetik I*, Theorie Werkausgabe (Frankfurt am Main: Suhrkamp, 1970), p. 511. All translations are my own.

The consequence, throughout the history of the term *allegory*, is a recurrent ambivalence in its aesthetic valorization. Allegory is frequently dismissed as wooden, barren (*kahl*), ineffective, or ugly, yet the reasons for its ineffectiveness, far from being a shortcoming, are of such all-encompassing magnitude that they coincide with the furthest-reaching achievements available to the mind and reveal boundaries that aesthetically more successful works of art, because of this very success, were unable to perceive. To remain with Hegel a moment longer, the aesthetic condemnation of allegory, which becomes evident in the assumed inferiority of Virgil with regard to Homer, is outdone, in Hegel's own allegory of history, by its assignation to the meta-aesthetic age of Christianity, thus making the triadic procession from Homer to Virgil to Dante characteristic for the history of art itself as the dialectical overcoming of art.[2] The theoretical discussion of the uncertain value of allegory repeats, in the *Aesthetics*, the theoretical discussion of the uncertain value of art itself. In the wavering status of the allegorical sign, the system of which the allegorical is a constitutive component is being itself unsettled.

Allegory is the purveyor of demanding truths, and thus its burden is to articulate an epistemological order of truth and deceit with a narrative or compositional order of persuasion. In a stable system of signification, such an articulation is not problematic; a representation is, for example, persuasive and convincing to the extent that it is faithful, exactly in the same manner that an argument is persuasive to the extent that it is truthful. Persuasion and proof should not, in principle, be distinct from each other, and it would not occur to a mathematician to call his proofs allegories. From a theoretical point of view, there ought to be no difficulty in moving from epistemology to persuasion. The very occurrence of allegory, however, indicates a possible complication. Why is it that the furthest-reaching truths about ourselves and the world have to be stated in such a lopsided, referentially indirect mode? Or, to be more specific, why is it that texts that attempt the articulation of epistemology with persuasion turn out to be inconclusive about their own intelligibility in the same manner and for the same reasons that produce allegory? A large number of such texts on the relationship between truth and persuasion exist in the canon of philosophy and of rhetoric, often crystallized around such traditional philosophical topoi as the relationship between analytic and synthetic judgments, between propositional and modal logic, between logic and mathematics, between logic and rhetoric, between rhetoric as *inventio* and rhetoric as *dispositio*, and so forth. In order to try to progress in the precise formulation of the difficulty, I turn to what I find to be a suggestive example, one of the later didactic texts written by Pascal for the instruction of the pupils at Port-Royal. The text, which dates from 1657 or 1658 (Pascal died in 1662), remained unpublished for a long time, but did not pass unnoticed, since Arnauld and Nicole incor-

---

2. Ibid., p. 512.

porated parts of it in the *Logique* of Port-Royal. It has since been mentioned by most specialists of Pascal and has been the object of at least one learned monograph.[3] The text is entitled *Réflexions sur la géométrie en général; De l'esprit géométrique et de l'Art de persuader,*[4] a title rendered somewhat oddly, but not uninterestingly, in one English edition of Pascal as *The Mind of the Geometrician*.[5] It is an exemplary case for our inquiry, since it deals with what Pascal calls, in the first section, "l'étude de la vérité" or epistemology and, in the second, "l'art de persuader" or rhetoric.

Ever since it was discovered, *Réflexions* has puzzled its readers. Arnauld and Nicole's way of excerpting from it to make it serve the more narrowly traditional Cartesian mold of the *Logique* considerably simplified and indeed mutilated its Pascalian complexity; the Dominican Father Touttée, who was the first to unearth it from among Pascal's papers, expressed great doubts about its internal coherence and consistency.[6] Despite strong internal evidence to the contrary, the text has often not been considered as a single entity divided in two parts, but as two entirely separate disquisitions; Pascal's early editors, Desmolets (in 1728) and Condoret (in 1776), gave it as separate fragments, and not until 1844 did it appear more or less in the now generally accepted form of one single unit divided into two parts.[7] The history of the text's philology curiously repeats the theoretical argument, which has compulsively to do with questions of units and pairs, divisibility, and heterogeneity.

The argument of the *Réflexions* is digressive, but not at all lacking in consistency. If it indeed reaches dead ends and breaking points, it does so by excess of

---

3. Jean-Pierre Schobinger, *Kommentar zu Pascals Reflexionen über die Geometrie im Allgemeinen* (Basel: Schwabe, 1974). The work consists of a translation into German of the original text, but contains an extensive line-by-line commentary, particularly valuable with regard to the history of the relationships between mathematical theory and epistemology in the seventeenth century.

4. The text appears in most current editions of Pascal's works. References are to Blaise Pascal, *Œuvres complètes*, ed. Louis Lafuma (Paris: Éditions du Seuil, Collection l'Intégrale, 1963), pp. 348–59.

5. *Great Shorter Works of Pascal*, trans. Emilie Caillet (Philadelphia: Westminster Press, 1948), pp. 189–211.

6. In a letter of 12 June 1711 to Pascal's nephew, Louis Périer, Father Touttée writes: "I have the honor to return the three manuscripts you were kind enough to send me. . . . I have one general observation to make, namely, that this text, which promises to discuss the method of the geometricians, indeed begins by doing so without, in my opinion, saying anything very remarkable, and then embarks on a long digression that deals with the two infinites, the infinitely large and the infinitely small that can be observed in the three or four things that make up nature. One fails to understand how this relates to the main topic of the text. This is why I think it opportune to cut the text in two and make it into two separate pieces, for they hardly seem to go together" (quoted in Schobinger, *Kommentar zu Pascals Reflexionen*, p. 110).

7. On the history of the edition of the text, see Blaise Pascal, *Œuvres complètes*, ed. J. Mesnard (Paris: Desclée de Brouwer, 1964 and 1970), summarized in Schobinger, *Kommentar zu Pascals Reflexionen*, pp. 108–14.

rigor rather than for lack of it. That such breaking points are reached, however, cannot be denied. Recent commentators have valiantly tried to patch up the most conspicuous holes by attributing them to historical indeterminations characteristic of Pascal's time and situation.[8] In a text that is historically as overdetermined as this one—and that contains echoes of an almost endless series of disputations which, in the wake of such philosophers as Descartes, Leibniz, Hobbes, and Gassendi, mark the period as one of intense epistemological speculation—the temptation is great to domesticate the more threatening difficulties by historicizing them out of consciousness. Even after this operation has been performed, some anomalies remain that pertain specifically to the nature rather than the state of the question. The most conspicuous break occurs in the second part, in the section on persuasion (p. 356). Pascal has asserted the existence of two entirely different modes by which arguments can be conducted. The first mode has been established in the first section, in polemical opposition to the scholastic logic of syllogisms, as the method of the geometricians, and it can be codified in the rules that Arnauld and Nicole incorporated in the *Logique*. When these rules are observed, it is the only mode to be both productive and reliable. Because of the fallen condition of man, however, it cannot establish itself as the only way. Though man is accessible to reason and convinced by proof, he is even more accessible to the language of pleasure and of seduction, which governs his needs and his passions rather than his mind. In their own realms, the language of seduction (*langage d'agrément*) and the language of persuasion can rule or even cooperate, but when natural truth and human desire fail to coincide, they can enter into conflict. At that moment, says Pascal, "a dubious balance is achieved between truth and pleasure [*vérité et volupté*] and the knowledge of the one and the awareness of the other wage a combat of which the outcome is very uncertain" (p. 356). Such dialectical moments are, as the readers of the *Pensées* well know, very common in Pascal and function as the necessary precondition for insights. No such resolution occurs at this crucial moment, however, although the efficacy of the entire text is

---

8. As one instance among many, Schobinger confronts the problem of the discrepancy between mathematical knowledge and belief, in Pascal, as it finds expression in the fluctuations of a terminology that is, at times, derived from the language of proof (in terms such as *raison, entendement, esprit*) and, at other times, from the language of affectivity (in terms such as *cœur, sentiment, instinct*). The topic, as is well known, leads to the famous opposition between "esprit de géométrie" and "esprit de finesse." He explains the difficulty as an evolution in Pascal's attitude toward Descartes. In the *Réflexions* (except for the theological section) Pascal still adheres to a dualism of mind and the senses, or of discursive and intuitive knowledge, that goes back to Descartes. Later, "in the *Pensées*, he refines this opposition into a new model for discursive thought. The *Réflexions* therefore correspond to a Cartesian phase in Pascal's thought whereas the *Pensées* are the result of a change and represent a move away from Descartes" (Schobinger, *Kommentar zu Pascals Reflexionen*, pp. 402–4). What is striking about a statement such as this (of which many equivalences can be found in the literature on Pascal) is not that it is right or wrong, but that, by stating an epistemological tension in terms of a historical narrative, it creates an appeasing delusion of understanding.

at stake. Pascal retreats in a phraseology of which it is impossible to say whether it is evasive or ironically personal: "Now, of these two methods, the one of persuasion, the other of seduction [*convaincre . . . agréer*], I shall give rules only for the former . . . [the geometrical persuasion]. Not that I do not believe the other to be incomparably more difficult, more subtle, more useful, and more admirable. So, if I do not discuss it, it is because of my inability to do so. I feel it to be so far beyond my means that I consider it entirely impossible. Not that I do not believe that if anyone is able to do so, it is people whom I know, and that no one has as clear and abundant insight into the matter as they do" (p. 356). The reference appears to be to Pascal's friend the Chevalier de Méré, who had already been present by polemical allusion at an earlier and delicate moment in the first part of the treatise,[9] thus enforcing the impression that, at the moment in the demonstration when we are the most in need of clear and explicit formulation, what we get is private obfuscation. For, as is clear from many testimonials and, among many other instances, from the prose of the *Lettres provinciales*, Pascal's claim at being incompetent in the rhetoric of seduction is certainly not made in good faith. The concluding paragraphs of the text never recover from this decisive break in a by no means undecisive argument. What is it, in this argument, that accounts for the occurrence of this disruption? What is it, in a rigorous epistemology, that makes it impossible to decide whether its exposition is a proof or an allegory? We have to retrace and interpret the course of the argument, as it develops in the first section of the *Réflexions* and as it finds its equivalent in the underlying logical and rhetorical structure of the *Pensées*, in order to answer this question.

"De l'esprit géométrique," part 1 of the *Réflexions*, starts out from a classical and very well known problem in epistemology: the distinction between nominal and real definition, *definitio nominis* and *definitio reo*. Pascal insists at once that the superiority and reliability of the geometrical (i.e., mathematical) method is established because "in geometry we recognize only those definitions that logicians call *definitions of name* [*définitions de nom*], that is to say, giving a name only to those things which have been clearly designated in perfectly known terms" (p. 349). Nothing could be simpler, in Pascal's exposition, than this process of denomination, which exists only as a kind of stenography, a free and flexible code used for reasons of economy to avoid cumbersome repetitions, and which in no way influences the thing itself in its substance or in its properties. Definitions of name are, says Pascal, "entirely free and never open to contradiction" (p. 349). They require some hygiene and some policing. One should avoid, for example,

---

9. On the relationship between Antoine Gombaud, Chevalier de Méré, and Pascal, see J. Mesnard, *Pascal et les Roannez*, vols. 1 and 2 (Paris: Desclée de Brouwer, 1965); F. Strowski, *Pascal et son temps* (Paris: Plon, 1907–8), vol. 2 (pp. 292–317), and also Schobinger, *Kommentar zu Pascals Reflexionen*, p. 330.

that the same signifier designate two distinct meanings, but this can easily be assured by public convention. Real definitions, on the other hand, are a great deal more coercive and dangerous: they are actually not definitions, but axioms or, even more frequently, propositions that need to be proven. The confusion between nominal and real definitions is the main cause of the difficulties and obscurities that plague philosophical disputation, and to keep the distinction between them clear and sharp is, in Pascal's own terms, "the (real) reason for writing the treatise, more than the subject with which I deal" (p. 351). The mind of the geometrician is exemplary to the extent that it observes this distinction.

Can it really do so? As soon as it is enunciated, the apparently simple definition of definition runs into complications, for the text glides almost imperceptibly from the discussion of nominal definition to that of what it calls "primitive words," which are not subject to definition at all, since their pretended definitions are infinite regresses of accumulated tautologies. These terms (which include the basic topoi of geometrical discourse, such as motion, number, and extension) represent the natural language element that Descartes scornfully rejected from scientific discourse, but which reappears here as the natural light that guarantees the intelligibility of primitive terms despite their undefinability. In geometrical (i.e., epistemologically sound) discourse, primitive words and nominal definition are coextensive and blend into each other: in this "judicious science . . . all terms are perfectly intelligible, either by natural light or by the definitions it produces" (p. 351).

But things are not quite so simple. For if primitive words possess a natural meaning, then this meaning would have to be universal, as is the science that operates with these words; however, in one of the sudden shifts so characteristic of Pascal and which sets him entirely apart from Arnauld's trust in logic, this turns out not to be the case. "It is not the case," says Pascal, "that all men have the same idea of the essence of the things which I showed to be impossible and useless to define . . . (such as, for example, time). It is not the nature of these things which I declare to be known by all, but simply *the relationship between the name and the thing*, so that on hearing the expression *time*, all turn (or direct) the mind toward the same entity [*tous portent la pensée vers le même objet*]" (p. 350). Here the word does not function as a sign or a name, as was the case in the nominal definition, but as a vector, a directional motion that is manifest only as a turn, since the target toward which it turns remains unknown. In other words, the sign has become a trope, a substitutive relationship that has to posit a meaning whose existence cannot be verified, but that confers upon the sign an unavoidable signifying function. The indeterminacy of this function is carried by the figural expression "porter la pensée," a figure that cannot be accounted for in phenomenal terms. The nature of the relationship between figure (or trope) and mind can only be described by a figure, the same figure that Pascal will use in the *Pensées* in order to describe figure: "Figure *porte* absence et présence, plaisir et déplaisir" (265/677,

p. 534);[10] this is a sentence to which we will have to return later on. This much, at least, is clearly established: in the language of geometry, nominal definition and primitive terms are coextensive, but the semantic function of the primitive terms is structured like a trope. As such, it acquires a signifying function that it controls neither in its existence nor in its direction. Another way of stating this is to say that the nominal definition of primitive terms always turns into a proposition that has to, but cannot, be proven. Since definition is now itself a primitive term, it follows that the definition of the nominal definition is itself a real, and not a nominal, definition. This initial complication has far-reaching consequences for the further development of the text.

The discussion of denomination and of definition leads directly into Pascal's more fundamental and systematic statement about the intelligibility and coherence of mind and cosmos: the principle of double infinity, which also underlies the theological considerations of the *Pensées*. From a traditional point of view, the interest of the *Réflexions* is that it spells out, more explicitly than can be the case in the apologetic and religious context of the *Pensées*, the link between this central principle, so often expressed, in Pascal himself and in his interpreters, in a tonality of existential pathos, and the geometrical or mathematical logic of which it is actually a version. The text helps to undo the tendentious and simplistic opposition between knowledge and faith which is often forced upon Pascal. The *logos* of the world consists of the "necessary and reciprocal link" that exists between the intrawordly dimensions of motion, number, and space (to which Pascal also adds time), the principle asserted in the only quotation from Scripture to appear in the text: "Deus fecit omnia in pondere, in numero, et mensura."[11]

Pascal is indeed in conformity with his age of science in making the cohesion of arithmetic, geometry, and rational mechanics the logical model for epistemological discourse. He is also in essential conformity with that age, the age of Leibniz and the development of infinitesimal calculus, in designating the principle of double infinity, the infinitely large and the infinitely small, as the "common property (of space, time, motion, and number) where knowledge opens up the mind to the greatest marvels in nature" (p. 351). Thus, when the burden of Pascal's text becomes the assertion of the infinite divisibility of space and of number (it being assumed that infinite expansion is readily granted, but that the mind resists the notion of infinite divisibility), one is not surprised to find the first four of the five arguments designed to overcome that resistance to be traditional assertions that

---

10. Pascal's *Pensées* exist in different editions with different identifying numbers. I quote the number of the Lafuma classification in the Éditions du Seuil volume, followed by the number of the Brunschvicg classification, and the page number in the Éditions du Seuil volume.

11. Wisdom 11:21. The assimilation of space to measure (*mensura*) and especially of motion to weight (*pondere*) raises questions leading into Pascal's scientific and experimental concerns with the problems of gravity.

do not stand in need of development. They reiterate such fundamental principles of calculus as the impossibility of comparing finite and infinite quantities and, in general, move between spatial and numerical dimensions by means of simple computation (as in the instance of the irrational number for the square root of two), or by experimental representations in space, without the intervention of discursive language (p. 353). The text starts to proliferate and to grow tense, however, when it has to counter an objection that is to be attributed to Méré and that compels Pascal to reintroduce the question of the relationship between language and cognition. Méré argued that it is perfectly possible in the order of space to conceive of an extension made up from parts that are themselves devoid of extension, thus implying that space can be made up of a finite quantity of indivisible parts, rather than of an infinity of infinitely divisible ones, because it is possible to make up numbers out of units that are themselves devoid of number. Méré uses the principle of homogeneity between space and number, which is also the ground of Pascal's cosmology, to put the principle of infinitesimal smallness into question. Pascal's retort (p. 353) marks the truly Pascalian moment in the demonstration. It begins by dissociating the laws of number from the laws of geometry, by showing that what applies to the indivisible unit of number, the *one*, does not apply to the indivisible unit of space. The status of the *one* is paradoxical and apparently contradictory: as the very principle of singleness, it has no plurality, no number. As Euclid said, *one* is not a number. It is a mere name given to the entity that does not possess the properties of number, a nominal definition of nonnumber. On the other hand, the one partakes of number, according to the principle of homogeneity enunciated by the same Euclid who decreed the one not to be a number. The principle of homogeneity ("magnitudes are said to be of the same kind or species when one magnitude can be made to exceed another by reiterated multiplication") is mathematically linked to the principle of infinity implicit in this proposition. *One* is not a number; this proposition is correct, but so is the opposite proposition, namely, that *one is* a number, provided it is mediated by the principle of homogeneity, which asserts that *one* is of the same species as number, as a house is not a city, yet a city is made up of houses that are of the same species as the city, since one can always add a house to a city and it remains a city. Generic homogeneity, or the infinitesimal, is a synecdochal structure. We again find in the fundamental model of Pascal's cosmos, which is based on tropes of homogeneity and on the notion of the infinite, a system that allows for a great deal of dialectical contradiction (one can say $1 = N$ as well as $1 \neq N$), but one that guarantees intelligibility.

The interest of the argument is, however, that it has to reintroduce the ambivalence of definitional language. The synecdochal totalization of infinitude is possible because the unit of number, the *one*, functions as a nominal definition. But, for the argument to be valid, the nominally indivisible number must be distinguished from the *really* indivisible space, a demonstration that Pascal can accomplish easily, but only because the key words of the demonstration—indivisible, spatial extension (*étendue*), species (*genre*), and definition—function as real, and not as nominal, definitions, as "définition de chose" and not as "définition de nom." The language almost forces this formulation upon Pascal, when he has to say: "cette dernière preuve est fondée sur la *définition* de ces deux *choses*, indivisible et étendue" or "Donc, il n'est pas de même genre que l'étendue, par la *définition* des *choses* du même genre" (p. 354; emphasis mine). The reintroduction of a language of *real* definition also allows for the next turn in the demonstration, which, after having separated number from space, now has to suspend this separation while maintaining it—because the underlying homology of space and number, the ground of the system, should never be fundamentally in question. There exists, in the order of number, an entity that is, unlike the *one*, heterogeneous with regard to number: this entity, which is the *zero*, is radically distinct from one. Whereas one is and is not a number at the same time, zero is radically not a number, absolutely heterogeneous to the order of number. With the introduction of zero, the separation between number and space, which is potentially threatening, is also healed. For equivalences can easily be found in the order of time and of motion for the zero function in number: instant and stasis (*repos*) are the equivalences that, thanks to the zero, allow one to reestablish the "necessary and reciprocal link" between the four intrawordly dimensions on which divine order depends. At the end of the passage, the homogeneity of the universe is recovered, and the principle of infinitesimal symmetry is well established. But this has happened at a price: the coherence of the system is now seen to be entirely dependent on the introduction of an element—the zero and its equivalences in time and motion—that is itself entirely heterogeneous with regard to the system and is nowhere a part of it. The continuous universe held together by the double wings of the two infinites is interrupted, disrupted *at all points* by a principle of radical heterogeneity without which it cannot come into being. Moreover, this rupture of the infinitesimal and the homogeneous does not occur on the transcendental level, but on the level of language, in the inability of a theory of language as sign or as name (nominal definition) to ground this homogeneity without having recourse to the signifying function, the real definition, that makes the zero of signification the necessary condition for grounded knowledge. The notion of language as sign is dependent on, and derived from, a different notion in which language functions as rudderless signification and transforms what it denominates into the linguistic equivalence of the arithmetical zero. It is as sign that language is capable of engendering the principles of infinity, of genus, species, and homogeneity, which allow for synecdochal totalizations, but none of these tropes could come about without the systematic effacement of the zero and its reconversion into a name. There can be no *one* without zero, but the zero always appears in the guise of a *one*, of a (some)thing. The name is the trope of the zero. The zero is always *called* a one, when the zero is actually nameless, "innommable." In the French language, as used by Pascal and his interpreters, this happens concretely in the confusedly alternate use of the two terms *zéro* and *néant*. The verbal, predicative form *néant*, with its gerundive ending, indicates not the zero, but rather the one, as the *limit* of the infinitely small, the almost zero that is the one. Pascal is not consistent in his use of *zéro* and *néant*; nor could he be if the system of the two infinites is to be enunciated at all. At the crucial point, however, as is the case here, he knows the difference, which his commentators, including the latest and most astute ones, always forget.[12] At the end of the most systematic exposition of the theory of the two infinites, at the conclusion of part 1 of the *Réflexions*, we find once again the ambivalence of the theory of definitional language, which we encountered at the start.

The unavoidable question will be whether the model established in this text, in which discourse is a dialectical and infinitesimal system that depends on its undoing in order to come into being, can be extended to texts that are not purely mathematical, but stated in a less abstract, more phenomenally or existentially perceivable form. One would specifically want to know whether the principle of homogeneity implicit in the theory of the two infinites, *as well as* the disruption of this system, can be retraced in the theological and subject-oriented context of the *Pensées*. Since this would involve an extensive reading of a major and difficult work, we must confine ourselves here to preliminary hints, by showing first of all how the principle of totalization, which is implicit in the notion of the infinite, underlies the dialectical pattern that is so characteristic of the *Pensées*. Once this is done, we should then ask whether this pattern is at all interrupted, as the numerical series are interrupted by zero, and how this disruption occurs. As a general precaution, we should be particularly wary not to decide too soon that this is indeed the case, not only because the consequences, from a theological and an epistemological point of view, are far-reaching, but also because the remarkable elasticity of the dialectical model, capable of recovering totalities threatened by the most

---

12. Louis Marin, in his outstanding book on Pascal and on the *Logic* of Port-Royal (*La Critique du discours* [Paris: Éditions de Minuit, 1975]), makes a considerable contribution to Pascal's philosophy of language and its relationship to theology. Chapter 8, "De la définition de nom" (pp. 239–69), is particularly relevant to our topic and constitutes one of the best expositions of the link between nominal definition and the theory of the two infinites, culminating in the following conclusion: "The group of elements that 'ground' scientific discourse in a principle of certainty that is not absolutely convincing . . . are the same as those which provoke this discourse to transgress its limitations, because they are its limits as illimitation. By obeying the law of double infinity, magnitudes can be accurately determined by means of computation and measure but, at the same time, they point toward something other than what they are, the transcendental limits of the magnitude which orders all magnitudes." When Marin then quotes paragraph 3 of Pensée 418/233, p. 550, which states that "the addition of the *one* to the infinite does not augment it" and concludes that "in this deprivation [*dénuement*] the totalization of the infinite signified = 0 fulfills itself," this would be a classical instance of the confusion of "néant" (or *one* as the infinitely small) with zero. In Pascal's system it is possible to say that néant = ∞ (or $1 = \infty$), but never that 0 (zero) = ∞.

radical contradictions, should not be underestimated. The Pascalian dialectic should be allowed to display the full extent of its feats, and, if a disjunction is to be revealed, it can only be done by following Pascal in pushing it to its eventual breaking point.

What is here called, for lack of a better term, a rupture or a disjunction is not to be thought of as a negation, however tragic it may be. Negation, in a mind as resilient as Pascal's, is always susceptible of being reinscribed in a system of intelligibility. Nor can we hope to map it out as one topos among topoi, as would be the case with regular tropes of substitution. It is possible to find, in the terminology of rhetoric, terms that come close to designating such disruptions (e.g., *parabasis* or *anacoluthon*), which designate the interruption of a semantic continuum in a manner that lies beyond the power of reintegration. One must realize at once, however, that this disruption is not topical, that it cannot be located in a single point—since it is indeed the very notion of point, the geometrical zero,[13] that is being dislodged—but that it is all-pervading. The anacoluthon is omnipresent, or, in temporal terms and in Friedrich Schlegel's deliberately unintelligible formulation, the parabasis is permanent. Calling this structure ironic can be more misleading than helpful, since *irony*, like *zero*, is a term that is not susceptible to nominal or real definition. To say then, as we are actually saying, that allegory (as sequential narration) is the trope of irony (as the one is the trope of zero) is to say something that is true enough but not intelligible, which also implies that it cannot be put to work as a device of textual analysis. To discover, in the *Pensées*, the *instances de rupture*, the equivalence of the zero in Pascal's theory of number, we can only reiterate compulsively the dialectical pattern of Pascal's own model or, in other words, read and reread the *Pensées* with genuine insistence. Pascal himself has formulated the principle of totalizing reading, in which the most powerful antinomies must be brought together, in the Pensée headed "Contradiction" (257/684, p. 533): "One can put together a good physiognomy only by reconciling all our oppositions. It does not suffice to follow a sequence of matched properties without reconciling contraries: in order to understand an author's meaning, one must reconcile all the contradictory passages [*pour entendre le sens d'un auteur il faut accorder tous les passages contraires*]." Applied to Scripture, which Pascal here has in mind, this reconciliation leads directly to the fundamental opposition that underlies all others: that between a figural and a true reading. "If one takes the law, the sacrifices, and the kingdom as realities, it will be impossible to coordinate all passages [of the Bible]; it is therefore necessary that they be mere figures" (p. 533). The question remains, of course, whether the pair figure/reality can or

---

13. On the concept of "point," see Schobinger (*Kommentar zu Pascals Reflexionen*, p. 365), who gives interesting quotations from Simon Stevin and from Mersenne discussing the assimilation of the geometrical "point" to the arithmetical zero.

cannot be itself thus reconciled, whether it is a contradiction of the type we encountered when it was said that one is a number and is not a number at the same
time, or whether the order of figure and the order of reality are heterogeneous.

For all the somber felicity of their aphoristic condensation, the *Pensées* are also
very systematically schematized texts that can be seen as an intricate interplay of
binary oppositions. Many of the sections are, or could easily be, designated by the
terms of these oppositions, as is the case for our first and simplest example, two
of the Pensées (125/92 and 126/93, p. 514), which could properly be entitled
"Nature" and "Custom": "What are our natural principles if not the principles we
have grown accustomed to? In children, they are the principles they have learned
from the customs of their fathers, like the hunt in animals. A different custom will
produce different natural principles. This can be verified by experience, by ob-
serving if there are customs that cannot be erased. . . . Fathers fear that the natural
love of their children can be erased. What kind of nature is this, that can thus be
erased? Custom is a second nature that destroys the first. But what is nature? Why
is custom not natural? I am very much afraid that this nature is only a first custom,
as custom is a second nature." This passage turns around a saying of common wisdom ("La coutume est une seconde nature"), as is frequently the case in Pascal,
and it thus sets up a very characteristic logical or, rather, rhetorical pattern. A set
of binary oppositions is matched in a commonsensical order in terms of their
properties: here, custom and nature are matched with the pairs first/second and
constant/erasable (*effaçable*), respectively. Nature, being a *first* principle, is constant, whereas custom, being second or derived from nature, is susceptible to
change and erasure. The schema, at the onset, is as follows:

nature	first	constant
custom	second	erasable

The pattern is put in motion by a statement (also based, in this case, on common
observation) that reverses the order of association of the entities and their properties. It is said that fathers fear, apparently with good reason, that natural feelings
of filial affection can be erased, thus coupling the natural with the erasable and,
consequently, with secondness. A first (nature) then becomes a first second, that
is, a second; a second (custom) becomes in symmetrical balance, a second first,
that is, a first:

The properties of firstness and secondness have changed places, which results in
the undoing or the deconstruction of the binary opposition from which we started.
It has now become impossible to decide whether a given experience can be called

natural or customary. Since they are able, in a chiasmic reversal, to exchange or cross over their properties, nature and custom have been brought together to the extent that their opposition has been inscribed into a system of exchange which is structured like a trope (chiasmus). Nature and custom are united within a single system, which, although experienced as negative by the author ("I am afraid that . . ."), is nevertheless a cognition.

The same pattern, with increased complications, reappears time after time and underlies some of the most famous and thematically suggestive of the Pensées. Consider, for example, the section on the nature of man (131/434, pp. 514–15). It starts out from an opposition that, this time, is historical and, to that extent, empirical: the philosophical debate—to which Pascal has gained access through his closest predecessors, Montaigne and Descartes—between skeptical and dogmatic philosophy, *pyrrhoniens* and *dogmatistes*. The establishment of the original grid, which was obvious in the case of nature and custom as first and second, is more complex in this case, in which skepticism and dogmatic faith have to be matched with truth and nature, respectively. The argument goes back to the example and the logic used by Descartes in the first two meditations.[14] It established the claim for the cognitive value of doubt by reference to the polarity of sleeping and waking, of dream and reality. One normally assumes that the condition of waking is the true condition of man, the first norm from which sleep and dream are derived and displaced, secondary versions. Sleep is grafted upon the condition of awakeness like a secondary upon a primary quality. The original pattern is as follows:

wake	perception	first
sleep	dream	second

Since we think that we are awake when we dream, it follows that the properties can be ordered according to the same symmetrical pattern we encountered in the Pensée on nature and custom. Like Keats at the end of the "Ode to a Nightingale," we should each ask: Do I wake or sleep? For it is no longer certain that our primary consciousness is awake at all, that consciousness is not a palimpsest of dreams, some of them individual, some shared with others, all grafted upon each other. "Is it not possible that this half of our life (day) is itself a mere dream on which the other dreams are grafted, and of which we will awake at death?" (p. 514). This suspicion, which undoes the natural polarities of day and night, wake and sleep, is clearly the product of the skeptical mind and justifies the pairing of skepticism with knowledge. The skeptical position always had knowledge on its side, and the only thing the dogmatists can oppose to this knowledge is the natural conviction that infinite doubt is intolerable. "What will man do in this condition? Will he doubt of everything, doubt that he is awake, that he is being

---

14. René Descartes, *Œuvres philosophiques*, ed. F. Alquié, 3 vols. (Paris: Garnier, 1967), 2:406.

pinched or burned, will he doubt that he doubts, doubt that he is? One cannot reach this condition, and I assert as a fact that there never has been a perfectly consistent and actual skeptic. Nature supports our feeble reason and shelters it from such extravagance" (p. 515). Skepticism and dogmatism are now firmly paired with truth and nature, respectively.

Skepticism   Truth
Dogmatism   Nature

But this original configuration is not a stable one. As is clear from the preceding quotation, one cannot be consistently skeptical, but it is just as impossible to be consistently natural, for however "extravagant" the skeptical position may be, it is nevertheless the only mode of truth accessible to us, and it deprives all claims to natural truth of authority. To the belief "that one cannot doubt natural principles," the skeptics counter "that the uncertainty of our origin includes that of our nature." This argument cannot be refuted: "The dogmatists have been trying to refute it ever since the world began."

The situation is not only unstable, but coercive as well. At this point in the *Pensées*, one moves from the logic of propositions, statements as to what is the case, to modal logic, statements of what should or ought to be the case. For one cannot remain suspended between the irreconcilable positions: it is clear that, by not choosing between the two poles of the polarities, one is adopting the skeptical position. The predicament is that of the undecidable: propositional logic is powerless to decide a conflict that has to find a solution, if this logic is to survive.

In a first dialectical reversal, the answer will be to give the predicament a name, which, in this case, will be "man," the being who stands in that predicament. "Man" is then not a definable entity, but an incessant motion beyond itself. "L'homme passe l'homme" says Pascal, in a phrase that has received many pseudo-Nietzschean interpretations of existential transcendence and transgression. Perhaps more important is the numerical formulation of the "definition" of man, which takes us back to the *Réflexions*. For it follows, says Pascal, that man is double, that the one is always already at least a two, a pair. Man is like the *one* in the system of number, infinitely divisible and infinitely capable of self-multiplication. He is another version of the system of the two infinites; immediately after having stated that man surpasses man, and that man is double, Pascal can add that man *infinitely* surpasses man, "l'homme passe *infiniment* l'homme." As a metaphor of number, man is one and is not one, is a pair and is infinite all at the same time.

The dialectic of the infinite, which starts in the initial doubt, is thus able to unfold itself consistently. For the double, and hence infinitesimal, condition of man, this becomes the key to the knowledge of man's nature. "For who fails to see that without the knowledge of this double condition of nature man was in an irrevocable ignorance of the truth of his nature?" (p. 515). This ruse of reason is purely Cartesian: doubt is suspended by the knowledge of doubt. One sees that the original structure, pairing skepticism with truth and dogmatism with nature, has been chiastically crossed, since now the true knowledge of radical skepticism is paired with nature, through the mediation of the concept of man, standing by implication for the system of double infinitude. The rhetorical pattern that underlies this system is the same as in the previous example.

It is legitimate to "pair" this Pensée with another and more rigorously schematized one, which states the same tension, but empties it of the existential pathos of totalization (122/416, p. 514). It is headed by the binary opposition "Grandeur et misère": "Since misery is derived from greatness, and greatness from misery, some have decided in favor of misery all the more decisively, since they have taken greatness to be the proof of misery, and others have decided for greatness with all the more power, since they derive it from misery itself. All they were able to say in support of greatness has served as an argument for the others to demonstrate misery, since the higher the station from which one falls the more miserable one will be, and vice versa. They are carried upon each other [portés les uns sur les autres] in a circle without end, it being certain that as men gain in enlightenment, they find both greatness and misery in themselves. In a word: man knows he is miserable. He is therefore miserable, since that is what he is, but he is also great because he knows it [En un mot, l'homme connaît qu'il est misérable. Il est donc misérable puisqu'il l'est, mais il est bien grand puisqu'il le connaît]."

The end of the text telescopes the chiasmus in a particularly condensed form, starting from the pairing of misery with (self-)knowledge and of greatness with being: "Man is great because man knows misery [l'homme connait qu'il est misérable]." The final sentence has reversed the pattern: misery is paired with being, in the tautology "il est misérable puisqu'il l'est," and greatness with knowledge, the self-knowledge of misery. The mediation is carried out by the apparently deductive prepositions in the sentence: "il est donc misérable puisqu'il l'est," where the cognitive power is carried by the logical articulations donc and puisque, and the ontological power by the tautology of the assertion. The dialectic has been flattened out into tautology, in the endlessly circular repetition of the same, and the teleological form of infinite transcendence has been replaced by this monotony. All the same, despite the thematic and tonal difference between the two Pensées on man, the rhetorical pattern remains the same, grounded in the infinitesimal symmetry of the chiasmic reversal. Here, in one of the bleakest of the Pensées, this pattern appears perhaps in the purest form.[15]

The transition from self-knowledge and anthropological knowledge to teleological knowledge often passes, in Pascal, through the dimension of the political.

---

15. See also Pensée 514/397, p. 513.

Louis Marin is right to insist on the close interconnection between epistemology, political criticism, and theology, in the sequence of *Pensées* entitled "Raison des effets."[16] This sequence deals primarily with a distinction between popular and scientific knowledge and thus returns to the question that underlies the *Réflexions* as well: the antinomy between natural language and metalanguage. The polarities in Pensées 90–101 (pp. 510–11)[17] oppose the language of the people (vox populi) to that of the mathematicians; moreover, Pensée 91/336 contains a good description of Pascal's own writing style, in its peculiar mixture of popular, nontechnical diction with redoutable critical rigor: one must have what Pascal calls "une pensée de derrière" (which sees behind the apparent evidence of things), yet speak like the people. Whereas the man of science possesses true knowledge (*episteme*), the people follow the vagaries of opinion (*doxa*). The starting position, then, will be:

| people | doxa | false |
| geometrician | episteme | true |

It would be a mistake, however, to dismiss popular opinion as simply false. In a way, the (popular) saying "Vox populi, vox dei" is sound, as are, according to Pascal, the various popular opinions of which he enumerates a rather baffling catalog of examples. This being the case, a first chiasmic reversal takes place, in which popular opinion has some claims to truth, and the mind of the geometrician, in his scorn for popular wisdom, some taint of falsehood.

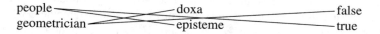

This first chiasmus, however, is only the beginning. Although it is true that the people have sound opinions, it is not really true that they possess the truth. For the people can be counted on to provide the wrong reasons for their sound opinions. "They believe," says Pascal, "that truth is to be found where it is not. There is truth in their opinions, but not where they imagine it to be." This knowledge of error, which is true, is no longer a popular knowledge, but the privileged knowledge of the man who has benefited from the critical rigors of scientific reasoning. A second reversal now associates popular opinion, which to some extent is true, with epistemological falsehood, whereas the knowledge of this falsehood is again true. "We have shown that men are vain in their respect for trivial matters; this vanity reduces all their opinions to nought. We have then shown these opinions to be altogether sound; consequently, the self-esteem of the people is quite legiti-

16. Marin, *La Critique du discours*, pp. 369–400.
17. The equivalent numbers in the Brunschvicg classification are 337–336–335–328–313–316–329–334–80–536–467–324.

mate, and the people are not at all as inestimable as one believes. And thus we have destroyed the opinion that destroyed the opinion of the people. But we must now destroy this final proposition and show that it remains true that the people are in error, although their opinions are sound, because they don't locate their truth where it belongs, and by thus locating it where it is not, their opinions are again very erroneous and very unsound" (p. 511).

Many more instances could be listed in an order than would cover the thematic scale of topoi taken up in the *Pensées*, from the most trivial to the most sublime. The same structure, the same "continual reversal from pro to contra [*renverse-ment continuel du pour au contre*]" (p. 511) would reappear in an endless set of variations on chiasmic crossings of binary oppositions. In the process, a wealth of thematic insights would indicate the universal effectiveness of what is a funda-mentally dialectical pattern of reasoning, in which oppositions are, if not recon-ciled, at least pursued toward a totalization that may be infinitely postponed, but that remains operative as the sole principle of intelligibility. Our question remains whether some of the texts from the *Pensées* explicitly refuse to fit this pattern— not because they are structured along a different tropological model (which would diversify but not necessarily invalidate the dialectical model), but because they disrupt the motion of what is demonstrably the same pattern. Consider the Pensée (103/298, p. 512) headed "Justice, power" ("Justice, force").

"It is just that what is just should be followed; it is necessary that what has the most power should be followed.

"Justice without power is impotent, power without justice is tyrannical.

"Justice without power is open to contradiction, because there always are wrongdoers. Power without justice stands accused. Justice and power must there-fore be brought together, by making the just strong and the strong just.

"Justice is subject to dispute. Power is easily recognizable and without dispute. Thus it has been impossible to give power to justice, because power has contra-dicted justice and said that it is unjust, and said that it is itself just.

"And thus, not being able to make the just strong, one has made the strong to be just.

"[*Ainsi*[18] *on n'a pu donner la force à la justice, parce que la force a contredit la justice et a dit qu'elle était injuste, et a dit que c'était elle qui était juste.*

"*Et ainsi, ne pouvant faire que ce qui est juste fût fort, on a fait que ce qui est fort fût juste*]."

It is at once clear, on hearing the passage, that, although the chiasmic structure is the same as before, the crossing is no longer symmetrical, since it takes place in one direction but not in the other. A new complication has been introduced and is observable in an opposition that gives each of the key words a double register that

---

18. The Éditions du Seuil Lafuma version of this Pensée says *Aussi* here; the Brunschvicg edition has *Ainsi.*

is no longer, as in the previous passages, an opposition between two modes of cognition. The opposition is stated at the start in the contrast between "il est juste" and "il est nécessaire," in which the first assertion depends on a propositional cognition, but the second on sheer quantitative power, as in the proverb "La raison du plus fort est toujours la meilleure" or, in English, "Might makes right." Propositional statements line up on the side of cognition, modal statements on the side of performance; they perform what they enunciate regardless of considerations of truth and falsehood. Consequently, all words used in the demonstration acquire this ambivalent status: the verb *suivre*, for instance, can be read in its deductive and cognitive sense, in which the necessity is the necessary deductiveness of reason, but it can also be read in the sense of pure coercive power, as in the phrase "la femme doit suivre son mari."

Suivre is thus distributed in its double register in the first two sentences of the Pensée. The same is true of justice, which can on the one hand be read as cognitive *justesse*, as the precision of rational argument, but which is clearly also to be read in the sense of the judicial praxis of a court of law. In this latter capacity, it clearly lacks the persuasive power of sheer argument which it possesses in the first sense; it is open to uncertainty and contradiction and therefore lacks power. For the proper of justice to be power, and for the proper of power to be justice, they must be able to exchange the attributes of necessity and of innocence which characterize them. Justice must become necessary by might, might innocent by justice. This would accomplish and demonstrate the homogeneity of propositional statements as cognition and of modal statements as performance. But, unlike all other previous examples from the *Pensées*, the exchange does not take place. Justice refuses to become *justesse*; it remains pragmatic and inconsistent, "sujet à dispute," unable to fulfill the criterion of necessity as cognitive persuasion. Might, however, has no difficulty whatever satisfying the criterion of necessity; it is "sans dispute" and can therefore *usurp* the consistency of cognition without giving anything in return. The usurpation occurs in the double register of the locution "sans dispute," a quality that pertains to mathematical proof as an indication of epistemological rigor, but which, as in "Right makes might," also pertains to force by sheer intolerance and tyranny. Force, which is pure performance, usurps the claim to epistemological rightness. It does so because it can become the subject of the sentence of enunciation and can be said to speak: "la force a contredit . . ." and "la force a dit . . ."; it can pronounce on the lack of epistemological "rightness" of justice, and it can proclaim its own epistemological infallibility. The performative declares itself declarative and cognitive. The "on" in the final sentence—"on a fait que ce qui est fort fût juste"—can only be "might," which belongs indeed to the order of the "faire" and not of "savoir." But the unilateral victory of force over justice, if it is to be enunciated, as is the case in this passage, still can only be stated in the mode of cognition and of deduction, as is evident from the use of the deductive "ainsi" coupled with "faire" in the sentence "ainsi on a fait. . . ." The status of this "ainsi" is now very peculiar, however, for the pure act of force is entirely arbitrary and not cognitively consequential at all. The "ainsi" does not belong to Descartes, but to any despot who happens to be in power.

The discomfort one should experience on the reading of this final sentence is the same one should experience on hearing the zero assimilated to the one and thus being reinscribed into a system of cognition in which it does not belong. For at the very moment that might has usurped, by imposition and not by transgression, the authority of cognition, the tropological field of cognition is revealed to be dependent on an entity, might, that is heterogeneous with regard to this field, just as the zero was heterogeneous with regard to number. The break is immediately reinscribed as the knowledge of the break in the "ainsi on a fait. . . ," but this "ainsi" must now be said to be ironical, that is to say, disruptive of its own deductive claim. The dialectic starts again, but it has been broken in a way that is essentially different from the transgressive reversals we encountered in the other instances. It is in the realm of practical and political justice, and not of Christian charity, that the equivalence of the mathematical zero reappears in the text of the *Pensées*. What is of considerable importance, from a linguistic point of view, is that the break that in the *Réflexions* was due to the complications of definition is now seen to be a function of the heterogeneity between cognitive and performative language. Language, in Pascal, now separates in two distinct directions: a cognitive function that is right (*juste*) but powerless, and a modal function that is mighty (*forte*) in its claim to rightness. The two functions are radically heterogeneous to each other. The first generates canonical rules of persuasion, whereas the second generates the eudaemonic values that are present as soon as one has to say that the claim to authority is made "at the *pleasure* of" the despot. The first is the language of truth and of persuasion by proof, the second the language of pleasure (*volupté*) and of persuasion by usurpation or seduction. We now know why it is that, in the second half of the *Réflexions*, Pascal had to dodge the question of the relationship between these two modes. To the extent that language is always cognitive and tropological as well as performative at the same time, it is a heterogeneous entity incapable of justice as well as of *justesse*. Even in the transcendental realm of revealed language in Holy Writ, the necessary choice between seduction and truth remains undecidable. Pascal's "definition" of figure retains this complication: when it is said that "Figure porte absence et présence," we recognize the infinitesimal structure of cognitive dialectics, but when it is also said that "Figure porte plaisir et déplaisir," it will be impossible to square, to inscribe the four terms *présence/absence* and *plaisir/déplaisir* into a homogeneous "geometrical" structure. The (ironic) pseudoknowledge of this impossibility, which pretends to order sequentially, in a narrative, what is actually the destruction of all sequence, is what we call allegory.

Phenomenality and Materiality in Kant

The possibility of juxtaposing ideology and critical philosophy, which is the persistent burden of contemporary thought, is pointed out, as a mere historical fact, by Michel Foucault in *Les Mots et les choses*. At the same time that French ideologues such as Destutt de Tracy are trying to map out the entire field of human ideas and representations, Kant undertakes the critical project of a transcendental philosophy which, says Foucault, marks "the retreat of cognition and of knowledge out of the space of representation."[1] Foucault's ensuing historical diagnosis, in which ideology appears as a belated manifestation of the classical spirit and Kant as the onset of modernity, interests us less than the interplay between the three notions: ideology, critical philosophy, and transcendental philosophy. The first term of this triad, "ideology," is the most difficult to control and one may hope that the interrelationship with the two others might be of some assistance.

A possible starting point can be found in the introduction to the third *Critique* in a difficult but important differentiation between transcendental and metaphysical principles. Kant writes as follows: "A transcendental principle is one by means

---

"Phenomenality and Materiality in Kant" was delivered as the fourth Messenger lecture at Cornell on 1 March 1983. It was published in Gary Shapiro and Alan Sica, eds., *Hermeneutics: Questions and Prospects* (Amherst: University of Massachusetts Press, 1984), pp. 121–44, and reprinted in Hugh J. Silverman and Gary E. Aylesworth, eds., *The Textual Sublime* (Albany: State University of New York Press, 1990), pp. 87–108. De Man signed and dated the manuscript of this essay 1 March 1983. All notes are de Man's, slightly modified.

1. Michel Foucault, *Les mots et les choses* (Paris: Gallimard, 1966), p. 255 [de Man's translation].

of which is represented, a priori, the universal condition under which alone things can be objects of our cognition. On the other hand, a principle is called metaphysical if it represents the a priori condition under which alone objects, whose concept must be given empirically, can a priori be further determined. Thus the principle of the cognition of bodies as substances and as changeable substances is transcendental if thereby it is asserted that their changes must have a cause; it is metaphysical if it asserts that their changes must have an *external* cause. For in the former case bodies need only be thought by means of ontological predicates (pure concepts of understanding), e.g., as substance, in order to permit the a priori cognition of the proposition; but in the latter case, the empirical concept of a body (as a movable thing in space) must lie at the base of the proposition, although once this basis has been laid down it can be seen completely a priori that the other predicate (motion by external causes) belongs to the body."[2]

The difference between transcendental and metaphysical concepts that concerns us is that the latter imply an empirical moment that necessarily remains *external* to the concept, whereas the former remain entirely interconceptual. Metaphysical principles lead to the identification and definition, to the knowledge, of a natural principle that is not itself a concept; transcendental principles lead to the definition of a conceptual principle of possible existence. Metaphysical principles state why and how things occur; to say that bodies move because of gravity is to reach a conclusion in the realm of metaphysics. Transcendental principles state the conditions that make occurrence possible at all: the first condition for bodies to be able to change is that such a thing as bodies and motion exist or occur. The condition of existence of bodies is called substance; to state that substance is the cause of the motion of bodies (as Kant does in the passage quoted) is to examine critically the possibility of their existence. Metaphysical principles, on the other hand, take the existence of their object for granted as empirical fact. They contain knowledge of the world, but this knowledge is precritical. Transcendental principles contain no knowledge of the world or anything else, except for the knowledge that metaphysical principles that take them for their object are themselves in need of critical analysis, since they take for granted an objectivity that, for the transcendental principles, is not a priori available. Thus the objects of transcendental principles are always critical *judgments* that take metaphysical knowledge for their target. Transcendental philosophy is always the critical philosophy of metaphysics.

---

2. Immanuel Kant, *Kritik der Urteilskraft*, vol. 10 of *Werkausgabe*, ed. Wilhelm Weischedel (Frankfurt am Main: Suhrkamp, 1978), p. 90. Subsequent references to this work cite two page numbers. The first refers to this edition; the second reference (here pp. 17–18) is to the English translation (*Critique of Judgment*, trans. J. H. Bernard [New York: Hafner Press, 1951]). I have occasionally made slight changes in the English version. References to other works by Kant are from the same Suhrkamp *Werkausgabe*; the translations are my own.

Ideologies, to the extent that they necessarily contain empirical moments and are directed toward what lies outside the realm of pure concepts, are on the side of metaphysics rather than critical philosophy. The conditions and modalities of their occurrence are determined by critical analyses to which they have no access. The object of these analyses, on the other hand, can only be ideologies. Ideological and critical thought are interdependent and any attempt to separate them collapses ideology into mere error and critical thought into idealism. The possibility of maintaining the causal link between them is the controlling principle of rigorous philosophical discourse: philosophies that succumb to ideology lose their epistemological sense, whereas philosophies that try to by-pass or repress ideology lose all critical thrust and risk being repossessed by what they foreclose.

The Kant passage establishes two other points. By speaking of a *causal* link between ideology and transcendental philosophy, one is reminded of the prominence of causality in Kant's example, the focus on the internal or external *cause* of the motion of bodies. The example of bodies in motion is indeed more than a mere example that could be replaced by any other; it is another version or definition of transcendental cognition. If critical philosophy and metaphysics (including ideologies) are causally linked to each other, their relationship is similar to the relationship, made explicit in the example, between bodies and their transformations or motions. Critical philosophy and ideology then become each other's motion: if an ideology is considered to be a stable entity (body, corpus, or canon), the critical discourse it generates will be that of a transcendental motion, of a motion whose cause resides, so to speak, within itself, within the substance of its own being. And if the critical system is considered stable in its principles, the corresponding ideology will acquire a mobility caused by a principle that lies outside itself; this principle, within the confines of the system thus constituted, can only be the principle of constitution, the architectonics of the transcendental system that functions as the cause of the ideological motions. In both cases, it is the transcendental system, as substance or as structure, that determines the ideology and not the reverse. The question then becomes how the substance or the structure of a transcendental discourse can be determined. To try to answer this question from the inside of the Kantian text is the tentative purpose of this still-introductory and expository paper.

The second point to be gained from the same passage has to do with the aesthetic. Immediately after distinguishing between transcendental and metaphysical principles, Kant goes on to distinguish between "the pure concept of objects of possible subjective cognition [*der reine Begriff von Gegenständen des möglichen Erfahrungserkenntnisses überhaupt*]" and "the principle of practical purposiveness which must be thought as the idea of the determination of a free will"; the distinction is a correlate of the prior more general distinction between transcendental and metaphysical principles. The distinction directly alludes to the division between pure and practical reason and corresponds to the major division in the corpus of Kant's works. One sees again how the third *Critique* corresponds to the necessity of establishing the causal link between critical philosophy and ideology, between a purely conceptual and an empirically determined discourse. Hence the need for a phenomenalized, empirically manifest principle of cognition on whose existence the possibility of such an articulation depends. This phenomenalized principle is what Kant calls the aesthetic. The investment in the aesthetic is therefore considerable, since the possibility of philosophy itself, as the articulation of a transcendental with a metaphysical discourse, depends on it. And the place in the third *Critique* where this articulation occurs is the section on the sublime; in the section on the beautiful, the articulation is said to be between understanding (*Verstand*) and judgment. In both cases, one meets with great difficulties but the motives for this are perhaps easier to perceive in the case of the sublime, possibly because reason is explicitly involved.

The complexity and possible incongruity of the notion of the sublime, a topic that no eighteenth-century treatise of aesthetics is ever allowed to ignore, makes the section of the third *Critique* that deals with it one of the most difficult and unresolved passages in the entire corpus of Kant's works. Whereas, in the section on the beautiful, the difficulties at least convey the illusion of being controlled, the same can hardly be said of the sublime. It is possible to formulate with some clarity what the project, the burden, of the section might be, and equally possible to understand what is at stake in its accomplishment. But it remains very difficult to decide whether or not the enterprise fails or succeeds. The complication is noticeable from the very start, in the introduction that distinguishes between the beautiful and the sublime. From the point of view of the main theme of the third *Critique*, the problem of teleological judgment or of purposiveness without purpose, the consideration of the sublime seems almost superfluous. "The concept of the sublime," says Kant, "is not nearly so important or rich in consequences as the concept of the beautiful and, in general, it displays nothing purposive in nature itself. . . ." "The idea of the sublime thus separates from that of a purposiveness of nature and this makes the theory of the sublime a mere appendix [*einen bloßen Anhang*] to the aesthetic judging of that purposiveness . . ." (p. 167; 84). After that modest beginning, however, it turns out that this outer appendage is in fact of crucial importance, because, instead of informing us, like the beautiful, about the teleology of nature, it informs us about the teleology of our own faculties, more specifically about the relationship between imagination and reason. It follows, in accordance with what was said before, that whereas the beautiful is a metaphysical and ideological principle, the sublime aspires to being a transcendental one, with all that this entails.

Contrary to the beautiful, which at least appears to be all of a piece, the sublime is shot through with dialectical complication. It is, in some respects, infinitely attractive but, at the same time, thoroughly repellent; it gives a peculiar kind of pleasure (*Lust*), yet it is also consistently painful; in less subjective, more structural terms, it is equally baffling: it knows of no limits or borders, yet it has to appear as a determined totality; in a philosophical sense, it is something of a monster, or, rather, a ghost: it is not a property of nature (there are no such things as sublime objects in nature) but a purely inward experience of consciousness (*Gemütsbestimmung*), yet Kant insists, time and again, that this noumenal entity has to be phenomenally represented (*dargestellt*); this is indeed an integral part, the crux, in fact, of the analytics of the sublime.

The question becomes whether the dialectical incompatibilities will find, in the concept of the sublime, a possibility of resolution. A first symptom that this may not simply and unambiguously be the case appears in an additional complication that makes the schema of the sublime distinct from that of the beautiful. One can grant that it is methodologically as legitimate to evaluate the impact on us of the sublime, as pleasure or as pain, in terms of quantity instead of, as is the case with the beautiful, in terms of quality. But, if this is indeed the case, why then can the analytics of the sublime not be closed off with the section on the mathematical sublime, centered on quantity and on number? Why the need for another section, nonexistent in the area of the beautiful, which Kant calls the *dynamic* sublime, and of which it will be difficult to say whether it still belongs to the order of quantity or of quality? Kant gives *some* explanation of why this is needed, but this explanation raises more questions than it answers (section 24). The sublime produces an emotional, agitated response in the beholder; this response can be referred back to the needs of knowledge (in the mathematical sublime) as well as to the needs of desire (*Begehrungsvermögen*) (in the dynamic sublime). In the realm of aesthetic judgment, both have to be considered regardless of purpose or interest, a requirement that can conceivably be met in the realm of knowledge but that is much less easy to fulfill in the realm of desire, all the more so since it is clearly understood that this desire has to be considered in itself, as subjective manifestation, and not as an objectified knowledge of desire. And indeed, when we reach the section on the dynamic sublime, we find something quite different from desire. The need for the additional subdivision, as well as the transition from the one to the other (from mathematical quantity to the dynamic), is by no means easy to account for and will demand an avowedly speculative effort of interpretation, of which it is not certain that it will succeed.

The antinomies at play in the mathematical sublime are clearly defined and so are the reasons of their relevance for aesthetic judgment. The mathematical sublime starts out from the concept of number. Its burden is that of calculus, as one would expect in a philosopher whose master's thesis dealt with Leibniz: it is the burden of realizing that finite and infinite entities are not susceptible of comparison and cannot both be inscribed within a common system of knowledge. As calculus the proposition is self-evident and, in the infinitesimal realm of number, "the power of number," says Kant, "reaches infinity" (p. 173; 89), it creates no difficulties: the infinitely large (or, for that matter, the infinitely small) can be conceptualized by means of number. But such a conceptualization is entirely devoid of phenomenal equivalences; in terms of the faculties, it is, strictly speaking, unimaginable. This is not, however, how the sublime has been defined. The sublime is not mere quantity or number, still less the notion of quantity as such (*Quantum*). Quantity thus conceived, and expressed by number, is always a relative concept that refers back to a conventional unity of measurement; pure number is neither large nor small, and the infinitely large is also the infinitely small: the telescope and the microscope, as instruments of measurement, are the same instrument. The sublime, however, is not "the large" but "the largest"; it is that "compared to which everything else is small." As such, it can never be accessible to the senses. But it is not pure number either, for there is no such thing as a "greatest" in the realm of number. It belongs to a different order of experience, closer to extension than to number. It is, in Kant's words, "absolute magnitude" (*die Größe*—or better, as in the beginning of the section, *das Größte schlechthin*), as far as consciousness can grasp it in an intuition (*so weit das Gemüt sie in einer Anschauung fassen kann*) (p. 173; 90). This phenomenalization cannot stem from number, only from extension. The sentence is another version of the original statement that the sublime is to be borderless (*unbegrenzt*) yet a totality: number is without limit, but extension implies the possibility of a determined totalization, of a contour. The mathematical sublime has to articulate number with extension and it faces a classical problem of natural philosophy. The fact that it is a recurrent philosophical theme does not make it any easier to solve, nor does it allow one to overlook the intricacies of the arguments by which the solution is attempted just because the burden of argument turns out to be familiar.

Kant tries to articulate number with extension by way of two demonstrations, the first epistemological, the second in terms of pleasure and pain. Neither of these arguments is truly conclusive. On the level of understanding, the infinity of number can be conceived as a purely logical progression, which is not in need of any spatial concretization. But, on the level of reason, this "comprehensio logica" is no longer sufficient. Another mode of understanding called "comprehensio aesthetica" is needed, which requires constant totalization or condensation in a single intuition; even the infinite "must be thought as entirely given, according to its totality" (p. 177; 93). But since the infinite is not comparable to any finite magnitude, the articulation cannot occur. It does not, in fact, ever occur and it is the *failure* of the articulation that becomes the distinguishing characteristic of the sublime: it transposes or elevates the natural to the level of the supernatural, perception to imagination, understanding to reason. This transposition, however, never allows for the condition of totality that is constitutive of the sublime, and it can therefore not supersede the failure by becoming, as in a dialectic, the knowledge of this failure. The sublime cannot be defined as the failure of the sublime, for this failure deprives it of its identifying principle. Neither could one say that, at this point, the sublime fulfills itself as desire for what it fails to be, since what it desires—totality—is not other than itself.

The same pattern returns with regard to pleasure and pain. It is clear that what the sublime achieves is not the task required by its own position (articulation of number and extension by ways of the infinite). What it achieves is the awareness of another faculty besides understanding and reason, namely, the imagination. Out of the pain of the failure to constitute the sublime by making the infinite apparent (*anschaulich*) is born the pleasure of the imagination, which discovers, in this very failure, the congruity of its law (which is a law of failure) with the law of our own suprasensory being. Its failure to connect with the sensory would also elevate it above it. This law does not reside in nature but defines man in opposition to nature; it is only by an act of what Kant calls "subreption" (p. 180; 96) that this law is fallaciously attributed to nature. But is not this subreption a mirror image of another, previous subreption by which the sublime subreptitiously posits itself by claiming to exist by dint of the impossibility of its own existence? The transcendental judgment that is to decide on the possibility of existence of the sublime (as the spatial articulation of the infinite) functions metaphorically, or ideologically, when it subreptitiously defines itself in terms of its other, namely, of extension and totality. If space lies outside the sublime and remains there, and if space is nevertheless a necessary condition (or cause) for the sublime to come into being, then the principle of the sublime is a metaphysical principle that mistakes itself for a transcendental one. If imagination, the faculty of the sublime, comes into being at the expense of the totalizing power of the mind, how can it then, as the text requires, be in contrastive harmony (p. 182; 97) with the faculty of reason, which delimits the contour of this totality? What the imagination undoes is the very labor of reason, and such a relationship cannot without difficulty be said to unite both of them, imagination and reason, in a common task or law of being. Kant's definition of aesthetic judgment as what represents the subjective play of the faculties (imagination and reason) as "harmonious through their very contrast" remains, at this point, quite obscure. Which accounts, perhaps, in part for the fact that a further elaboration is needed in which the relationship between the same two powers of the mind will be somewhat less enigmatically represented; this can occur, however, only after moving from the mathematical to the dynamic sublime.

The difficulty can be summarized in a shift in terminology that occurs later in the text but that directly alludes to the difficulties we already encounter in the mathematical sublime. In section 29, in the general remark upon the exposition of the aesthetic judgment, appears the most concise but also the most suggestive definition of the sublime as "an object (of nature) the representation [*Vorstellung*] of which determines consciousness [*Gemüt*] to *think* the unattainability of nature as a sensory representation [*Darstellung*] of ideas" (p. 193; 108; emphasis mine). The key word, for our present purpose, in this quotation in which every word is rich in innumerable questions, is the word *denken* in the phrase "die Unerreich-barkeit der Natur als Darstellung zu *denken*." A few lines later, Kant speaks of the necessity "to *think* nature itself in its totality, as the sensory representation of something that lies beyond the senses, without being able to accomplish this representation *objectively* [*die Natur selbst in ihrer Totalität, als Darstellung von etwas Übersinnlichem, zu* denken, *ohne diese Darstellung* objektiv *zu Stande bringen zu können*]" (p. 194; 108; emphasis Kant's). Still a few lines later, the word *denken* is singled out and contrasted with knowing: "die Natur als Darstellung derselben [i.e., die Idee des Übersinnlichen] nicht *erkennen*, sondern nur *denken* können..." How are we to understand the verb "to think" in these formulations, in distinction from knowing? The way of knowledge, of *Erkenntnis*, has not been able to establish the existence of the sublime as an intelligible concept. This may be possible only by ways of *denken* rather than *erkennen*. What would be an instance of such thinking that differs from knowing? Was heißt denken?

Still in the mathematical sublime, in section 26, next to the epistemology and the eudaemony of the sublime, appears another description of how an infinite quantity can become a sensory intuition in the imagination, or how, in other words, the infinity of number can be articulated with the totality of extension (p. 173; 89). This description, which is formal rather than philosophical, is a great deal easier to follow than the subsequent arguments. In order to make the sublime appear in space we need, says Kant, two acts of the imagination: apprehension (*apprehensio*) and comprehension or summation (*comprehensio aesthetica*), *Auffassung* and *Zusammenfassung* (p. 173; 90). Apprehension proceeds successively, as a syntagmatic, consecutive motion along an axis, and it can proceed ad infinitum without difficulty. Comprehension, however, which is a paradigmatic totalization of the apprehended trajectory, grows increasingly difficult as the space covered by apprehension grows larger. The model reminds one of a simple phenomenology of reading, in which one has to make constant syntheses to comprehend the successive unfolding of the text: the eye moves horizontally in succession whereas the mind has to combine vertically the cumulative understanding of what has been apprehended. The comprehension will soon reach a point at which it is saturated and will no longer be able to take in additional apprehensions: it cannot progress beyond a certain magnitude which marks the limit of the imagination. This ability of the imagination to achieve syntheses is a boon to the understanding, which is hardly conceivable without it, but this gain is countered by a corresponding loss. The comprehension discovers its own limitation, beyond which it cannot reach. "[The imagination] loses as much on the one side as it gains on the other" (p. 174; 90). As the paradigmatic simultaneity substitutes for the syntagmatic succession, an economy of loss and gain is put in place which functions with predictable efficacy, though only within certain well-defined limits. The exchange from part to whole generates wholes that turn out to be only parts. Kant gives the example of the Egyptologist Savary, who observed that, in order to perceive the magnitude of the pyramids, one could be neither too far away nor too close. One is reminded of Pascal: "Bornés en tout genre, cet état qui tient le milieu entre deux extrêmes, se trouve en toutes nos puissances. Nos sens n'aperçoivent rien d'extrême, trop de bruit nous assourdit, trop de lumière éblouit, trop de distance et trop de proximité empêche la vue. Trop de longueur et trop de brièveté de discours l'obscurcit, trop de vérité nous étonne..."[3] It is not surprising that, from considerations on vision and, in general, on perception, Pascal moves to the order of discourse, for the model that is being suggested is no longer, properly speaking, philosophical, but linguistic. It describes not a faculty of the mind, be it as consciousness or as cognition, but a potentiality inherent in language. For such a system of substitution, set up along a paradigmatic and a syntagmatic axis, generating partial totalizations within an economy of profit and loss, is a very familiar model indeed—which also explains why the passage seems so easy to grasp in comparison with what precedes and follows. It is the model of discourse as a tropological system. The desired articulation of the sublime takes place, with suitable reservations and restrictions, within such a purely formal system. It follows, however, that it is conceivable only within the limits of such a system, that is, as pure discourse rather than as a faculty of the mind. When the sublime is translated back, so to speak, from language into cognition, from formal description into philosophical argument, it loses all inherent coherence and dissolves in the aporias of intellectual and sensory appearance. It is also established that, even within the confines of language, the sublime can occur only as a single and particular point of view, a privileged place that avoids both excessive comprehension and excessive apprehension, and that this place is only formally, and not transcendentally, determined. The sublime cannot be grounded as a philosophical (transcendental or metaphysical) principle, but only as a linguistic principle. Consequently, the section on the mathematical sublime cannot be closed off in a satisfactory manner and another chapter on the dynamics of the sublime is needed.

According to the principles of the quadrivium, the further extension of the system number-extension should have been motion, and we could have expected a kinetic rather than a dynamic sublime. But the kinetics of the sublime are treated at once, and somewhat surprisingly, as a question of *power*: the first word of section 28 (p. 184; 99) (on the dynamics of the sublime) is *Macht*, soon followed by violence (*Gewalt*) and by the assertion that violence is the only means by which to overcome the resistance of one force to another. A classical way to have moved from number to motion would have been by way of a kinetics of physical bodies, a study, as, for example, in Kepler, of the motion of heavenly bodies in function of gravity as acceleration. Gravity can also be considered a force or a power, next to being a motion—as in Wordsworth's line: "no motion has she now, no force"—

---

3. Blaise Pascal, *Pensées*, ed. Louis Lafuma (Paris: Éditions du Seuil, Collection l'Intégrale, 1963), Pensée 199, p. 527.

and the passage from a kinesis to a dynamics of the sublime could be treated in terms of mathematical and physical concepts. Kant does not pursue this line of thought and at once introduces the notion of might in a quasi-empirical sense of assault, battle, and fright. The relationship between the natural and the aesthetic sublime is treated as a scene of combat in which the faculties of the mind somehow have to overpower the forces of nature.

The necessity of extending the model of the mathematical sublime, the system of number-extension, to the model of the dynamic sublime as the system number-motion, as well as the interpretation of motion as empirical power, is not accounted for in philosophical terms in the analytics of the sublime, nor can it, especially in its latter aspect (the empiricization of force into violence and battle), be explained by purely historical reasons. The only way to account for it is as an extension of the linguistic model beyond its definition as a system of tropes. Tropes account for the occurrence of the sublime but, as we saw, in such a restrictive and partial way that the system could not be expected to remain quiescent within its narrow boundaries. From the pseudocognition of tropes, language has to expand to the activity of performance, something of which language has been known to be capable well before Austin reminded us of it. The transition from the mathematical to the dynamic sublime, a transition for which the justification is conspicuously lacking in the text (section 28 begins most abruptly with the word "Power" [*Macht*]), marks the saturation of the tropological field as language frees itself of its constraints and discovers within itself a power no longer dependent on the restrictions of cognition. Hence the introduction, at this point in the text, of the concept of morality, but on the level of practical rather than pure reason. The articulation between pure and practical reason, the raison d'être of the third *Critique*, occurs in the widening definition of language as a performative as well as a tropological system. The *Critique of Judgment* therefore has, at its center, a deep, perhaps fatal, break or discontinuity. It depends on a linguistic structure (language as a performative as well as a cognitive system) that is not itself accessible to the powers of transcendental philosophy. Nor is it accessible, one should hasten to add, to the powers of metaphysics or of ideology, which are themselves precritical stages of knowledge. Our question, then, becomes whether and where this disruption, this disarticulation, becomes apparent in the text, at a moment when the aporia of the sublime is no longer stated, as was the case in the mathematical sublime and in the ensuing general definitions of the concept, as an explicit paradox, but as the apparently tranquil, because entirely unreflected, juxtaposition of incompatibles. Such a moment occurs in the general remark or recapitulation (section 29) that concludes the analytics of the sublime.

The chapter on the dynamics of the sublime appears as another version of the difficulties encountered in the mathematical sublime rather than as their further development, let alone their solution. Except for the introduction of the moral dimension, hard to account for in epistemological or aesthetic terms, this chapter differs most from the preceding inquiry by concentrating on affect rather than on reason (as in the mathematical sublime) or on understanding (as in the analytics of the beautiful). The preeminence of the faculty of the imagination is maintained, as is the question of its relationship to reason, but this dialectic of reason and imagination is now mediated by affects, moods and feelings, rather than by rational principles. The change results in a restatement and refinement rather than in a transformation of the principle of the sublime. The admirably concise and previously quoted definition given at the beginning of the "General Remarks" benefits from the references to mood and to affectivity but does not differ in substance from similar developments that occurred in the preceding paragraphs. Nor is it, for all its controlled concentration, in essence less obscure than the previous formulations.

The chapter also contains, somewhat abruptly, a reminder that, in a transcendental aesthetic of judgment, objects in nature susceptible of producing sublime effects have to be considered in a radically nonteleological manner, completely detached from any purpose or interest that the mind may find in them. Kant adds that he had previously reminded the reader of this necessity, but it is not clear to what passage he alludes. He is rather restating a general principle that underlies the entire enterprise and that was first formulated, with all desirable clarity, at the onset of the analytics of the beautiful under the modality of quality (p. 116; 38). This time, however, Kant relates the principle of disinterestedness specifically to objects in nature and takes for his example two landscapes: "If, then, we call the sight of the starry heaven *sublime*, we must not place at the foundation of judgment concepts of worlds inhabited by rational beings and regard the bright points, with which we see the space above us filled, as their suns moving in circles purposively fixed with reference to them; but we must regard it, just as we see it [*wie man ihn sieht*], as a distant, all-embracing vault [*ein weites Gewölbe*]. Only under such a representation can we range that sublimity that a pure aesthetic judgment ascribes to this object. And in the same way, if we are to call the sight of the ocean sublime, we must not think of it as we ordinarily do, as implying all kinds of knowledge (that are not contained in immediate intuition). For example, we sometimes think of the ocean as a vast kingdom of aquatic creatures, or as the great source of those vapors that fill the air with clouds for the benefit of the land, or again as an element that, though dividing continents from each other, yet promotes the greatest communication between them; all these produce merely teleological judgments. To find the ocean nevertheless sublime we must regard it as poets do [*wie die Dichter es tun*], merely by what the eye reveals [*was der Augenschein zeigt*]—if it is at rest, as a clear mirror of water only bounded by the heavens; if it is stormy, as an abyss threatening to overwhelm everything" (p. 196; 110-11).

The passage is remarkable in many respects, including its apparent anticipation of many such passages soon to be found in the works of romantic poets and already present, in many cases, in their eighteenth-century predecessors. But it is just as necessary to distinguish it from these symbolic landscapes as to point out the similarities. The predominant perception, in the Kant passage, is that of the heavens and the ocean as an architectonic construct. The heavens are a vault that covers the totality of earthy space as a roof covers a house. Space, in Kant as in Aristotle, is a house in which we dwell more or less safely, or more or less poetically, on this earth. This is also how the sea is perceived or how, according to Kant, poets perceive it: its horizontal expanse is like a floor bounded by the horizon, by the walls of heaven as they close off and delimit the building.

Who, one may wonder, are the poets who thus perceive the world in an architectonic rather than in a teleological way and how can the architectonic then be said to be opposed to the teleological? How are we to understand the term *Augenschein* in relation to the other allusions to sensory appearance that abound in the attempts to define or to describe the sublime? It is easier to say what the passage excludes and how it differs from others than to say what it is, but this may well be in accordance with Kant's insistence (pp. 195-96; 109) on the primarily *negative* mode of the imagination. Certainly, in our tradition, the first poet we think of as having similar intuitions is Wordsworth, who, in the nest-robbing episode in *The Prelude*, evoked the experience of dizziness and absolute fright in the amazing lines: "The sky was not a sky / Of earth, and with what motion moved the clouds!" Here, too, the sky is originally conceived as a roof or vault that shelters us, by anchoring us in the world, standing on a horizontal plane, *under* the sky, reassuringly stabilized by the weight of our own gravity. But, if the sky suddenly separates from the earth and is no longer, in Wordsworth's terms, a sky *of* earth, we lose all feeling of stability and start to fall, so to speak, skyward, away from gravity.

Kant's passage is *not* like this because the sky does not appear in it as associated in any way with shelter. It is not the construct under which, in Heidegger's terms, we can dwell (*wohnen*). In a lesser-known passage from the *Logic* Kant speaks of "a wild man who, from a distance, sees a house of which he does not know the use. He certainly observes the same object as does another, who knows it to be definitely built and arranged to serve as a dwelling for human beings. Yet in formal terms this knowledge of the selfsame object differs in both cases. For the first it is mere intuition [*bloße Anschauung*], for the other both intuition and concept."[4] The poet who sees the heavens as a vault is clearly like the savage, and unlike Wordsworth. He does not see prior to dwelling, but merely sees. He does not see in order to shelter himself, for there is no suggestion made that he could in any way be threatened, not even by the storm—since it is pointed out that he

---

4. Kant, *Logik*, in *Werkausgabe*, 6:457.

remains safely on the shore. The link between seeing and dwelling, *sehen* and *wohnen*, is teleological and therefore absent in pure aesthetic vision.

Or, still in association with Wordsworth, one thinks of the famous passage from "Tintern Abbey":

> And I have felt
> A presence that disturbs me with the joy
> Of elevated thoughts; a sense sublime
> Of something far more deeply interfused
> Whose dwelling is the light of setting suns,
> And the round ocean and the living air
> And the blue sky, and in the mind of man: . . .

The sublimity of the round ocean, horizon-bound as a vast dome, is especially reminiscent of the Kant passage. But the two invocations of sublime nature soon diverge. Wordsworth's sublime is an instance of the constant exchange between mind and nature, of the chiasmic transfer of properties between the sensory and the intellectual world that characterizes his figural diction, here explicitly thematized in the "motion and spirit that impels / All thinking things, all objects of all thoughts / And rolls through all things." No mind is involved in the Kantian vision of ocean and heaven. To the extent that any mind, that any judgment, intervenes, it is in error—for it is not the case that heaven is a vault or that the horizon bounds the ocean like the walls of a building. That is how things are to the eye, in the redundancy of their appearance to the eye and not to the mind, as in the redundant word *Augenschein,* to be understood in opposition to Hegel's *Ideenschein,* or sensory appearance of the idea; *Augenschein,* in which the eye, tautologically, is named twice, as eye itself and as what appears to the eye.

Kant's architectonic world is not a metamorphosis of a fluid world into the solidity of stone, nor is his building a trope or a symbol that substitutes for the actual entities. Heaven and ocean as building are a priori, previous to any understanding, to any exchange or anthropomorphism which will allow Wordsworth to address, in book 5 of *The Prelude*, the "speaking face" of nature. There is no room for address in Kant's flat, third-person world. Kant's vision can therefore hardly be called literal, which would imply its possible figuralization or symbolization by an act of judgment. The only word that comes to mind is that of a *material* vision, but how this materiality is then to be understood in linguistic terms is not, as yet, clearly intelligible.

Not being part of trope or figuration, the purely aesthetic vision of the natural world is in no way solar. It is not the sudden discovery of a true world as an unveiling, as the a-letheia of Heidegger's *Lichtung*. It is not a solar world and we are explicitly told that we are not to think of the stars as "suns moving in circles." Nor are we to think of them as the constellation that survives at the apocalyptic end of Mallarmé's *Coup de Dés*. The "mirror" of the sea surface is a mirror without depth, least of all the mirror in which the constellation would be reflected. In this mode of seeing, the eye is its own agent and not the specular echo of the sun. The sea is called a mirror, not because it is supposed to reflect anything, but to stress a flatness devoid of any suggestion of depth. In the same way and to the same extent that this vision is purely material, devoid of any reflexive or intellectual complication, it is also purely formal, devoid of any semantic depth and reducible to the formal mathematization or geometrization of pure optics. The critique of the aesthetic ends up, in Kant, in a formal materialism that runs counter to all values and characteristics associated with aesthetic experience, including the aesthetic experience of the beautiful and of the sublime as described by Kant and Hegel themselves. The tradition of their interpretation, as it appears from near contemporaries such as Schiller on, has seen only this one, figural, and, if you will, "romantic" aspect of their theories of the imagination, and has entirely overlooked what we call the material aspect. Neither has it understood the place and the function of formalization in this intricate process.

The vision of heaven and world entirely devoid of teleological interference, held up here as a purely sublime and aesthetic vision, stands in direct contradiction to all preceding definitions and analyses of the sublime given in section 24 on until this point in section 29. Still, in the condensed definition that appears in the same chapter the stress falls on the sublime as a concrete representation of ideas (*Darstellung von Ideen*). As in the Wordsworth passage from "Tintern Abbey," the articulation of physical motion with the movements of the affects and of practical moral judgment has to encompass natural and intellectual elements under one single unifying principle, such as the sublime. And there has been so much emphasis, from the start, on the fact that the sublime does not reside in the natural object but in the mind of man (*Gemütsbestimmungen*) that the burden of the argument, much rather than emphasizing the purely inward, noumenal nature of the sublime, becomes the need to account for the fact that it nevertheless occurs as an outward, phenomenal manifestation. Can this in any way be reconciled with the radical materiality of sublime vision suddenly introduced, as if it were an afterthought, at this point in the argument? How is one to reconcile the concrete representation of ideas with pure ocular vision, *Darstellung von Ideen* with *Augenschein*?

The analytics of the sublime (like those of the beautiful) are consistently stated in terms of a theory of the faculties combined, in the dynamics of the sublime, with a theory of moral affect. "A feeling for the sublime in nature cannot well be thought without combining therewith a mood of *consciousness* which is akin to the *moral*" (p. 194; 109; emphasis mine). In the case of the beautiful, this moral component was also present, though in a much more subdued form. It manifested itself as the autonomy of aesthetic pleasure with regard to sensuous pleasure, a form of freedom and thus, in Kant's system, where morality is always linked to liberty, at least potentially a form of moral judgment. But in the case of the sublime, the tie with morality is much more explicit, for morality is involved, not as play, but as law-directed labor (*gesetzliches Geschäft*). The only restriction that keeps the sublime from passing entirely into the camp of morality is that the faculty involved in it is not reason, or at least not an unmediated manifestation of reason, but that the sublime is represented by the imagination itself, as a tool of reason. In the laborious, businesslike world of morality, even the free and playful imagination becomes an instrument of work. Its task, its labor, is precisely to translate the abstractions of reason back into the phenomenal world of appearances and images whose presence is retained in the very word imagination, *Bild* in the German *Einbildungskraft.*

Why this incarnation of the idea has to occur is accounted for in various ways. It is, first of all, a quasi-theological necessity that follows necessarily from our fallen condition. The need for aesthetic judgment and activity, although it defines man, is the expression of a shortcoming, of a curse rather than of an excess of power and inventiveness. There would be no need for it "if we were creatures of pure intellect or even capable of displacing ourselves mentally in such a condition" (p. 197; 111). The same inherent inferiority of the aesthetic (or, more precisely, of the aesthetic as symptomatic of an inherent shortcoming in us) becomes visible with regard to moral judgment. Morality and the aesthetic are both disinterested, but this disinterestedness becomes necessarily polluted in aesthetic representation: the persuasion that, by means of their very disinterestedness, moral and aesthetic judgments are capable of achieving is necessarily linked, in the case of the aesthetic, with positively valorized sensory experiences. The moral lesson of the aesthetic has to be conveyed by seductive means which, as we know, can reach far enough to make it necessary to read "Kant avec Sade" rather than the reverse. Instead of purely intellectual beauty, we can only produce the beauty of the imagination. How this occurs is the object of a crucial and difficult paragraph (p. 195; 109) in which the articulation of the imagination with reason, the assumedly "harmonious" relationship between reason and imagination wishfully promised at an earlier stage, is described in detail.

The passage introduces what a few pages later will be defined as a modulation between two moods or affects, the passage from shocked surprise (*Verwunderung*) to tranquil admiration (*Bewunderung*). The initial effect of the sublime, of a sudden encounter with colossal natural entities such as cataracts, abysses, and towering mountains, is one of shock or, says Kant, astonishment that borders on terror (*Verwunderung, die an Schreck grenzt*). By a play, a trick of the imagination, this terror is transformed into a feeling of tranquil superiority, the admiration one expresses for something or for someone one can afford to admire peacefully, because one's own superiority is not really in question. The better one thinks of him, the better one has to think of oneself. How enviable a peace of mind thus achieved in the recognition of another's worth as confirmation of one's own! Moral nobility is the best ego booster available—though Kant is not so blind as not to know of its cost in hidden terror.

He had not always held that the serenity of admiration, the tranquillity of spent emotion, is the highest of qualities. In the early, precritical essay on the sublime and the beautiful from 1764,[5] he had stated in peremptory fashion that the humor of the phlegmatic had to be rejected out of hand as having not the slightest possible relationship with beauty or sublimity, in any form or shape. It was said to be utterly devoid of any interest whatsoever. Its equivalent in terms of national stereotypes is that of the Dutch, described as a phlegmatized kind of German interested only in the dreariest of commercial and moneymaking activities. I have never felt more grateful for the fifty or so kilometers that separate the Flemish city of Antwerp from the Dutch city of Rotterdam. Considerations on feminine languor and passivity, unfavorably contrasted with male energy, make for equally difficult reading in the early Kant essay. By the time of the *Critique of Judgment,* however, things have changed a great deal. "For (which seems strange) the absence of affection (apatheia, phlegma in significatu bono) in a mind that follows consistently its unalterable ground rules, is sublime, and in a far more outstanding way, because it is backed by the satisfaction of pure reason" (p. 199; 113). The tranquillity thus achieved receives the predicate of nobility, or a morally elevated state of mind that will then subreptitiously be transferred to objects and things such as "a building, a garment, literary style, bodily presence, etc." How is it, then, that the imagination can achieve the nobility of such loss of pathos, of such a serenity?

It does so by an essentially negative way, which corresponds philosophically to the elevation of the imagination from a metaphysical (and, hence, ideological) to a transcendental (and, hence, critical) principle. As long as the faculty of the imagination is considered empirically—and one is reminded that, in the late Kant, the presence of this empirical moment characterizes the metaphysical dimensions of the mind—it is free and playful, closer to what then in English is called "fancy" rather than what is called "imagination." By sacrificing, by giving up this freedom, in a first negative moment of shocked, but pleasurable surprise, the imagination allies itself with reason. Why this is so is not at once clear; in affective terms, it takes on the form of a reconquered mastery, a reconquered superiority over a nature of which the direct threat is overcome. The free, empirical reaction of the imagination, when confronted with the power and might of nature, is to indulge, to enjoy the terror of this very magnitude. Taming this delectable, because imaginary, terror—the assumption always being that the person is not directly threatened, or at the very least separated from the immediate threat by a reflexive moment—and preferring to it the tranquil satisfaction of superiority, is to submit

---

5. Kant, *Betrachtungen über das Gefühl des Schönen und Erhabenen*, in *Werkausgabe*, 2:875.

the imagination to the power of reason. For the faculty that establishes the superiority of the mind over nature is reason and reason alone; the imagination's security depends on the actual, empirical physical attraction and, when this situation is threatening, it swings toward terror and toward a feeling of free submission to nature. Since, however, in the experience of the sublime, the imagination achieves tranquillity, it submits to reason, achieves the highest degree of freedom by freely sacrificing its natural freedom to the higher freedom of reason. "Thereby," says Kant, "it achieves a gain in power that is larger than what it sacrifices" (p. 195; 109). The loss of empirical freedom means the gain in critical freedom that characterizes rational and transcendental principles. Imagination substitutes for reason at the cost of its empirical nature and, by this anti- or unnatural act, it conquers nature.

This complicated and somewhat devious scenario accomplishes the aim of the sublime. The imagination overcomes suffering, becomes apathetic, and sheds the pain of natural shock. It reconciles pleasure with pain and in so doing it articulates, as mediator, the movement of the affects with the legal, codified, formalized, and stable order of reason. Imagination is not nature (for, in its tranquillity, it determines itself as larger and mightier than nature), but, unlike reason, it remains in contact with nature. It is not idealized to the point of becoming pure reason, for it has no knowledge of its actual predicament or of its actual strategies and remains pure affect rather than cognition. It becomes adequate (*angemessen*) to reason on the basis of its inadequacy (*Unangemessenheit*) to this same reason in its relation to nature. "In elevating this reflection of the aesthetic judgment to the point where it becomes adequate to reason [*zur Angemessenheit mit der Vernunft*], without, however, reaching a definite concept of reason, the object is nevertheless represented, despite the objective inadequacy of the imagination, even in its greatest extension, to reason [*Unangemessenheit der Einbildungskraft . . . für die Vernunft*] as subjectively purposive" (pp. 195–96; 109–10)—and thus, we may add, as pertaining both to reason and to practical judgment.

However complex this final formulation may sound, it is clarified and made persuasive by the road that leads up to it and that is by no means unfamiliar. Even as uninspired a paraphrase as the one I have given should reveal that we are hardly dealing with a tight analytical argument (as was the case, for example, in the distinction between transcendental and metaphysical principles from which we started out). What we have here is less authoritative but a great deal more accessible. For one thing, instead of being an argument, it is a story, a dramatized scene of the mind in action. The faculties of reason and of imagination are personified, or anthropomorphized, like the five squabbling faculties hilariously staged by Diderot in the *Lettre sur les sourds et les muets*,[6] and the relationship between

---

6. Denis Diderot, *Lettre sur les sourds et les muets*, in *Œuvres complètes*, ed. Roger Lewinter (Paris: Le Club français du livre, 1969–73), 2:573–74.

them is stated in delusively interpersonal terms. What could it possibly mean, in analytical terms, that the imagination sacrifices itself, like Antigone or Iphigenia— for one can only imagine this shrewd and admirable imagination as the feminine heroine of a tragedy—for the sake of reason? And what is the status of all this heroism and cunning which allows it to reach apathia, to overcome pathos, by ways of the very pathos of sacrifice? How can faculties, themselves a heuristic hypothesis devoid of any reality—for only people who have read too much eighteenth-century psychology and philosophy might end up believing that they have an imagination or a reason, the same way they have blue eyes or a big nose— how can faculties be said to *act*, or even to act freely, as if they were conscious and complete human beings? We are clearly not dealing with mental categories but with tropes, and the story Kant tells us is an allegorical tale. Nor are the contents of this tale at all unusual. It is the story of an exchange, of a negotiation in which powers are lost and gained in an economy of sacrifice and recuperation. It is also a story of opposite forces, nature and reason, the imagination and nature, tranquillity and shock, adequacy (*Angemessenheit*) and inadequacy, that separate, fight, and then unite in a more or less stable state of harmony, achieving syntheses and totalizations that were missing at the beginning of the action. Such personified scenes of consciousness are easily identified: they are not actually descriptions of mental functions but descriptions of tropological transformations. They are not governed by the laws of the mind but by the laws of figural language. For the second time in this text (the first time being in the interplay between apprehension and comprehension in the mathematical sublime) we have come upon a passage that, under the guise of being a philosophical argument, is in fact determined by linguistic structures that are not within the author's control. What makes this intrusion of linguistic tropes particularly remarkable is that it occurs in close proximity, almost in juxtaposition to the passage on the material architectonics of vision, in the poetic evocation of heaven and ocean, with which it is entirely incompatible.

For we are now confronted with two completely different notions of the architectonic—a concept that appears under that name in Kant's own text. The architectonic vision of nature as a building is, in Kant, as we saw, entirely material, emphatically not tropological, entirely distinct from the substitutions and exchanges between faculties or between mind and nature that make up the Wordsworthian or the romantic sublime. But the architectonic is also at times defined by Kant, though not in the third *Critique*, in entirely different terms, much closer to the allegory of the faculties and the tale of recovered tranquillity we have just been reading, much closer as well to the *edle Einfalt* and *stille Größe* of Winckelmann's neoclassicism. Near the end of the *Critique of Pure Reason*, a chapter entitled "The Architectonics of Pure Reason" defines the architectonic as the organic unity of systems, "the unity of miscellaneous cognitions brought together under one idea" and greatly favored, by Kant, over what he calls the "rhapsody" of mere speculation devoid of *esprit de système*. That this unity is conceived in organic terms is apparent from the recurring metaphor of the body, as a totality of various limbs and parts (*Glieder,* meaning members in all the senses of the word, as well as, in the compound *Gliedermann,* the puppet of Kleist's Marionettentheater). "The whole," says Kant, "is articulated [*articulatio— gegliedert*] and not just piled on top of [*gehäuft*] each other; it can grow from the inside out but not from the outside in. It grows like an animal body, not by the addition of new limbs [*Glieder*] but, without changing the proportions, by making each individual member stronger and more efficient for its own purpose."[7] One will want to know what becomes of this Aristotelian, zoomorphic architectonic when it is being considered, in the third *Critique*'s passage on heaven and ocean, in a nonteleological, aesthetic perspective. For one thing, it does not imply a collapse of the architectonic in the rhapsodic, a disintegration of the building; sea and heaven, as the poets see them, are more than ever buildings. But it is no longer at all certain that they are still articulated (*gegliedert*). After lingering briefly over the aesthetic vision of the heavens and the seas, Kant turns for a moment to the human body: "The like is to be said of the sublime and the beautiful in the human body. We must not regard as the determining grounds of our judgment the concepts of the purposes which all our limbs serve [*wozu alle seine Gliedmaßen da sind*] and we must not allow this unity of purpose to influence our aesthetic judgment (for then it would no longer be pure) . . ." (p. 197; 111). We must, in short, consider our limbs, hands, toes, breasts, or what Montaigne so cheerfully referred to as "Monsieur ma partie," in themselves, severed from the organic unity of the body, the way the poets look at the oceans severed from their geographical place on earth. We must, in other words, disarticulate, mutilate the body in a way that is much closer to Kleist than to Winckelmann, though close enough to the violent end that happened to befall both of them. We must consider our limbs the way the primitive man considered the house, entirely severed from any purpose or use. From the phenomenality of the aesthetic (which is always based on an adequacy of the mind to its physical object, based on what is referred to, in the definition of the sublime, as the concrete representation of ideas—*Darstellung der Ideen*) we have moved to the pure materiality of *Augenschein,* of aesthetic vision. From the organic, still asserted as architectonic principle in the *Critique of Pure Reason,* to the phenomenological, the rational cognition of incarnate ideas, which the best part of the Kant interpretation in the nineteenth and twentieth century will single out, we have reached, in the final analysis, a materialism that, in the tradition of the reception of the third *Critique,* is seldom or never perceived. To appreciate the full impact of this conclusion one must remember that the entire project of the third *Critique,* the full investment in the aesthetic, was to achieve the articulation

---

7. Kant, *Kritik der reinen Vernunft,* in *Werkausgabe,* 4:696.

that would guarantee the architectonic unity of the system. If the architectonic then appears, very near the end of the analytics of the aesthetic, at the conclusion of the section on the sublime, as the material disarticulation not only of nature but of the body, then this moment marks the undoing of the aesthetic as a valid category. The critical power of a transcendental philosophy undoes the very project of such a philosophy leaving us, certainly not with an ideology—for transcendental and ideological (metaphysical) principles are part of the same system—but with a materialism that Kant's posterity has not yet begun to face up to. This happens not out of a lack of philosophical energy or rational power, but as a result of the very strength and consistency of this power.

What, finally, will be the equivalence of this moment in the order of language? Whenever the disruption asserted itself, in the passage in the nonteleological vision of nature and of the body and also, less openly but not less effectively, in the unexplained necessity of supplementing the consideration of the mathematical sublime with a consideration of the dynamic sublime, in the blank between section 27 and section 28 (as we refer to a blank between stanzas 1 and 2 of the Lucy poem "A slumber did my spirit seal . . ." or between parts 1 and 2 of the Boy of Winander poem), whenever, then, the articulation is threatened by its undoing, we encountered a passage (the section on apprehension, the section on the sacrifice of the imagination) that could be identified as a shift from a tropological to a different mode of language. In the case of the dynamic sublime, one could speak of a shift from trope to performance. In this case, the nonteleological apprehension of nature, a somewhat different pattern emerges. To the dismemberment of the body corresponds a dismemberment of language, as meaning-producing tropes are replaced by the fragmentation of sentences and propositions into discrete words, or the fragmentation of words into syllables or finally letters. In Kleist's text, one would isolate the dissemination of the word *Fall* and its compounds throughout as such a moment when the aesthetic dance turned into an aesthetic trap, as by the addition of one single mute letter which makes *Fall* (fall) into *Falle* (trap).[8] No such artful moments seem to occur, at first sight, in Kant. But just try to translate one single somewhat complex sentence of Kant, or just consider what the efforts of entirely competent translators have produced, and you will soon notice how decisively determining the play of the letter and of the syllable, the way of saying (*Art des Sagens*) as opposed to what is being said (*das Gesagte*)—to quote Walter Benjamin—is in this most unconspicuous of stylists. Is not the persuasiveness of the entire passage on the recovery of the imagination's tranquillity after the shock of sublime surprise based, not so much on the little play acted out by the senses, but on the proximity between the German words for surprise and admiration, *Verwunderung* and *Bewunderung*? And are we not made to assent to the more

---

8. See Paul de Man, "Aesthetic Formalization: Kleist's *Über das Marionettentheater*," in *The Rhetoric of Romanticism* (New York: Columbia University Press, 1984).

than paradoxical but truly aporetic incompatibility between the failure of the imagination to grasp magnitude with what becomes, in the experience of the sublime, the success of this same imagination as an agent of reason, are we not made to assent to this because of a constant, and finally bewildering alternation of the two terms, *Angemessen(heit)* and *Unangemessen(heit),* to the point where one can no longer tell them apart? The bottom line, in Kant as well as in Hegel, is the prosaic materiality of the letter and no degree of obfuscation or ideology can transform this materiality into the phenomenal cognition of aesthetic judgment.

Sign and Symbol in Hegel's *Aesthetics*

The ideological shrillness of the polemics that surround the advent of literary theory in our time cannot entirely conceal that these debates, however ephemeral and ad hominem they may be, are the external symptom of tensions that originate at the furthest remove from the stage of public debate. Yet their apparent remoteness from common experience does not make them less pressing. What is at stake in these exchanges is the compatibility between literary experience and literary theory. There is something bleakly abstract and ugly about literary theory that cannot be entirely blamed on the perversity of its practitioners. Most of us feel internally divided between the compulsion to theorize about literature and a much more attractive, spontaneous encounter with literary works. Hence the relief one feels whenever a method of literary study is proposed that allows for a measure of theo-

When "Sign and Symbol in Hegel's *Aesthetics*" was published in *Critical Inquiry* 8:4 (summer 1982): 761–75, de Man appended the following prefatory note as an unnumbered footnote on the first page: "This paper is part of a work in progress on the relationship between rhetorical, aesthetic, and ideological discourse in the period from Kant to Kierkegaard and Marx. It was prepared for delivery as the Renato Poggioli Lecture in Comparative Literature (Harvard University, 1980). I have left unchanged the traces it bears of this occasion as well as the all too hasty presentation of the more technical issues involved especially in the reading of par. 20 from the *Encyclopedia of the Philosophical Sciences*. I wish to thank Raymond Geuss of the University of Chicago Department of Philosophy for his generous and astute reading of the manuscript. It has allowed me to correct inaccuracies and to prevent unnecessary ambiguities. His cogent objections to my reading of par. 20 of the *Encyclopedia* have helped me to strengthen an argument which I hope to have the opportunity to develop in further discussion." All notes are de Man's, slightly modified.

91

retical rigor and generality (and which is therefore, to speak from an academic point of view, teachable) while leaving intact, or even enhancing, the aesthetic appreciation or the potential for historical insight that the work provides. This is the satisfaction with which one encounters the work of a master of literary history such as Renato Poggioli or Ernst-Robert Curtius or a master of formal and structural analysis such as Reuben Brower or Roman Jakobson: the rigor of the method confirms the beauty of its object. But in the craggy field of literary theory one should not be too easily satisfied with one's own satisfaction. Prudence is the main virtue of theoretical discipline, and prudence dictates suspicion when one feels too pleased with a methodological solution. The alacrity with which one rushes, as by instinct, to the defense of aesthetic values indicates that the source of one's suspicion should be the compatibility of the aesthetic dimensions of literature with whatever it is that its theoretical investigation discloses. If it is indeed the case that a difficulty exists between the aesthetics and the poetics of literature and that this difficulty is inherent in the matter itself, then it would be naive to believe that one can avoid or dodge the task of its precise description.

It is not easy to discover the element, in literature, that can be suspected of interfering with its aesthetic integrity. The urge to conceal it is inscribed, so to speak, in the situation, and this urge is probably strong enough to block direct access to the problem. One has to turn, therefore, to the canonical texts of aesthetic theory that offer the strongest reasoned defense for the equation of art with aesthetic experience. For reasons that have to do with this particular occasion but hardly stand in need of a less personal justification, Hegel's *Aesthetics* offers perhaps the most arduous challenge to such an enterprise. Nowhere else do the structure, the history, and the judgment of art seem to come as close to being systematically carried out, and nowhere else does this systematic synthesis rest so exclusively on one definite category, in the full Aristotelian sense of the term, called the aesthetic. Under a variety of names, this category never ceased to be prominent in the development of Western thought, so much so that its being left nameless until the end of the eighteenth century is a sign of its overwhelming presence rather than of its nonexistence. And although the posthumous collection of Hegel's *Lectures on Aesthetics*, suffering as it does from the stylistic infelicities of magisterial lecture courses recorded by overloyal disciples, is not exactly a reader's delight, nor even, to judge from bibliographical evidence, frequently read at all, its influence on our way of thinking about and teaching literature is still all-pervasive. Whether we know it, or like it, or not, most of us are Hegelians and quite orthodox ones at that. We are Hegelian when we reflect on literary history in terms of an articulation between the Hellenic and the Christian Era or between the Hebraic and the Hellenic world. We are Hegelian when we try to systematize the relationships between the various art forms or genres according to different modes of representation or when we try to conceive of historical periodization as a development, progressive or regressive, of a collective or individual consciousness. Not that such concerns belong exclusively to Hegel; far from it. But the name "Hegel" stands here for an all-encompassing vessel in which so many currents have gathered and been preserved that one is likely to find there almost any idea one knows to have been gathered from elsewhere or hopes to have invented oneself. Few thinkers have so many disciples who never read a word of their master's writings.

In the case of the *Aesthetics*, the persistent power of philosophical synthesis is concentrated in the work's ability to bring together, under the common aegis of the aesthetic, a historical causality with a linguistic structure, an experiential and empirical event in time with a given, nonphenomenal fact of language. In Hegel's well-known and in essence unchallenged division of the history of art into three phases, two of these phases are designated by historical terms—the classic and the Romantic (which in Hegel designates any post-Hellenic, i.e., Christian art)— whereas the third period is designated by the term "symbolic," which we now associate with linguistic structures and which stems not from historiography but from the practice of law and of statecraft. The theory of the aesthetic, as a historical as well as a philosophical notion, is predicated, in Hegel, on a theory of art as symbolic. The famous definition of the beautiful as "the sensory appearance [or manifestation] of the idea [*das sinnliche Scheinen der Idee*]" does not only translate the word "aesthetics" and thus establish the apparent tautology of aesthetic art (*die schönen Künste* or *les beaux-arts*), but it could itself best be translated by the statement: the beautiful is symbolic. The symbol is the mediation between the mind and the physical world of which art manifestly partakes, be it as stone, as color, as sound, or as language. Hegel says so in no uncertain terms in the section on symbolic art. After having stated casually that the symbol can be considered a sign (*das Symbol ist nun* zunächst *ein Zeichen*), he goes on to distinguish between the symbolic and the semiotic function and leaves no doubt as to what side of this dichotomy art is on: "In the case of art, we cannot consider, in the symbol, the arbitrariness between meaning and signification [which characterizes the sign], since art itself consists precisely in the connection, the affinity, and the concrete interpenetration of meaning and of form."[1] Aesthetic theory and art history are thus the two complementary parts of a single *symbolon*. Whoever dares, today more than ever, to challenge this article of faith in any of its numerous guises should not expect to get away with it unscathed.

Hegel's *Aesthetics* thus appears to be, traditionally enough, a theory of symbolic form. Yet a disturbing element of personal inadequacy in Hegel himself seems to prevent the tradition of the *Aesthetics'* interpretation from resting con-

---

1. G. W. F. Hegel, *Werke in zwanzig Bänden* (Frankfurt am Main: Suhrkamp, 1979), vol. 13, *Vorlesungen über die Ästhetik I*, p. 395; all further references to this volume, abbreviated *Ästh.*, and to vols. 8 and 10 (*Enzyklopädie der philosophischen Wissenschaften I* and *III*), abbreviated *Enz. I* or *III*, will be included in the text; my translations.

tent in this assurance. For one thing, next to the familiar-sounding assertion, which we think we easily enough understand, that art partakes of the beautiful and is therefore a sensory manifestation of the idea, stands, in the same text, Hegel's more disturbing statement that art is, irrevocably, for us a thing of the past. Would this then mean that the sensory manifestation of the idea is no longer accessible to us in this form, that we are no longer able to produce truly symbolic forms of art? And is it not something of an irony of literary history and a concrete disavowal of Hegel that he declared art to have ended at the very moment that a new modernity was about to discover and to refine the power of the symbol beyond anything that Hegel's somewhat philistine taste could ever have imagined? It must have been a poor symbolist indeed who thus declared nineteenth-century Romanticism and symbolism stillborn when it was about to write a new chapter in a history which he proclaimed to be over.

The contemporary interpretation of the *Aesthetics*, even when it emanates from writers favorably inclined toward Hegel such as Hans-Georg Gadamer, for instance, or Theodor W. Adorno, keeps encountering this difficulty and finds Hegel useless for the understanding of post-Hegelian art and literature. His theory of art as symbol may have prefigured some of what was to come, but his lack of sympathy for his own contemporaries makes him shortsighted and inadequate for the all-important task of our own self-definition, of understanding our own modernity. The attitude is well exemplified in the statement of an astute and sensitive interpreter of nineteenth-century literature who certainly cannot be reproached for an overhasty dismissal of Hegel. In a volume entitled *Poetics and Philosophy of History*, Peter Szondi (who, until his untimely death, directed the seminar for comparative literature at the Free University of Berlin) describes the feeling one cannot help but share upon coming to the section in the *Aesthetics* where Hegel discusses the actual symbolic forms or genres: metamorphosis, allegory, metaphor, image, parable, and so on.[2]

> The literary scholar who expects to be instructed by Hegel's aesthetics has up till then had to content himself with philosophical concepts, mythological representations, and archaic architecture. He expects, at long last, to find what he has been looking for—but a great disappointment awaits him [*es wartet eine große Enttäuschung auf ihn*]. One will have to say, without further ado, that this is one of the least inspired sections in the entire work. [P. 390]

> From the point of view of contemporary poetics, which certainly tends more and more to view imagery and metaphor as an essential trait or even as the essence of the poetic, Hegel's considerations [on metaphor and

---

2. Peter Szondi, *Poetik und Geschichtsphilosophie I* (Frankfurt am Main: Suhrkamp, 1974); all further references will be included in the text; my translations.

on figuration] must seem truly shallow [*recht äußerlich*]. . . . He does not reach an adequate understanding of metaphor and simile. . . . [P. 395]

When Proust compares a moon which is already visible in daylight to an actress who has entered the theater well before making her entrée on the stage, and who, not yet made up or dressed, merely watches her fellow players, then we may well ask if it is legitimate, in a case like this, to distinguish between the abstract and the concrete, between meaning and image. The secret meaning of such comparisons must be sought in the discovery of analogies, of correspondences—the very *correspondances* which Baudelaire celebrates in his famous poem. To the poetic outlook they appear as the guarantee of the unity of the world. . . . One can certainly not reproach Hegel for his inability to notice such correspondences (although they do not appear only in modern poetry), but one cannot deny that it is his inadequate conception of the essence of language which is the cause of his failure. [P. 396]

From this point on, we can begin to see the limitations of Hegel's aesthetics. [P. 390]

Hegel, then, is a theoretician of the symbol who fails to respond to symbolic language. This does not allow us to dismiss his aesthetics entirely, since he was at least on the right track, but it allows us to say that we no longer need him, since we have traveled so much further along the same road. And it is certainly true that Hegel's theory of the symbolic seems halfhearted compared to that of contemporaries such as Georg Friedrich Creuzer (whom he mentions critically), Friedrich Schelling (whom he does not mention at all in that context), or Friedrich Schlegel (about whom he never has a kind word to say). Could it be that Hegel is saying something more complex about the symbol and about language than what we recognize in him as so familiar to us, but that part of what he has to say is something that we cannot or will not hear because it upsets what we take for granted, the unassailable *value* of the aesthetic? The answer to this question takes us on a circuitous route, first away from and then back to the *Aesthetics*, a route on which I only have time to point out some stations in an itinerary that is not, I am afraid, an entirely easy walk.

Hegel's assertion that art belongs unreservedly to the order of the symbolic is made in the context of a distinction between symbol and sign that in the realm of art does not seem to apply. A great deal hinges on this distinction, which recurs, though not very conspicuously, throughout the Hegelian corpus, most explicitly in a paragraph of the earlier *Encyclopedia of the Philosophical Sciences* of 1817 (the *Aesthetics* is from 1830). It occurs in a section where Hegel is concerned with the distinctions between the faculties of the intellect, more specifically, the distinction between perceiving, imagining (or representing), and thinking (*Anschauung*, *Vorstellung*, and *Denken*); the discussion of language is a subsection of the discussion of representation. Here Hegel offers a characterization of the sign which stresses the arbitrariness of the relationship between the sensory component necessarily involved in any signification and the intended meaning. The red, white, and green flag of Italy bears no actual relationship to the color of the country, which, as seen from the air, is predominantly ochre in color; only very naive children are supposed to be cute enough to be amazed that Italy actually does not have the same uniform color it has in their atlas. The symmetrical obverse of this observation is that of Roland Barthes reflecting on the naturalization of the signifier in his analysis of an advertisement for spaghetti, in which the white pasta, the red tomatoes, and the green peppers are so irresistibly effective because they convey, at least to the non-Italian, the illusion of devouring, of interiorizing the very essence of *italianité*—and very cheaply at that. As such, in its arbitrariness, the sign, says Hegel,

> differs from the symbol, a perception whose own determination [or meaning] more or less corresponds, essentially and conceptually, to the content it expresses as a symbol, whereas, in the case of the sign, the proper content of the perception [the red, white, and green of the flag] and the content of which it is a sign [Italy] have nothing to do with each other. [*Enz. III*, par. 458, p. 270]

There is nothing unusual about this characterization of the sign since the stress on its arbitrariness has numberless antecedents well before Ferdinand de Saussure. Somewhat less common are the value judgments Hegel derives from his analysis; although it would not be correct to say that Hegel valorizes the sign over the symbol, the reverse would be even less true. "Das Zeichen," says Hegel, "muß für etwas Großes erklärt werden [the sign must be proclaimed to be something great]." What is it, then, that is so "great" about the sign? To the extent that the sign is entirely independent with regard to the objective, natural properties of the entity toward which it points and instead posits properties by means of its own powers, the sign illustrates the capacity of the intellect to "use" the perceived world for its own purposes, to efface (*tilgen*) its properties and to put others in their stead. This activity of the intellect is both a freedom, since it is arbitrary, and a coercion, since it does violence, as it were, to the world. The sign does not *actually* say what it means to say, or, to drop the misleading anthropomorphic metaphor of a *speaking* sign endowed with a voice, the predication involved in a sign is always citational. When I say, "The red, white, and green flag is Italian," this predicative sentence is always what in scholastic terminology is called an *actus signatus*: it presupposes an implicit subject (or I) which frames the statement and makes it into a quotation: *I* say (or I declare, or I proclaim) that the red, white, and green flag is Italian—a specification which does not have to occur when, in ordinary conversation, I say, "The city of Rome and the Apennines are Italian." The sign is so "great," so crucially important, because it touches upon the question of the relationship between subject and predicate in any declarative sentence. From the question of the sign we are taken, then, by the logic of the passage itself, to the question of the subject—a topic on which Hegel has a great deal to say, perhaps most strikingly of all in a much earlier section of the *Encyclopedia*.

Paragraph 20 of the *Encyclopedia* has to do with the definition of thinking or with the conditions necessary for a science of logic. It states Hegel's equivalence of the Cartesian cogito by establishing the link between the general predicates of thought and the thinking subject. In order to understand thought, to think about thought, thought has to be represented, and this representation can only be that of the thinking subject: "the simple expression of the existing subject as thinking subject is I," says Hegel in a passage rich in Fichtean resonances. But this relatively straightforward and traditional—Cartesian, if you wish, or, at any rate, specular conception of the subject—leads at once to less predictable complications. The thinking subject is to be kept sharply distinguished from the perceiving subject, in a manner that is reminiscent of (or that anticipates) the distinction we have just encountered in the differentiation between sign and symbol. Just as the sign refuses to be in the service of sensory perceptions but uses them instead for its own purposes, thought, unlike perception, appropriates the world and literally "subjects" it to its own powers. More specifically, thought subsumes the infinite singularity and individuation of the perceived world under ordering principles that lay claim to generality. The agent of this appropriation is language. "Since language," says Hegel, "is the labor of thought, we cannot say anything in language that is not general"—a sentence with which Kierkegaard will take issue, in an ironic mode, in *Fear and Trembling*. Thus the sign, random and singular at its first position, turns into symbol just as the I, so *singular* in its independence from anything that is not itself, becomes, in the general thought of logic, the most inclusive, plural, general, and impersonal of subjects.

As such, it is also the most disinterested and self-effacing of subjects. Certainly, since the validity of thought resides in its generality, we cannot be interested, in thought, in the private, singular opinions of the thinker but will expect from him a more humble kind of philosophical self-forgetting. "When Aristotle," says Hegel, "demands [from the philosopher] that he live up to the dignity of his calling, then this dignity consists of his ability to discard particular opinions . . . and to leave things to be what they are in their own right" (*Enz. I*, par. 23, p. 80). When philosophers merely state their opinion, they are not being philosophical. "Since language states only what is general, I cannot say what is only my opinion [*so kann ich nicht sagen was ich nur meine*]." The German version is indispensable here since the English word "opinion," as in public opinion (*öffentliche Meinung*), does not have the connotation of "meaning" that is present, to some degree, in the German verb *meinen*. In Hegel, the assimilation of "meaning" to "me" (or I) is built into the system, since the generality of thought is also the appropriation, the making mine of the world by the I. It is, therefore, not only legitimate but necessary to hear, in the German word *meinen* (as in the sentence "Ich kann nicht sagen was ich nur meine") a connotation of *meinen* as "to make mine," a verbalization of the possessive pronoun *mein*. But that makes the innocuous pronouncement about the philosopher who, in humble self-effacement, has to progress beyond his private opinion, into a very odd sentence indeed: "Ich kann nicht sagen was ich (nur) meine" then means "I cannot say what I make mine" or, since to think is to make mine, "I cannot say what I think," and, since to think is fully contained in and defined by the I, since Hegel's *ego cogito* defines itself as mere *ego*, what the sentence actually says is "I cannot say I"—a disturbing proposition in Hegel's own terms since the very possibility of thought depends on the possibility of saying "I."

Lest this itinerary by way of the signifier *meinen* appear too arbitrary to be taken seriously, the sequel to the passage makes explicit what one can already choose to hear in the original sentence. Hegel goes on to discuss the logical difficulty inherent in the deictic or demonstrative function of language, in the paradox that the most particular of designations such as "now," "here," or "this" are also the most powerful agents of generalization, the cornerstones of this monument of generality that is language—a paradox perhaps inherent in the Greek word *deiktik-os*, which means "to point to" as well as "to prove" (as in the French word *démontrer*). If this is so for adverbs or pronouns of time and place, it is even more so for the most personal of personal pronouns, the word "I" itself. "All other humans have in common with me to be I, as all *my* feelings, representations, and so on, have in common with each other to be distinctively *my own*." The word "I" is the most specifically deictic, self-pointing of words, yet it is also "the most entirely abstract generality." Hegel can therefore write the following quite astonishing sentence: "When I say 'I,' I *mean* myself as *this* I to the exclusion of all others; but what I say, I, is precisely anyone; any I, as that which excludes all others from itself [*ebenso, wenn ich sage: 'Ich,' meine ich mich als diesen alle anderen Ausschließenden; aber was ich sage, Ich, ist eben jeder*]" (*Enz. I*, par. 20, p. 74). In this sentence, the otherness of *jeder* does not designate in any way a specular subject, the mirror image of the I, but precisely that which cannot have a thing in common with myself; it should be translated, in French, not as *autrui*, not even as *chacun*, but as *n'importe qui* or even *n'importe quoi*. The contradiction between *sagen* and *meinen*, between "to say" and "to mean," between *dire* and *vouloir dire*, is an explicitation of the previous sentence, "Ich kann nicht sagen was ich (nur) meine," and a confirmation that it also has to be read, next to its ordinary meaning, in the sense of "*I cannot say I*."

Thus, at the very onset of the entire system, in the preliminary consideration of the science of logic, an inescapable obstacle threatens the entire construction that follows. The philosophical I is not only self-effacing, as Aristotle demanded, in the sense of being humble and inconspicuous, it is also self-effacing in the much more radical sense that the position of the I, which is the condition for thought,

implies its eradication, not, as in Fichte, as the symmetrical position of its negation but as the undoing, the erasure of any relationship, logical or otherwise, that
could be conceived between what the I is and what it says it is. The very enterprise
of thought seems to be paralyzed from the start. It can only get under way if the
knowledge that renders it impossible, the knowledge that the linguistic position
of the I is only possible if the I forgets what it is (namely, I), if this knowledge is
itself forgotten.

The way in which the passage we are reading (par. 20 of the *Encyclopedia*) forgets its own statement is by describing the predicament it states, which is a logical
difficulty devoid of any phenomenal or experiential dimension, as if it were an
event in time, a narrative, or a history. At the beginning of the paragraph, after
having apodictically asserted that the act of thought predicates generality, Hegel
adds, as if it were a word of caution, that these assertions cannot, at this point, be
proven. We should nevertheless not consider them, he says, as his own opinions
(*meine Meinungen*) but should take them to be facts. We can verify these facts by
way of the experience of our own thought, by testing them, trying them out on
ourselves. But this experimentation is only accessible to those "who have acquired a certain power of attention and abstraction," that is to say, who are capable
of thought. The proof of thought is possible only if we postulate that what has to
be proven (namely, that thought is possible) is indeed the case. The figure of this
circularity is time. Thought is proleptic: it projects the hypothesis of its possibility
into a future, in the hyperbolic expectation that the process that made thought possible will eventually catch up with this projection. The hyperbolic I projects itself
as thought in the hope of re-cognizing itself when it will have run its course. This
is why thought (*denken*) is ultimately called by Hegel *Erkenntnis* (which implies
recognition) and is considered to be superior to knowledge (*wissen*). At the end of
the gradual progression of its own functioning, as it moves from perception to representation and finally to thought, the intellect will refind and recognize itself. A
great deal is at stake in this anagnorisis which constitutes the plot and the sus-
pense of Hegel's history of the mind. For if "the action of the intellect as mind is
called recognition" in an all-inclusive sense, and if the mind has invested, so
to speak, all its chances in this future possibility, then it matters greatly whether
or not there will be something there to be recognized when the time comes.
"The principal question for modern times depends on this," says Hegel, "namely,
whether a genuine recognition, that is, the recognition of the truth, is possible"
(*Enz. III*, par. 445, p. 242). The truth is all around us; for Hegel, who, in this respect, is as much of an empiricist as Locke or Hume, the truth is what happens, but
how can we be certain to recognize the truth when it occurs? The mind has to recognize, at the end of its trajectory—in this case, at the end of the text—what was
posited at the beginning. It has to recognize itself as itself, that is to say, as I. But
how are we to recognize what will necessarily be erased and forgotten, since "I"
is, per definition, what *I* can never say?

One understands the necessity for the mind to shelter itself from self-erasure, to resist it with all the powers of the intellect. This resistance takes a multitude of forms, among which the aesthetic is not the least efficacious. For it is not difficult to see that the problem can be recast in terms of the distinctiveness between sign and symbol. As we saw, the I, in its freedom from sensory determination, is originally similar to the sign. Since, however, it states itself as what it is not, it represents as determined a relationship to the world that is in fact arbitrary, that is to say, it states itself as symbol. To the extent that the I points to itself, it is a sign, but to the extent that it speaks of anything but itself, it is a symbol. The relationship between sign and symbol, however, is one of mutual obliteration; hence the temptation to confuse and to forget the distinction between them. The temptation is so strong that Hegel himself, who knows the necessity for this distinction with all possible clarity, cannot resist it and falls back into the confusion he has denounced, offering a theory of art as symbol which, except for being somewhat halfhearted, is quite traditional. But this does not prevent the symbol from being, in Hegel's own terms, an ideological and not a theoretical construct, a defense against the logical necessity inherent in a theoretical disclosure.

This ideology of the symbol is very familiar to us in the commonplaces of our own historical discourse on literature. It dominates, for example, the discussion of Romanticism in its relation to its neoclassical antecedents as well as to its heritage in modernity. It determines the polarities that shape the value judgments implicated in these discussions: such familiar oppositions as those between nature and art, the organic and the mechanical, pastoral and epic, symbol and allegory. These categories are susceptible to infinite refinement, and their interplay can undergo numberless combinations, transformations, negations, and expansions. The commanding metaphor that organizes this entire system is that of interiorization, the understanding of aesthetic beauty as the external manifestation of an ideal content which is itself an interiorized experience, the recollected emotion of a bygone perception. The sensory manifestation (*sinnliches Scheinen*) of art and literature is the outside of an inner content which is itself an outer event or entity that has been internalized. The dialectics of internalization make up a rhetorical model powerful enough to overcome national and other empirical differences between the various European traditions. Attempts, for instance, to mediate between Hegel and English Romantics such as Wordsworth, Coleridge, and Keats often turn around the distinctive topoi of internalization: secularized versions of the Fall and the Redemption of man as a *process* of consciousness, for example, or the subjectivism associated, at least since Kant, with the problematics of the sublime. In all these instances, Hegel can be invoked as the philosophical counterpart of what occurs with greater delicacy in the figural inventions of the poets. For Hegel is indeed, from the relatively early *Phenomenology* to the late *Aesthetics*, prominently the theoretician of internalization, of *Er-innerung* as the ground of the aesthetic as well as of the historical consciousness. *Erinnerung*, recollection as the inner gathering and preserving of experience, brings history and beauty together in the coherence of the system. It is also an integral part of the ideology of the symbol which Hegel both espouses and undoes. The question remains, however, whether the external manifestation of the idea, when it occurs in the sequential development of Hegel's thought, indeed occurs in the mode of recollection, as a dialectic of inside and outside susceptible to being understood and articulated. Where is it, in the Hegelian system, that it can be said that the intellect, the mind, or the idea leaves a material trace upon the world, and how does this sensory appearance take place?

The answer takes a hint from the same section (par. 458, p. 271) near the end of the *Encyclopedia,* in a discussion on the structure of the sign, with which we began. Having stated the necessity to distinguish between sign and symbol and alluded to the universal tendency to conflate one with the other, Hegel next makes reference to a faculty of the mind which he calls *Gedächtnis* and which "in ordinary [as opposed to philosophical] discourse is often confused with recollection [*Erinnerung*], as well as with representation and imagination"—just as sign and symbol are often used interchangeably in such modes of ordinary parlance as literary commentary or literary criticism (*Enz. III*, par. 458, p. 271). *Gedächtnis,* of course, means memory in the sense that one says of someone that he has a good memory but not that he has a good remembrance or a good recollection. One says, in German, "er hat ein gutes Gedächtnis," and not, in that same sense, "eine gute Erinnerung." The French *mémoire,* as in Henri Bergson's title *Matière et mémoire,* is more ambivalent, but a similar distinction occurs between *mémoire* and *souvenir; un bon souvenir* is not the same as *une bonne mémoire.* (Proust struggles with the distinction in his attempts to distinguish between *mémoire volontaire*—which is like *Gedächtnis*—and *mémoire involontaire,* which is rather like *Erinnerung.*) The surprise, in Hegel, is that the progression from perception to thought depends crucially on the mental faculty of memorization. It is *Gedächtnis,* as a subspecies of representation, which makes the transition to the highest capacity of the thinking intellect: the echo of *denken* preserved in the word *Gedächtnis* suggests the close proximity of thought to the capacity of remembering by memorization. In order to understand thought, we must first understand memory, but, says Hegel, "to understand the place and the meaning of memory in the systematic study of the intellect and in its organic connection with thought is one of the most readily ignored and most difficult points in the study of the mind" (*Enz. III*, par. 464, p. 283). Memorization has to be sharply distinguished from recollection and from imagination. It is entirely devoid of images (*bildlos*), and Hegel speaks derisively of pedagogical attempts to teach children how to read and write by having them associate pictures with specific words. But it is not devoid of materiality altogether. We can learn by heart only when all meaning is forgotten and words read as if they were a mere list of names. "It is well known," says Hegel, "that one knows a text by heart [or by rote] only when one no longer associates any meaning with the words; in reciting what one thus knows by heart one necessarily drops all accentuation."

We are far removed, in this section of the *Encyclopedia* on memory, from the mnemotechnic icons described by Frances Yates in *The Art of Memory* and much closer to Augustine's advice about how to remember and to psalmodize Scripture. Memory, for Hegel, is the learning by rote of *names*, or of words considered as names, and it can therefore not be separated from the notation, the inscription, or the writing down of these names. In order to remember, one is forced to write down what one is likely to forget. The idea, in other words, makes its sensory appearance, in Hegel, as the material inscription of names. Thought is entirely dependent on a mental faculty that is mechanical through and through, as remote as can be from the sounds and the images of the imagination or from the dark mine of recollection, which lies beyond the reach of words and of thought.

The synthesis between name and meaning that characterizes memory is an "empty link [*das leere Band*]" and thus entirely unlike the mutual complementarity and interpenetration of form and content that characterizes symbolic art (*Enz. III*, par. 463, p. 281). It is not aesthetic in the ordinary or in the classically Hegelian sense of the word. However, since the synthesis of memory is the only activity of the intellect to occur as sensory manifestation of an idea, memory is a truth of which the aesthetic is the defensive, ideological, and censored translation. In order to have memory one has to be able to forget remembrance and reach the machinelike exteriority, the outward turn, which is retained in the German word for learning by heart, *aus-wendig lernen*. "It is in names that we think," says Hegel (*Enz. III*, par. 462, p. 278); names, however, are the hieroglyphic, silent inscriptions in which the relationship between what one perceives and what one understands, between the written letter and the meaning, is only exterior and superficial. "Visible, written language," says Hegel, "relates to voice, to sounded language, only as a sign" (*Enz. III*, par. 459, p. 277). In memorization, in thought, and, by extension, in the sensory manifestation of thought as an "art" of writing, "we are dealing only with signs [*wir haben es überhaupt nur mit Zeichen zu tun*]." Memory effaces remembrance (or recollection) just as the I effaces itself. The faculty that enables thought to exist also makes its preservation impossible. The art, the *techné*, of writing which cannot be separated from thought and from memorization can only be preserved in the figural mode of the symbol, the very mode it has to do away with if it is to occur at all.

No wonder, then, that Hegel's *Aesthetics* turns out to be a double and possibly duplicitous text. Dedicated to the preservation and the monumentalization of classical art, it also contains all the elements which make such a preservation impossible from the start. Theoretical reasons prevent the convergence of the apparently historical and the properly theoretical components of the work. This results in the enigmatic statements that have troubled Hegel's readers, such as the assertion that art is for us a thing of the past. This has usually been interpreted and criticized or, in some rare instances, praised as a historical diagnosis disproven or borne out by actual history. We can now assert that the two statements "art is for us a thing of the past" and "the beautiful is the sensory manifestation of the idea" are in fact one and the same. To the extent that the paradigm for art is thought rather than perception, the sign rather than the symbol, writing rather than painting or music, it will also be memorization rather than recollection. As such, it belongs indeed to a past which, in Proust's words, could never be recaptured, *retrouvé*. Art is "of the past" in a radical sense, in that, like memorization, it leaves the interiorization of experience forever behind. It is of the past to the extent that it materially inscribes, and thus forever forgets, its ideal content. The reconciliation of the two main theses of the *Aesthetics* occurs at the expense of the aesthetic as a stable philosophical category. What the *Aesthetics* calls the beautiful turns out to be, also, something very remote from what we associate with the suggestiveness of symbolic form.

Before dismissing it as simply, or merely, ugly, one should perhaps bear in mind what Proust has to say in *Swann's Way* about symbols, which, unlike metaphors, do not mean what they say. "Such symbols are not represented symbolically [*le symbole (n'est) pas représenté comme un symbole*] since the symbolized thought is not expressed but the symbol represented as real, as actually inflicted or materially handled [*puisque la pensée symbolisée (n'est) pas exprimée, mais (le symbole représenté) comme réel, comme effectivement subi ou matériellement manié*]." This symbol that is not symbolic is much like the theory of the aesthetic which, in Hegel, is no longer aesthetic, like the subject which has to say "I" but can never say it, the sign which can only survive as a symbol, a consciousness (or subconsciousness) which has to become like the machine of mechanical memory, a representation which is in fact merely an inscription or a system of notation. Such signs, says Proust, may have a special beauty, "une étrangeté saisissante," which will be appreciated only much later, at a degree of aesthetic and theoretical remove so advanced as to be always "of the past" and not our own.

The passage in Proust from which I am quoting deals with Giotto's allegories of the Vices and of the Virtues in the frescoes of the Arena Chapel at Padua. If we then wonder, as we should, where it is, in Hegel's *Aesthetics*, that the theory of the sign manifests itself materially, we would have to look for sections on art forms which Hegel explicitly says are not aesthetic or beautiful. Such is the case for the brief chapter, at the end of the section on symbolic art, on allegory. Allegory, in conforming with the received opinion of Hegel's day, which was, not unproblematically, associated with Goethe, is dismissed as barren and ugly (*kahl*). It belongs to the belated, self-consciously symbolic modes (Hegel calls them "comparative") which, "instead of presenting things or meanings according to their adequate reality, *only* present them as an image or a parable" and which are therefore "inferior genres [*untergeordnete Gattungen*]" (*Ästh.*, p. 488). Before allowing Hegel's dismissal to dismiss the problem, one should remember that, in a truly dialectical system such as Hegel's, what appears to be inferior and enslaved (*untergeordnet*) may well turn out to be the master. Compared to the depth and beauty of recollection, memory appears as a mere tool, a mere slave of the intellect, just as the sign appears shallow and mechanical compared to the aesthetic *aura* of the symbol or just as prose appears like piecework labor next to the noble craft of poetry—just as, we may add, neglected corners in the Hegelian canon are perhaps masterful articulations rather than the all too visible synthetic judgments that are being remembered as the commonplaces of nineteenth-century history.

The section on allegory, apparently so conventional and disappointing, may well be a case in point. Allegory, says Hegel, is primarily a personification produced for the sake of clarity, and, as such, it always involves a subject, an I. But this I, which is the subject of allegory, is oddly constructed. Since it has to be devoid of any individuality or human specificity, it has to be as general as can be, so much so that it can be called a "grammatical subject." Allegories are allegories of the most distinctively linguistic (as opposed to phenomenal) of categories, namely, grammar. On the other hand, allegory fails entirely in its purpose if one is unable to recognize the abstraction that is being allegorized; it has to be, in Hegel's words, *erkennbar*. Therefore, specific predicates of the grammatical subject will *have to be* enunciated, despite the fact that these specifications are bound to conflict with the generality, the pure grammaticality, of the "I": our reading of paragraph 20 of the *Encyclopedia* threatens the stability of the predicative sentence "I am I." What the allegory narrates is, therefore, in Hegel's own words, "the separation or disarticulation of subject from predicate [*die Trennung von Subjekt und Prädikat*]." For discourse to be meaningful, this separation has to take place, yet it is incompatible with the necessary generality of all meaning. Allegory functions, categorically and logically, like the defective cornerstone of the entire system.

We would have to conclude that Hegel's philosophy, which, like his *Aesthetics*, is a philosophy of history (and of aesthetics) as well as a history of philosophy (and of aesthetics)—and the Hegelian corpus indeed contains texts that bear these two symmetrical titles—is in fact an allegory of the disjunction between philosophy and history, or, in our more restricted concern, between literature and aesthetics, or, more narrowly still, between literary experience and literary theory. The reasons for this disjunction, which it is equally vain to deplore or to praise, are not themselves historical or recoverable by ways of history. To the extent that they are inherent in language, in the necessity, which is also an impossibility, to connect the subject with its predicates or the sign with its symbolic significations, the disjunction will always, as it did in Hegel, manifest itself as soon as experience shades into thought, history into theory. No wonder that literary theory has such a bad name, all the more so since the emergence of thought and of theory is not something that our own thought can hope to prevent or to control.

Hegel on the Sublime

Just as the place of aesthetics in the canon of Hegel's works and in the history of its reception remains hard to interpret, the place of the sublime within the more restricted corpus of the *Aesthetics* itself is equally problematic. The fact that the same observation, with proper qualifications, applies to Kant as well compounds the difficulty. The ensuing uncertainties help to account for the numberless confusions and misguided conflicts that clutter the stage of contemporary theoretical discourse on or around literature. One striking example of such a confusion is the principle of exclusion that is assumed to operate between aesthetic theory and epistemological speculation, or, in a symmetrical pattern, between a concern with aesthetics and a concern with political issues.

The confusion has curious consequences. Derrida's name, for instance—to take an example that is both timely and closely familiar—is anathema to a number of literary academics, not so much because of his declared political opinions or positions, but because he has arrived at these positions by way of a professional philosopher's skills and interests; the same people who consider his influence nefarious can be quite tolerant toward writers or critics who are more flamboyantly radical in politics but who stay away from the technical vocabulary of philosophical cognition. On the other hand, Derrida is treated with a great deal of suspicion, if not downright hostility, by political activists, Marxist or other, for no other rea-

"Hegel on the Sublime" was published in Mark Krupnick, ed., *Displacement, Derrida and After* (Bloomington: Indiana University Press, 1983), pp. 139–53. It was delivered as the third Messenger lecture at Cornell on 28 February 1983. All notes are de Man's, slightly modified.

son than that the canon on which he works remains "confined to philosophical and literary texts" and, hence, "confined to concepts and to language rather than to social institutions." Reactionaries deny him access to the aesthetic because he is too much of a philosopher, while proponents of political activism deny him access to the political because he is too concerned with questions of aesthetics. In both cases the aesthetic functions as the principle of exclusion: aesthetic judgment, or the lack of it, excludes the philosopher from access to literature, and the same aesthetic judgment, or the excess of it, excludes him from the political world. These symmetrical gestures, even if one does not approve of them, appear commonplace and easy to understand. Yet intellectual history, let alone actual philosophy, tells a very different story.

In the history of aesthetic theory since Kant, aesthetics, far from being a principle of exclusion, functions as a necessary, though problematic, articulation. In Kant, the articulation of the first *Critique* with the second, of the schemata of theoretical reason with those of practical reason, has to occur by way of the aesthetic, successful or not. Aesthetic theory is critical philosophy to the second degree, the critique of the critiques. It critically examines the possibility and the modalities of political discourse and political action, the inescapable burden of any linkage between discourse and action. The treatment of the aesthetic in Kant is certainly far from conclusive, but one thing is clear: it is epistemological as well as political through and through. That several intellectual historians, American as well as European, have been able to claim the reverse and to assert that the aesthetic in Kant is "free from cognitive and ethical consequences," is their problem, not Kant's.

Hegel, on the same question, is even more explicit. The link between politics, art, and philosophy, by way of a philosophy of art or aesthetics, is built into his system, not in the unreflected sense that aesthetics is concerned with the political as its subject matter, but in the much further-reaching sense that, here again, the trajectory from political to intellectual reality, the passage, in Hegel's terminology, from the objective to the absolute spirit, passes by necessity through art and through the aesthetic as critical reflection on art. At this crucial junction between the most advanced stage of political thought, in the attempt to conceive of the state as historical act, and philosophical thought, Hegel, in the *Encyclopedia of the Philosophical Sciences*, situates art. How this is to be understood is certainly not a simple matter, neither in itself nor in the history of Hegel reception as it has come down to us and as Hegel is read today; it depends on the reading of Hegel's own treatment of the aesthetic in the late *Lectures on Aesthetics*. But one thing can be ascertained from the start: by dint of the structure of the Hegelian system, the consideration of aesthetics only makes sense in the context of the larger question of the relationship between the order of the political and the order of philosophy. This would imply that since in Hegel the aesthetic belongs to a more advanced but proximate stage of speculative thought than political reflection, truly productive political thought is accessible only by way of critical aesthetic theory. The last thing this sentence means, in Hegelian or in any other terms, is that political wisdom belongs to what we ordinarily call aestheticism. What it might mean, to return to our initial example, is that someone like Derrida is politically effective because of, and not in spite of, his concentration on literary texts. This would be borne out by the historical fact that some of the most incisive contributions to political thought and political action have come from "aesthetic" thinkers. Marx himself, whose *German Ideology* is a model of critical procedure along the lines of Kant's third *Critique,* is a case in point—as are, closer to our own times, the writings of Walter Benjamin, Lukács, Althusser, and Adorno. But the work of what are then called "aesthetic thinkers" bears little resemblance to what nineteenth- and twentieth-century literary history identifies as aestheticism, for the work of these thinkers precludes, for example, any valorization of aesthetic categories at the expense of intellectual rigor or political action, or any claim for the autonomy of aesthetic experience as a self-enclosed, self-reflexive totality.

These preliminary remarks lead up to the task of interpreting Hegel's *Lectures on Aesthetics.* Despite the considerable amount of philosophical and critical talent that has been mobilized in its behalf, this task has proved to be very difficult. In no instance has it been possible to reach a consistent reading, especially when, as is the case for Heidegger and for Adorno, the reading of the *Aesthetics* has to become part of a general critical reading of Hegel himself by way of such key concepts as that of *Aufhebung* or of the dialectic itself. For, at first sight, the *Aesthetics* appear as the most blandly orthodox and dogmatic of the late writings, at a moment when the magisterial exposition of the system seems to have reached a stage of deadly mechanical didacticism. One either has to reduce the *Aesthetics,* as Heidegger does, to the gnomic wisdom of its most enigmatic pronouncements— the end of art, the sensory appearance of the idea—and treat it as the mute sphinx that ends all conversation, or, like Adorno and some of his followers, one has to consider it as the Achilles' heel of an entire system, in the very specific sense that the *Aesthetics* would be the place where the inadequacy of Hegel's theory of language would be revealed. The dispersal over the entirety of the collected works of an implicit conception of language that is never formulated weighs heavily on the enterprise and privileges passages and texts in which such a theory, by coming closest to being stated, would finally reveal its shortcomings. Peter Szondi, a literary historian who was himself close to Adorno, locates such a place in the *Aesthetics,* in Hegel's discussion of allegory and metaphor: "[Hegel's] often derogatory characterization of [these] poetic resources [allegory and metaphor] allows us to see why they lay almost entirely beyond his understanding. In asking for these reasons, the limits of Hegel's aesthetics also become visible. . . . It is Hegel's inadequate conception of the nature of language that is to be blamed [for his failure]."[1] The importance of the *Aesthetics* as a possible point of entry into a critique of the dialectic stands clearly revealed in this quotation. For if the inadequacy of the *Aesthetics* is due to an inadequate theory of language, then this is bound to contaminate the logic, the phenomenology of cognition, and ultimately all the essential claims of the system. It is the considerable merit of this approach to have directed attention to what are indeed the determining issues and even the determining passages involved in the interpretation of the *Aesthetics*.

A reading thus sensitized to linguistic terminology and to the problematics of language can hope to displace the received ideas, oracular or dogmatic, by which the interpretation of the *Aesthetics* had been brought to a standstill. It also allows for an extension of the textual corpus from the *Aesthetics* to considerations on language that occur elsewhere in Hegel's works, in the *Encyclopedia*, the *Science of Logic*, or the *Phenomenology of the Spirit*. It allows for a linkage between the theory of language, of the subject, and of sensory perception. Finally, it should clarify the relationship of art and literature to the dimension of pastness that is a necessary component of any discourse involving history. If art, the sensory or (better) the phenomenal manifestation of the idea, belongs for us, as the *Aesthetics* asserts, to the past, then this pastness is to be a function of its phenomenality, of its mode of appearance. Where and how is it, then, in the system of Hegel's writings as a whole, that the idea appears, and why does this specifically aesthetic moment belong necessarily to the past?

The *Aesthetics* seems to provide only banal and empirical answers to these questions. In the wake of Winckelmann and Schiller, it historicizes the problem in the ideologically loaded genealogy of the modern as derived from the classical, Hellenic past, thus creating an illusion of misplaced concreteness that is responsible for a great deal of poor historiography from the early nineteenth century to the present. These historical fallacies run parallel to a concept of language in which the all-important distinction between the symbolic and the semiotic aspects of language is eroded. Since this happens most distinctively in the *Aesthetics*, one sees the need for a detour out of this work into other Hegel texts in which the discussion of the same issue is less blurred by romantic ideology.

This allows for a more precise answer to the question about the appearance of the idea. Most clearly in the *Encyclopedia*, but in the *Logic* as well, the idea makes its appearance on the mental stage of human intelligence at the precise moment when our consciousness of the world, which faculties such as perception or imagination have interiorized by way of recollection (*Erinnerung*), is no longer experienced but remains accessible only to memorization (*Gedächtnis*). At that moment, and at no other, can it be said that the idea leaves a material trace, accessible to the senses, upon the world. We can perceive the most fleeting and imagine

---

1. Peter Szondi, *Poetik und Geschichtsphilosophie I* (Frankfurt am Main: Suhrkamp, 1974), pp. 390, 396; my translation.

the wildest things without any change occurring to the surface of the world, but from the moment we memorize, we cannot do without such a trace, be it as a knot in our handkerchief, a shopping list, a table of multiplication, a psalmodized singsong or plain chant, or any other memorandum. Once such a *notation* has occurred, the inside-outside metaphor of experience and signification can be forgotten, which is the necessary (if not sufficient) condition for thought (*Denken*) to begin. The aesthetic moment in Hegel occurs as the conscious forgetting of a consciousness by means of a materially actualized system of notation or inscription.

This conclusion is derived from a section of the *Encyclopedia* entitled "Psychology" that follows upon the section entitled "Consciousness." Nothing even remotely similar seems to be stated in the public theses or arguments of the *Aesthetics*. Lest we assume that the later, professorial Hegel was so busy thinking that he "forgot" his former more speculative self—a supposition that flatters the source of our livelihood way beyond its deserts—such inconsistencies in a systematic philosopher are unlikely; they tend to memorize their own writings very thoroughly. Much more likely is the assumption that similar or equivalent assertions actually occur in the *Aesthetics* but that, for a variety of reasons, the passages in which they occur have been overlooked, misunderstood, or censored. If Hegel's theory of memorization has any merit at all, the pressure of its power would indeed have to make itself felt in the *Aesthetics*, in however oblique or disguised a way. Chapter 2 of the section on symbolic art entitled "Die Symbolik der Erhabenheit" (The symbolics of the sublime),[2] a chapter that immediately precedes the section on comparative art forms singled out by Peter Szondi as the nether point of Hegel's aesthetic sensibilities, is one of the places in the *Aesthetics* where it surfaces.

The first hint one gets of this is in Hegel's rather shabby treatment of Kant early on in the chapter. We are told that Kant's treatment of the sublime is longwinded but still of some interest—and the reasons given for this interest are altogether cogent. But by putting so much emphasis on the particularity of the affects in which he rightly chose to locate it, Kant has trivialized the sublime. It is open to question whether Hegel does justice here to Kant's concept of affect (*Gemüt*), but one can surmise the reasons for his impatience with Kant's interest in affect and mood. For if the aesthetic, in Hegel, is indeed akin, in some way or another, to memorization, then it has little concern for particularized emotions, and any self-conscious sentimentalization had better be checked from the start.

More revealing, perhaps, though still merely formal, is the place Hegel allots to the sublime in the dialectical continuum of the various art forms. "We find the sublime first and in its original form primarily in the Hebraic state of mind and in the sacred texts of the Jews" (p. 480). The association of the sublime with the po-

---

2. G. W. F. Hegel, *Vorlesungen über die Ästhetik I*, vol. 13, *Werke* (Frankfurt am Main: Suhrkamp, 1970), pp. 466–546. All further references to this work are cited in the text.

etry of the Old Testament is a commonplace, especially in Germany after Herder, but Hegel's reasons are of interest. Hebraic poetry is sublime because it is icono-clastic; it rejects art as plastic or architectural representation, be it as temple or as statue. "Since it is impossible to conceive of an image of the divine that would in any degree be adequate, there is no place for the plastic arts in the sublime sacred art of the Jews. Only the poetry of a representation that manifests itself by means of the *word* will be acceptable" (p. 480; emphasis mine). In its explicit separation from anything that could be perceived or imagined, the word indeed appears here as the inscription which, according to the *Encyclopedia*, is the first and only phe-nomenal manifestation of the idea. Monuments and statues made of stone and metal are only pre-aesthetic. They are sensory appearances, all right, but not, or not yet, appearances *of the idea*. The idea appears only as written inscription. Only the written word can be sublime, to the precise extent that the written word is neither representational, like a perception, nor imaginative, like a phantasm.

The section on the sublime confirms this formal affirmation and develops some of its implications and consequences. In the process, it soon becomes ap-parent that the sublime in Hegel differs considerably from the post-Longinian sublime of those of his predecessors, to borrow a suggestive listing from Meyer Abrams's very useful chapter on the sublime in *The Mirror and the Lamp*, such as John Dennis, Bishop Lowth, and Herder,[3] a tradition which has survived in the American interpretation of Romanticism in Wimsatt, Abrams, Bloom, Hartman, and Weiskel; it was finally ironized, though not necessarily exorcised, in Neil Hertz's remarkable essay "Lecture de Longin"[4]—which remains conveniently hidden from the tradition by appearing, of all places, in Paris, where no one can appreciate what is at stake in this closely familial romance. The most conspicu-ous, though not the most decisive, of these differences resides in the disappear-ance of the familiar oppositions between poetry and prose, or between the sublime and the beautiful. The sublime for Hegel *is* the absolutely beautiful. Yet nothing sounds less sublime, in our current use of the term, than the sublime in Hegel. That it marks an open break with the linguistic model of the symbol that pervades all sections of the *Aesthetics* is visible from the start; already in the introductory section on Kant it is said that in the sublime "the actual *symbolic* character" of the work of art vanishes (p. 468). What this involves, however, becomes clear only as the inner logic of the passage is allowed to unfold.

The moment Hegel calls sublime is the moment of radical and definitive sepa-ration between the order of discourse and the order of the sacred. The necessity to

---

3. M. H. Abrams, *The Mirror and the Lamp* (New York: Oxford University Press, 1953), pp. 72–78.

4. Neil Hertz, "Lecture de Longin," *Poétique* 15 (1973): 292–306. An English translation of Hertz's essay was published in the March 1983 issue of *Critical Inquiry*. [Reprinted in Neil Hertz, *The End of the Line* (New York: Columbia University Press, 1985).]

isolate such a moment is forced upon him by the concept of language as symbol to which the *Aesthetics* is firmly committed—without which, indeed, no such topic as the aesthetic could come into being. The phenomenality of the linguistic sign can, by an infinite variety of devices or turns, be aligned with the phenomenality, as knowledge (meaning) or sensory experience, of the signified toward which it is directed. It is the phenomenalization of the sign that constitutes signification, regardless of whether it occurs by way of conventional or by way of natural means. The term phenomenality here implies not more and not less than that the process of signification, in and by itself, can be known, just as the laws of nature as well as those of convention can be made accessible to some form of knowledge.

The constraint to abandon this claim arises, in Hegel, from the classical and, in this case, Kantian critical process to discriminate between modes of cognition and to separate the knowledge of the natural world from the knowledge of how knowledge is achieved, the separation between mathematics and epistemology. In the history of art, it corresponds to the moment when the infinite diffusion and dispersal of what Hegel calls the "single substance" (*die eine Substanz*) that stands beyond the antinomy of light and the shapeless singularizes itself in the designation of this absolute generality as the sacred or as god. It is the passage from pantheistic to monotheistic art, the passage, in Hegel's picture-book but by no means innocent history, from Indian to Mohammedan poetry. The relationship between pantheism and monotheism in the history of art and religion (since, up to this point, it would be impossible to distinguish between them) is like the relationship between natural science and epistemology: the concept of mind (be it as Locke's understanding, Kant's *Vernunft*, or Hegel's Spirit) is the monotheistic principle of philosophy as the single field of unified knowledge. The monotheistic moment (which in Hegel is not or not yet the sublime) is essentially verbal and coincides with the fantastic notion that *die eine Substanz* could be given a name—such as, for instance, *die eine Substanz*, or the One, or Being, or Allah, or Yahweh, or I— and that this name could then function symbolically, yielding knowledge and discourse. From this moment on, language is the deictic system of predication and determination in which we dwell more or less poetically on this earth. In conformity with his tradition and with his place in the ongoing discourse of philosophy, Hegel understands this moment as a relationship between mind and nature constituted by negation. But behind this familiar and historically intelligible dialectical model stands a different reality. For it is one thing to assert that absolute knowledge accomplishes its labor by way of negation, another thing entirely to assert the possibility of negating the absolute by allowing it, as in this passage, to enter into an unmediated relationship with its other. If "mind" and "nature" stand, in fact, for the absolute and its other, then Hegel's narrative resembles that of dialectical sublation or upheaval (*Aufhebung*) only on a first level of understanding.

The difficulty of the passage—the section entitled "Die Kunst der Erhabenheit" and the subsequent chapter, "The conscious symbolism of comparative art forms" (pp. 479–539)—stems indeed from the interference of a dialectical with another, not necessarily compatible, pattern of narration. When we read of a hidden god who has "withdrawn into himself and thus asserted his autonomy against the finite world, as pure interiority and substantive power," or hear that in the sublime, the divine substance "becomes truly manifest" (p. 479) against the weakness and the ephemerality of its creatures, then we easily understand the pathos of this servitude as praise of divine power. The language of negativity is then a dialectical and recuperative moment, akin to similar turns that Neil Hertz has located in Longinus's treatise. Hegel's sublime may stress the distance between the human discourse of the poets and the voice of the sacred even further than Longinus, but as long as this distance remains, as he puts it, a *relationship* (pp. 478, 481), however negative, the fundamental analogy between poetic and divine creation is preserved. Yet the narrative generated on the level of the dialectic does not correspond to the implicit narrative of the section. To be *erhaben* (sublime) is not the same, it appears, as to be *erhoben* or *aufgehoben*, however close the two words may be in sound and despite Hegel's occasional substitution of one term for the other (as at the bottom of p. 483). If one considers the one example of sublimity that Hegel and Longinus share in common, the *fiat lux* from Genesis, then the complexity of the passage begins to appear (pp. 481, 484). Hegel quotes "And God said, let there be light: and there was light" to illustrate that the relationship between God and man is no longer natural or genetic, and that God cannot be considered as a progenitor. For *zeugen* (to engender) Hegel wishes to substitute *schaffen* (to create), but creation then has a stronger negative connotation than the term normally implies; no polarity of young/old or male/female should suggest a familial hierarchy. The hierarchy is much starker. Creation is purely verbal, the imperative, pointing, and positing power of the word. The word speaks and the world is the transitive object of its utterance, but this implies that what is thus spoken, and which includes us, is not the subject of its speech act. Our obedience to the word is mute: "the word . . . whose command to be also and actually posits what is without mediation and in *mute* obedience" (p. 480; emphasis mine). If the word is said to speak through us, then we speak only as a ventriloquist's dummy, also and especially when we pretend to talk back. If we say that language speaks, that the grammatical subject of a proposition is language rather than a self, we are not fallaciously anthropomorphizing language but rigorously grammatizing the self. The self is deprived of any locutionary power; to all intents and purposes it may as well be mute.

Yet *das Daseiende* that language produces speaks, and even writes, a great deal in Hegel, and in an interesting variety of ways. First of all, it quotes. Scripture quotes Moses who quotes God and it makes use, in Genesis, of the fundamental rhetorical modes of representation: mimesis, in Plato's sense, as reported speech (*erlebte Rede*), as in the sentence "And God said 'Let there be light,'" as well as, closely intertwined with the former, diegesis or indirect speech (*erzählte Rede*), as

in the sentence: "And God called the light day. . . ." At this level, the distinction
between the two modes of locution is not important, since mimesis and diegesis
are part of the same system of representation; the mimesis can always be considered as encased in a third-person narrative (and he said ". . ."). But none of these
utterances is mute in the sense of being merely passive or devoid of reflexive
knowledge. Quotations can have considerable performative power; indeed, a case
could be made that only quotations have such power. Even hidden quotations
are not mute: a plagiarizer who gets caught may be dumb but he (or she) is no
dummy. They are, however, devoid of positional power: to quote the marriage
vows allows one to perform a marriage but not to posit marriage as an institution.
And quotations certainly carry a considerable cognitive weight: if, as Longinus
implies, the sublime poet here is Moses himself, then the question of the veracity
of Moses' testimonial is bound to arise, that is to say, a cognitive critical inquiry is
inevitably linked to the assertion of linguistic positional force. This accounts for
the fact that in a statement such as "Let there be . . . ," *light* is indeed the privileged
object of predication, rather than life (Let there be life) or humanity (Let there be
woman and man). "Light" names the necessary phenomenality of any positing
(*setzen*). The convergence of discourse and the sacred, which, in the choice of example and in Hegel's commentary on it, is not in question, occurs by way of phenomenal cognition. No matter how strongly the autonomy of language is denied,
as long as the language can declare and know its own weakness and call itself
mute, we remain in a Longinian mode. Pascal's paradox applies: "In a word, man
knows that he is miserable. Thus, he is miserable since that is what he is. But he is
very great inasmuch as he knows it." A dialectized sublime is still, as in Longinus,
an intimation of poetic grandeur and immortality.

   A little further in the text, Hegel mentions another example of the sublime also
taken from Scripture, this time from the Psalms. In this case, the rhetorical mode
is not a mimesis-diegesis system of representation but direct apostrophe. And
what is said in apostrophe is curiously different from what is shown and told in
representation, although—or rather because—it also has to do with light: "Light is
your garment, that you wear; you stretch out the heavens like a curtain. . . ."[5] The
juxtaposition of the two quotations, marked, however discreetly, by the symmetrical position of God and man ("von Seiten Gottes her" [p. 481] and "von Seiten des
Menschen" [p. 484]), is quite amazing. The garment is a surface (*ein äußeres
Gewand*), an outside that conceals an inside. One can understand this, as Hegel
does, as a statement about the insignificance of the sensory world as compared to
the spirit. Unlike the *logos*, it does not have the power to posit anything; its power,
or only discourse, is the knowledge of its weakness. But since this same spirit
also, without mediation, *is* the light (p. 481), the combination of the two quota-

---

5. Hegel quotes from the Lutheran Bible. The King James Version is much less assertive: "Who
coverest thyself with light as with a garment . . ." (Ps. 104:2).

tions states that the spirit posits itself as that which is unable to posit, and this dec-
laration is either meaningless or duplicitous. One can pretend to be weak when
one is strong, but the power to pretend is decisive proof of one's strength. One can
know oneself, as man does, as that which is unable to know, but by moving from
knowledge to position, all is changed. Position is all of a piece, and, moreover, unlike thought, it actually occurs. It becomes impossible to find a common ground
for or between the two quotations, "Let there be light" and "Light is your garment." To pretend, as Hegel does, that the first, which could be called Longinian,
corresponds to the sublime as seen from the perspective, or the side, of God (*von
Seiten Gottes*), whereas the second corresponds to the sublime as seen from the
perspective of man, does not, of course, mitigate or suspend the incompatibility.
Within the monotheistic realm of *die eine Substanz*, no such thing as a human perspective could exist independently of the divine, nor could one speak of a "side"
of the gods (as one speaks of the "côté de chez Swann"), since the *parousia* of the
sacred allows for no parts, contours, or geometry. The only thing the misleading
metaphor of a two-sided world accomplishes is to radicalize the separation between sacred and human in a manner that no dialectic can surmount (*aufheben*).
Such is indeed the declared thesis of the chapter, but it can only be read if one dis-
pels the pathos of negation that conceals its actual force.

It is not insignificant that the reading only emerges from a combination of two
rhetorical modes, that of representation and that of apostrophe. Paradoxically, the
assumption of praise, in the Psalms, undoes the ground for praise established in
Genesis. Apostrophe is the mode of praise par excellence, the figure of the ode.
The strength of Hegel's choice of example makes clear that what the ode praises is
not what it addresses ("la prise de Namur," Psyche or God)—for the light that
allows the addressed entity to appear is always a veil—but that it always praises
the veil, the device of apostrophe as it allows for the illusion of address. Since
the ode, unlike the epic (which belongs to representation), knows exactly what it
does, it does not praise at all, for no figure of speech is ever praiseworthy in itself.
The passage reveals the inadequacy of the Longinian model of the sublime as representation. Apostrophe is not representation; it occurs independently of any
report, be it as quotation or narration, and when it is put on a stage, it becomes
ludicrous and cumbersome. Whereas representation can be shown to be a form
of apostrophe, the reverse is not true. Apostrophe is a figure or a trope, as is
clear from Hegel's next quotation from the Psalms, in which the garment becomes
face: "Thou hidest thy face, they are troubled" (*Verbirgst du dein Angesicht, so
erschrecken sie*—Ps. 104:29). The light from "Licht ist dein Kleid" is preserved
in the German word *Angesicht*. The trope of face-giving (*prosoponpoiein*) is a
particularly effective way by which to be drawn into the entire transformational
system of tropes. When language functions as trope, and no longer only as representation, the limits of the Longinian sublime as well as of its considerable powers

of recuperation, including the power of self-ironization,[6] are reached. As the section develops, the divergence between Hegel and Longinus becomes nearly as absolute as the divergence between man and God that Hegel calls sublime. Yet the two discourses remain intertwined as by a knot that cannot be unraveled. The heterogeneity of art and of the sacred, first introduced as a moment in an epistemological dialectic, is rooted in the linguistic structure in which the dialectic is itself inscribed.

In Hegel, too, there appears to be, at this point, a recuperative corollary to the declared otherness of the divine. It takes the form of a reassertion of human autonomy as ethical self-determination, "the judgment concerning good and evil; and the decision for the one over the other is now displaced in the subject itself" (p. 485). Out of this originates "a positive relationship to God" in the form of a legal system of reward and punishment. Before blaming or congratulating Hegel for this conservative individualism, one should try to understand what is involved in this passage from the aesthetic theory of the sublime to the political world of the law. Recuperation is an economic concept that allows for a mediated passage or crossing between negative or positive valorization: Pascal's Pensée on human grandeur and misery that has just been quoted is a good example of how an absolute lack can be turned into an absolute surplus. But the definitive loss of the absolute experienced in the sublime puts an end to such an economy of value and replaces it with what one could call a critical economy: the law (*das Gesetz*) is always a law of differentiation (*Unterscheidung*), not the grounding of an authority but the unsettling of an authority that is shown to be illegitimate. The political in Hegel originates in the critical undoing of belief, the end of the current theodicy, the banishment of the defenders of faith from the affairs of the state, and the transformation of theology into the critical philosophy of right. The main monarch to be thus dethroned or desacralized is language, the matrix of all value systems in its claim to possess the absolute power of position. *Setzen* becomes *das Gesetz* as the critical power to undo the claim to power, not in the name of absolute or relative justice, but by its own namelessness, its own ordinariness. To pursue this would take us into the two treatises that have to be considered conjointly and in the wake of the *Aesthetics*: the *Principles of the Philosophy of Law* and the *Lectures on the Philosophy of Religion*. What matters for our topic is that the necessity to treat these two alien political forces, law and religion, is established in the *Aesthetics*, and specifically in the aesthetics of the sublime. That this would have been taken to state the reverse of what it states confirms the strength of Hegel's analysis; the same fate will soon befall similar assertions in Kierkegaard and Marx and, in our own times, in Walter Benjamin.

There can be no better preparation for a critical reading of the Philosophies of

---

6. Hertz, "Lecture de Longin," pp. 305–6.

Law and Religion than the immediate sequel to the theory of the sublime in what Hegel somewhat cryptically calls "comparative" art forms. The separation, still suspended in deliberate ambivalence in the sublime, now carries out the law of its occurrence into its next stage. Language as symbol is replaced by a new linguistic model, closer to that of the sign and of trope, yet distinct from both in a way that allows for a concatenation of semiotic and tropological features. This complication is reflected in the curious combination of art forms that make up this section: some of them, like metaphor, allegory, and something called image (*Bild*), are more or less straightforward tropes, but others, such as fable, proverb, and parable, are minor literary genres that seem to be of an entirely different order. What is being undone, in each of these instances and cumulatively in their succession, is not the dual structure of signification as a combination of sign and meaning which the symbol is assumed to overcome. Rather, it is the homology, in each of the particular genres of tropes, of the structure that defines them with the structure that defines the symbol. Hegel first makes the point by way of a traditional inside/outside polarity. Even the symbol does not simply coincide with the entity it symbolizes; it requires the mediation of an understanding to cross the borderline that keeps it "outside" this entity. The relationship between sign and meaning, however, in the symbol, is dialectical. But now "this exteriority, since it was already latently [*an sich*] available in the symbol, must also be posited" (*Diese Äußerlichkeit aber, da sie an sich im Symbolischen vorhanden ist, muß auch gesetzt werden*). This *Gesetz der Äußerlichkeit* implies that the principle of signification is now itself no longer animated by the tensions between its dual poles, but that it is reduced to the preordained motion of its own position. As such, it is no longer a sign-producing function (which is how Hegel valorized the sign in the *Encyclopedia*), but the quotation or repetition of a previously established semiosis. Neither is it a trope, for it cannot be closed off or replaced by the knowledge of its reduced condition. Like a stutter, or a broken record, it makes what it keeps repeating worthless and meaningless. The passage is itself the best illustration of this. Completely devoid of aura or *éclat*, it offers nothing to please anyone: it deeply distresses the aesthetic sensibilities of a symbolist like Peter Szondi, but it also spoils the fun of playful semioticians and reduces to nought the pretensions of the solemn ones, including the pathos of rhetorical analysis. Such passages are, of course, the ones to look out for in as pathos-laden a canon as Hegel's.

The spatial metaphor of exteriority (*Äußerlichkeit*) is not adequate to describe the knowledge that follows from the experience of the sublime. The sublime, it turns out, is self-destroying in a manner without precedent at any of the other stages of the dialectic. "The difference between the present stage (that of the comparative art forms) and the sublime . . . is that the sublime relationship is completely eliminated [*vollständig fortfällt*]." There is nothing left to lift up or to uplift. This is the case with very few, if any, other key terms in Hegel's vocabulary, in the *Aesthetics* or elsewhere. One sees perhaps better what is implied by stating the process in temporal terms. This may also establish contact with the theory of symbol and sign, of subject and memorization, that was derived from the reading of section 20 of the *Encyclopedia*.

The alignment of literal and figural discourse in a figuration, by way (for example) of resemblance in the case of a metaphor, is now called by Hegel a *comparison*. The emphasis falls on the deliberate and conscious nature of this gesture. The juxtaposition of the two aspects of the figure is neither a genuine relationship nor a contractual convention, but an arbitrary positioning (*Nebeneinandergestelltsein*, p. 487). The function of art is to make it appear as a discovery, when it is in fact preestablished by the one who claims to discover it. The illusion of discovery is consciously and cunningly contrived by means of a faculty Hegel calls *Witz* and which is very remote from natural genius in Kant or Schiller. Wit discovers nothing that is new or that was hidden; it invents only in the service of redundancy and reiteration. In temporal terms, it projects into the future what belongs to the past of its own invention and repeats as if it were a finding what it knew all along. This apparent reversal of past and present (metalepsis) is in fact no reversal at all, for the symmetrical equivalence of the sacrificed future is not an understood, but a trivialized, past. Yet this bleak and disappointing moment, in all its sobriety, is also the moment in the *Aesthetics* when we come closest to the fundamental project of speculative philosophy. As we know from section 20 of the *Encyclopedia*, the starting point of philosophy, "the simple expression of the existing subject as thinking subject" (I, p. 72), is equally arbitrary and pretends to verify its legitimacy in the sequential unfolding of its future until it reaches the point of self-recognition. Like the work of art, the subject of philosophy is a reconstruction a posteriori. Poets and philosophers share this lucidity about their enterprise.

Rather than putting it in terms that suggest deceit and duplicity, one could say that the poet, like the philosopher, must *forget* what he knows about his undertaking in order to accede to the discourse to which he is committed. Like all writers who happen to think wittily of some figure of language and then keep it embalmed, so to speak, in the coffin of their memory (or, in some cases, in an actual wooden box) until the day they will compose the text that proclaims to discover what they themselves had buried, poets know their figures only by rote and can use them only when they no longer remember or understand them. No actual bad faith is involved in such a process unless, of course, one claims transcendental merits for a move that pertains to the ethics of survival rather than of heroic conquest. At the end of the section in the *Aesthetics* on symbolic form, after the reversal of the sublime, writing is structured like memorization, or, in the terminology of Hegel's system, like thought. To read poets or philosophers thoughtfully, on the level of their thought rather than of one's or their desires, is to read them by rote. Every poem (*Gedicht*) is a *Lehrgedicht* (p. 541), whose knowledge is forgotten as it is read.

We can put this in still another way, providing a suitably arbitrary link with the political themes mentioned at the beginning of this paper. Hegel describes the inexorable progression from the rhetoric of the sublime to the rhetoric of figuration as a shrinkage from the categories of critical language that are able to encompass entire works, such as genre, to terms that designate only discontinuous segments of discourse, such as metaphor or any other trope. His own language becomes increasingly contemptuous of these subparts of the aesthetic monument. He calls them inferior genres (*untergeordnete Gattungen*), only (*nur*) images or signs "deprived of spiritual energy, depth of insight, or of substance, devoid of poetry or philosophy." They are, in other words, thoroughly prosaic. They are so, however, not because of some initial shortcoming in the poet who uses these art forms rather than the major representational genres—epic, tragedy—but as the consequence of an inherent linguistic structure that is bound to manifest itself. In this entire development, there is no moment that could be reduced to avoidable accidents or contingencies, least of all the moment when poetic skills are shown to be themselves contingent and accidental. The infrastructures of language, such as grammar and tropes, account for the occurrence of the poetic superstructures, such as genres, as the devices needed for their oppression. The relentless drive of the dialectic, in the *Aesthetics*, reveals the essentially prosaic nature of art; to the extent that art is aesthetic, it is also prosaic—as learning by rote is prosaic compared to the depth of recollection, as Aesop is prosaic compared to Homer, or as Hegel's sublime is prosaic compared to Longinus's. The prosaic, however, should not be understood in terms of an opposition between poetry and prose. When the novel, as in Lukács's interpretation of nineteenth-century realism, is conceived as an offspring, however distant or elegiac, of the epic, then it is anything but prosaic in Hegel's sense. Nor would Baudelaire's prose versions of some of the poems of *Les Fleurs du Mal* be prosaic as compared to the metered and rhymed diction of the originals; all one could say is that they bring out the prosaic element that shaped the poems in the first place. Hegel summarizes his conception of the prosaic when he says: "It is in the slave that prose begins" (*Im Sklaven fängt die Prosa an* [p. 497]). Hegel's *Aesthetics*, an essentially prosaic discourse on art, is a discourse of the slave because it is a discourse of the figure rather than of genre, of trope rather than of representation. As a result, it is also politically legitimate and effective as the undoer of usurped authority. The enslaved place and condition of the section on the sublime in the *Aesthetics*, and the enslaved place of the *Aesthetics* within the corpus of Hegel's complete works, are the symptoms of their strength. Poets, philosophers, and their readers lose their political impact only if they become, in turn, usurpers of mastery. One way of doing this is by avoiding, for whatever reason, the critical thrust of aesthetic judgment.

Kant's Materialism

The reception of Kant's third *Critique* or *Critique of Judgment* (1790) represents a baffling episode in the intellectual history of the nineteenth and twentieth centuries, an episode that is far from finished or even from having begun to be mapped out. Richard Klein took Frank Lentricchia's comments for his starting point, but the notion that, in Kant, the realm of the aesthetic is "free from cognitive and ethical consequences"[1] or that the aesthetic experience is "barred from the truth of the phenomenal world"[2] can hardly be laid at Lentricchia's doorstep. It echoes a well-established opinion among American historians of the Enlightenment, of Romanticism, and of the transition from the one to the other—the genealogy which allows for a lineage that is supposed to lead from Kant, by ways of Schiller and Coleridge, to decadent formalism and aestheticism. The extreme version, bordering on caricature, of this filiation, the juxtaposition of Kant and Oscar Wilde, is a commonplace of literary history that can be found, among other places, in Meyer Abrams's *The Mirror and the Lamp*.[3] In careless hands, this sort of thing results in a misunderstanding of the category of the aesthetic as well as of the present-day concern with language and poetic form. It inspires a false diagnosis of the part played by aesthetic theory in contemporary thought, overestimating

---

"Kant's Materialism" was delivered at a session ("Kant and the Problem of the Aesthetic") of the 1981 Modern Language Association convention in New York. Notes were supplied by the editor.

1. Frank Lentricchia, *After the New Criticism* (Chicago: University of Chicago Press, 1980), p. 19.
2. Ibid., p. 41.
3. M. H. Abrams, *The Mirror and the Lamp* (New York: Oxford University Press, 1953), p. 328.

the apparent frivolity of the aesthetic and, hence, its vulnerability to moral censure, and underestimating its powers of cognition and deep complicity with the phenomenalist epistemology of realism. It suggests, at any rate, a hasty and superficial reading of the third *Critique*.

This inadequacy can hardly be blamed only on the skills, the knowledge, or the ideological bias of the interpreters. *The Critique of Judgment* is an exceptionally difficult and eccentric text, not the least because it is so immensely suggestive at any particular point, in each and every example or proposition it sets up, that one constantly responds to local solicitations which Kant himself leaves suspended with what amounts, considering how tantalizing they are, to mental cruelty. While by and large attending to its particular business, the text proliferates into so many diverse directions that this business constantly threatens to be forgotten. How is one to leave alone such remarks, dropped en passant, as that one should perhaps someday pay attention to the metaphors of grounding that abound in philosophical discourse (section 59) or that one should meditate on the parasitic grafting of one tree species onto another and study the pathological but pharmaceutically beneficial tumors that this produces (section 64)? One can certainly see why so many interpreters have lost sight of the forest for the trees—have concentrated, for instance, on purposiveness without purpose at the expense of the teleological judgment it makes possible, or on the notion of the aesthetic as free play at the expense of the aesthetic as pure reason.

All commentators on Kant seem to have felt that the third *Critique* constitutes something of a crux on which the unity of the canon depends, that its critical power reaches further than that of pure and practical reason and threatens the stability of those categories. Michel Foucault, as one instance among many, diagnoses this critical thrust by setting up a contrast between Kant and Destutt de Tracy, between critical philosophy and ideology. In contrast to the pre-Marxian ideologues, who proceeded according to a naive scheme of analytical judgment from the simple to the manifold, Kant marks "the retreat of cognition and of knowledge out of the space of representation."[4] But Kant's critique of representation is then said to engender a new tension between the transcendental order of negative cognition, in which a high degree of formalization is necessary, and the singularity of the empirical world, which demands formalization in order to be known but refuses it because this singularity is the very element that made the critique of the classical models of cognition necessary. In his reference to Edmund Burke, for example, Kant indeed finds fault with the methodology of empiricism: "One will never be able to reach the a priori principle, objective or subjective, that underlies judgments of taste by tracking down the empirical laws that govern the fluctuations of our moods"; instead, one should

---

4. Michel Foucault, *Les Mots et les choses* (Paris: Gallimard, 1966), p. 255.

accede to "a higher investigation, a transcendental explication [*Erörterung*] of this faculty."[5]

How is one to understand the critique of representation in passages such as these, together with the affirmation of its continued necessity? Is this reaffirmation, as Foucault and many other commentators seem to imply, a return of the empirical, in the sense in which we speak today of a return of the repressed? Can one speak of a Kantian idealism without taking into account the simultaneous activity, in his text, of a materialism much more radical than what can be conveyed by such terms as "realism" or "empiricism"? And how would this affect the methodological formalism now under attack as a direct descendant of Kantian aesthetics? The magnitude of the questions obviously precludes the possibility of a succinct or simple answer.

One of the privileged places in which to start looking for some of the answers is the section in the third *Critique* on the sublime. There are good theoretical as well as practical reasons for this choice, since the sublime is indeed where the congruity (*Angemessenheit*, p. 195) of the aesthetic to the order of pure reason is being established, in distinction from the beautiful, which belongs to the order of mere intelligence (*Verstand*). The selection of sections 28 and 29 as the main text for this communication is primarily based on the fact that it serves Hegel as the starting point for his own considerations on the sublime in *Lectures on Aesthetics*.

Hegel observes that, for all its long-windedness (as he puts it), Kant's way of distinguishing between the beautiful and the sublime still holds some interest for him. What can still interest us in Hegel's rather condescending expression of interest is his assertion (out of which will then develop his own highly interesting version of the sublime) that the experience and the discourse of the sublime are no longer symbolic: "[in der Erhabenheit] verschwindet der eigentlich symbolische Charakter [der Kunst]."[6] The symbolic was founded on a degree of congruence between formal structure and intellectual content; Hegel finds fault with Kant for having understood this reduction of the sublime as a return to the triviality of subjective moods, affects and faculties of the mind which he, Kant, fails to inscribe within the dialectical progression of cognition. He repeats, in a way, the reproach of empiricism that Kant levied at Burke. The loss of the symbolic, the loss of adequation of sign to meaning, is a necessary negative moment; Kant and Hegel are in agreement on this. But this loss is also threatening enough to invest the modality of its recuperation with considerable significance. And here Kant and Hegel

---

5. Immanuel Kant, *Kritik der Urteilskraft*, vol. 10 of *Werkausgabe*, ed. Wilhelm Weischedel (Frankfurt am Main: Suhrkamp, 1978), p. 203. Subsequent references to this work appear in the text. Reference to other works by Kant is from the same Suhrkamp *Werkausgabe* and is given by volume and page number.

6. G. W. F. Hegel, *Werke in zwanzig Bänden* (Frankfurt am Main: Suhrkamp, 1970), vol. 13, *Vorlesungen über die Ästhetik I*, p. 468.

don't tell the same story, and Kant's version has come down to us, in the tradition, in an even more distorted way than Hegel's.

The analyses of the sublime demand a two-part division that is not needed in the case of the beautiful. Besides the considerations of quantity as the mathematical sublimity of infinite grandeur, the analysis of the sublime also has to consider motion. The sublime thus reestablishes contact with the classical philosopheme that Kant inherits from Leibniz, in which the homogeneity between space and number, between geometry and calculus, is to be established by ways of infinitesimal motion. This rational objective is reached, in Kant, by ways of the affectivity of the subject.

The section on the mathematical sublime establishes the loss of the symbolic in the failure to represent, by sensory means, the infinite powers of inventive articulation of which the mind is capable. The faculty of *imagination* is itself beyond images; *Einbildungskraft* is *bildlos*, and the absurdity of its own name records its failure. How this failure can then be said to be, in a sense, overcome or defeated is the topic of the next section, entitled "Of the dynamic sublimity of nature" (sections 28 and 29).

The kinetics of the sublime are treated at once, and somewhat surprisingly, as a question of *power*: the first word of section 28 is *Macht*, soon followed by violence (*Gewalt*) and by the assertion that violence is the only means by which to overcome the resistance of one power with regard to another. A classical way to have moved from number to motion would have been by ways of a kinetics of physical bodies, a study, as in Kepler, for instance, of the motion of heavenly bodies in function of gravity as acceleration. But gravity can also be considered as a force or a power and the passage from a kinesis to what Kant calls a dynamics could be argued in terms of mathematical or physical concepts. For reasons that have to do with the teleology of his own text, Kant does not pursue this line of thought and at once introduces the notion of power in the empirical (but *is* it still empirical?) sense of assault, battle, and fright. The relationship between the aesthetic and the natural sublime is treated as a fight between antagonists rather than a discussion among scientists, in which the faculties of the mind somehow have to overpower, to be *überlegen* (superior) to, the power of nature. Hegel also conserves this notion of supremacy (*Überlegenheit*) in the passage from symbolic language to the language of the sublime.

It is therefore certainly not inconsistent if the same paragraph contains what appears to be a somewhat disquieting praise of the warrior over the statesman, the kind of statement one is more likely to expect from Nietzsche than from Kant. "In the comparison of the statesman with the general, people may well argue at length which of the two deserves the most respect; the aesthetic judgment, however, decides in favor of the latter" (p. 187). As always in Kant, one should not jump to conclusions; we know from his political writings that he is certainly not speaking of a superiority of war over peace or advocating military rather than civilian government. He *is* speaking, rather, of the spontaneous *affect* that prompts admiration for heroes in battle, the impulse that makes one at most love Aeneas but admire Achilles, that makes politicians envious of those who are allowed to wear a uniform. The point of the example is to separate affective from rational judgments. For the victory of the sublime over nature is the victory of one emotion (admiration, respect, etc.) over another emotion, such as fear. This language of the affections is what gives Kant's discourse some of the triviality of the particular, which often becomes audible in the ostensible silliness of some of his examples and illustrations, though never of his arguments. This blandness is hard to interpret, though it is possible, and even necessary, to develop a taste for it.

But what exactly is affectivity in Kant? It is easier to say what it is not: certainly not Shaftesbury's enthusiasm, nor the valorization of an inwardness which, in the Augustinian and pietistic tradition, unites the voice of consciousness (in all the meanings of the word) with the discourse of feeling, a tonality associated with Rousseau and with pre-Romanticism. Kant carefully distinguishes between affects and passions (*Leidenschaften*), which belong for him to the order of arbitrary and coercive desire: "in the affect, the freedom of the soul may be curtailed, but in a state of passion, it is eliminated altogether [*aufgehoben*]" (p. 198n). Kant's discussion of the affects does not start out from the inner experience of a subject, from the kind of interpretive sensitivity, the affective cogito that one can capture in Montaigne, in Malebranche, or in the Romantics. Kant is never as bland as when he discusses the emotions. He frequently seems to be using the dictionary rather than his own experience as a starting point, and he is often guided by external resemblances between words rather than by the inner resonances of emotion. Thus an important distinction between the emotion of surprise (*Verwunderung*), which is fleeting and transitory, and that of admiration (*Bewunderung*, p. 199), which is lasting, obviously owes more to the external resemblance between the two words than to a phenomenology of inner experience. Such a reduction from symbolic feeling to mere words, such a loss of pathos, of theatricality, and of self-reflection, is not easy to interpret and very easy to misjudge.

In the attempt to interpret this crucial point—and it *is* crucial, since the articulation of reason with practical morality and, hence, with political and legal wisdom, passes through the affectivity of the sublime—one can get some assistance from an early, precritical text of Kant on the same topic, written more than twenty-five years before the third *Critique* and entitled *Observations on the Sentiment of the Beautiful and the Sublime* (*Beobachtungen über das Gefühl des Schönen und Erhabenen*, 1764). This text, which reads at times like a collection of eighteenth-century provincial platitudes, is not to be dismissed lightly, especially not as an auxiliary to reading the section of the *Critique of Judgment* with which we are here concerned. Kant elaborates a contrastive typology of sublime and beautiful states of mind, values, and characteristics with a categorical self-assurance that borders on the ludicrous: we learn, among other things, that blue eyes and blond hair are beautiful, brown hair and black eyes sublime; that the Italians are beautiful and the English sublime; or, not unexpectedly, that men are sublime whereas women are beautiful, though women with brown hair, black eyes, and, insists Kant, with a pale complexion would at least be able to make a sublime impression, presumably on men. I spare you Kant's considerations on non-European nations, which, at the present date, are a little difficult to read—though not all that different from what Bougainville, but not Diderot, was saying around the same time. These distressing commonplaces are not to be blamed on the manner and the method of exposition, which remain of considerable interest throughout. The text proceeds by the enumeration of highly stylized character sil-houettes or caricatures (Kant refers to Hogarth), somewhat in the manner, though without the wit or the nuance, of la Bruyère—whose name is mentioned and whose device of designating set types by conventional names is at times being used. The typology, however, is never based on actual observation but entirely on words. Kant starts out from the verbal fund of the ordinary German language to set up elaborate classifications that need no further justification than their existence in the vocabulary, in the *Wortschatz* (or thesaurus), of common speech. Page after page consists of the listing, as mere *langue*, of terms which, in the realm of affect, are separated from each other by slight but decisive distinctions. One brief paragraph, taken almost at random, turns, in a few lines, on the succinct definition of such closely related words as *Fratzen*, *Phantast*, *Grillenfänger*, *läppisch*, *Laffe*, *Geck*, *abgeschmackt*, *aufgeblasen*, *Narr*, *Pedant*, and *Dunse*. The words are considered in themselves, without any concern for connotation, etymol-ogy, or figurative and symbolic overtone. In these pages, the symbolism of lan-guage, in Hegel's terms, has indeed entirely disappeared.

The loss of the symbolic is coupled with a thematic emphasis that becomes particularly noticeable in the section which establishes distinctions between beau-tiful and sublime feelings in terms of the four temperaments or humors. The sub-lime, we are told, is melancholic, whereas the beautiful is sanguine. But the mood of melancholy, described at length and with several specifications that will reap-pear, in less naive language, in the section on the dynamics of the sublime in the third *Critique*, is by no means a mood of narcissistic self-fascination. That there is nothing languid about it becomes even clearer when Kant specifies that the corre-sponding excess, in the case of melancholy, is adventurousness (*Abenteuer-lichkeit*). Sublime melancholy is also not incompatible with the sublime anger of the choleric temper. But there is one of the four temperaments that can never be either beautiful or sublime: Kant disposes contemptuously of the phlegmatic in one brief paragraph: "Since the phlegmatic contains none of the ingredients of the beautiful or the sublime to any observable degree, this aspect of the psyche does not belong among our considerations" (2:845). The equivalence of this *degré zéro* of emotion in the realm of national characteristics is the Dutch who, according to Kant, are phlegmatized Germans, interested only in money and totally devoid of any feeling for beauty or sublimity whatsoever. I have never felt more grateful for the hundred or so kilometers that separate Antwerp from Rotterdam.

More of all this than meets the hasty eye returns in the third *Critique*, also in the "general remark" that concludes the analyses of the beautiful and the sublime. The similarities are close enough to make any clear discrepancy between the two texts remarkable. Such a discrepancy occurs in a reference to the phlegmatic as loss or absence of affect (*Affektlosigkeit*), which, in the *Critique*, in sharp opposition to the early *Observations*, turns out to be associated with the highest form of the sublime. Enthusiasm, says Kant, may be aesthetically but not rationally sublime; it may have power, but it is blind. "This may appear odd," he continues, "but even the absence of emotion (*apatheia, phlegma in significatu bono*), when found in a mood that adheres emphatically and insistently to its principles, cannot only be sublime but most admirably so, because it will have the approval of pure reason on its side. This mood is the only one that can be called noble. The same quality can later also be applied to such things as, for example, a building, a dress, a style, a bodily stance, etc." (p. 199). What makes the sublime compatible with reason is its independence from sensory experience; it is beyond the senses, *übersinnlich*. This is what makes the junction of cognition with morality possible. A curious misprint, in the first edition of the third *Critique*, spelled *Sittlichkeit* for *Sinnlichkeit* (p. 202), thus confusing with one stroke of the typesetter what it took Kant thirty years of philosophizing to tear asunder. The error was corrected in the second edition, but many interpretations of the third *Critique read* as if the correction had never been made. "The inscrutability of the idea of freedom," says Kant, "bars the way to any attempt to represent it in a positive manner" (p. 202).

The passage is remarkable in still another respect. The supersensory moment in the dynamics of the aesthetic does not isolate the sublime in an otherworldly realm. It *applies*, as Kant puts it, to a variety of objects; art is the *techné* of a sublime that can only be found, in pure form, in nature in the raw. One of the examples given is that of a building: the *techné* of art is architectonic. The early *Observations* as well as the late *Critique* use the same pair of examples to designate the sublime work of art: the pyramids of Egypt and Saint Peter's Basilica in Rome. We have been led from our original question—what is the affect in Kant?—to a new question: what is the architectonic in Kant? The question, as you know, has also preoccupied Derrida in the fourth and final section of his reading of the third *Critique* entitled "Le colossal" (now in *La Vérité en peinture*).

The passage just quoted, on the potential nobility of buildings, occurs among several dictionary distinctions between related but opposed shades of affectivity: enthusiasm and apathy, admiration and surprise, enthusiasm and idolatry (*Schwärmerei*), madness (*Wahnsinn*) and grotesquerie (*Wahnwitz*). The distinctions are part of a larger subdivision between alert, combative sentiments (*Affekte von der* wackern *Art*) decreed to be sublime, and languid, yielding modes (*Affekte von der* schmelzenden *Art*) that can at best lay claim to beauty. Kant develops the distinction at some length in what amounts to a sermon in praise of heroic virility. This virtue contrasts favorably with qualities that will later be associated, in Goethe, Schiller, and still in Hegel, with the beautiful soul. Languid moods are found, says Kant, in novels and in *comédies larmoyantes* (*weinerlich*), in contrast to the nobility, to (in Winckelmann's words) the *edle Einfalt* and the *stille Größe* of the architectural crypts and temples.

Especially if one juxtaposes this passage to the section of the *Observations* entitled "Of the differences between the sublime and the beautiful in the opposition between the sexes," the interpretation of the architectonic as a principle of masculine virility, as pure macho of the German variety (whatever the word may be), seems inevitable. But to quote Derrida: "When erection is at stake, one should never be too much in a hurry—one should let things take their course [*il faut laisser la chose se faire*]."[7] This piece of good advice should be heeded, among other "things," with regard to Kant's and Derrida's texts. If erection is indeed "la chose," then it is likely to be anything but what one—or should I say men?—think(s) it to be.

What is it for Kant? We receive a hint in a passage which tells us how to look at the sublime, how to read judiciously, like the poets ("wie die Dichter es tun"): "If we call sublime the sight of a star-studded sky, we must not base this judgment on a notion of the stars as worlds inhabited by rational beings, in which the luminous points are their suns, moving purposefully and for their benefit. We must instead consider the sky as we see it [*wie man ihn sieht*], as a wide vault that contains everything. This is the only way to conceive of the sublime as the source of pure aesthetic judgment. The same is true of the sea: we must not look upon the ocean with the enriching knowledge that makes us conceive it as, for example, the vast habitat of nautical animals, or as the water supply from which, by evaporation and for the benefit of the land, clouds are being seeded, or even as an element that keeps continents apart, yet enables communication between them. All these are teleological judgments. Instead, one must see the ocean as poets do, as the eye seems to perceive it [*nach dem was der Augenschein zeigt*], as a transparent mirror when it is at peace, circumscribed only by the sky, and, when it is in motion, as an abyss that threatens to swallow everything" (p. 196).

Kant's architectonic vision here appears in its purest form. But a misguided imagination, distorted by a conception of romantic imagery, runs the risk of setting the passage awry. It may appear to be about nature in its most all-encompassing magnitude but, in fact, it does not see nature as nature at all, but as a construction, as a house. The sky is seen as a vault or a roof, and the horizon as the enclosure by this roof of the surface on which we dwell. Aesthetic space, in Kant as in Aristotle, is a house in which we dwell more or less safely, depending on the

---

7. Jacques Derrida, *La Vérité en peinture* (Paris: Flammarion, 1978), p. 144.

weather of the times. Similar intuitions are familiar to us from Wordsworth, as when we are told, in the nest-robbing episode from *The Prelude,* that ". . . the sky was not a sky / Of earth" or when, in a more tranquil mood, "Tintern Abbey" speaks of a "dwelling" that is ". . . the light of setting suns / And the *round* ocean and the living air / And the blue sky. . . ." But the reference to Wordsworth can also be misleading, for what Kant is definitely *not* evoking is a vision "into the life of things," a "presence" or "a sense / Of something far more deeply interfused / Where dwelling is the light . . . and in the mind of man." Wordsworth's interiorized sublime is not architectonic but, at most, "the picture *of the mind.*" No mind, no inside to correspond to an outside, can be found in Kant's scene. To the extent that any mind or judgment are present at all, they are in error: it is false to think of the sky as a roof or of the ocean as bounded by the horizon of the sky.

Neither is the vision a sensation, a primary or secondary understanding in Locke's sense: the eye, left to itself, entirely ignores understanding; it only notices appearance (it is *Augenschein*) without any awareness of a dichotomy between illusion and reality—a dichotomy which belongs to teleological and not to aesthetic judgment. In other words, the transformation of nature into a building, the transformation of sky and ocean into vault and floor, is not a trope. The passage is entirely devoid of any substitutive exchange, of any negotiated economy, between nature and mind; it is free of any facing or defacing of the natural world. Kant is as remote as possible from Wordsworth's mind looking "upon the speaking *face* of earth and heaven"; or of Baudelaire in "Le Voyage" "berçant notre infini sur le fini des mers"; it is in no way possible to think of this stony gaze as an address or an apostrophe. The dynamics of the sublime mark the moment when the infinite is frozen into the materiality of stone, when no pathos, anxiety, or sympathy is conceivable; it is, indeed, the moment of a-pathos, or apathy, as the complete loss of the symbolic.

One will object here that the evocation of the sea, with its mirror and the terror of its abyss, is the very figure of the mind, the consciousness of fear and mortality assuaging the affect of terror. But this, again, is reading the Kant passage as if it were Wordsworth's *The Prelude*, Shelley's "The Triumph of Life," or Baudelaire's "L'homme et la mer" ("La mer est son miroir . . ."), or even Mallarmé's "Hérodiade," all poems organized around the trope of a metamorphosis of the abysmal terror, with its vertiginous yielding, its descent into the maelstrom, into the hardness of reflection. But Kant's passage is not a metamorphosis, but the mere sequence of two random events. Within the logic of the text, the vision of the sea as part of a bounded space in no way depends on the opposition between mirror and abyss. Such depth perception is entirely absent from the flatness of the discourse. Since the observer is presumably safely on land, the fear that the strong sea may swallow him is exactly as false, and for the same reason, as the illusion that the sky is the limit of the water. Poets, in Kant, do not embark on the high seas.

The language of the poets therefore in no way partakes of mimesis, reflection, or even perception, in the sense which would allow a link between sense experience and understanding, between perception and apperception. Realism postulates a phenomenalism of experience which is here being denied or ignored. Kant's looking at the world just as one sees it ("wie man ihn sieht") is an absolute, radical formalism that entertains no notion of reference or semiosis. Yet it is this entirely a-referential, a-phenomenal, a-pathetic formalism that will win out in the battle among affects and find access to the moral world of practical reason, practical law, and rational politics. To parody Kant's stylistic procedure of dictionary definition: the radical formalism that animates aesthetic judgment in the dynamics of the sublime is what is called materialism. Theoreticians of literature who fear they may have deserted or betrayed the world by being too formalistic are worrying about the wrong thing: in the spirit of Kant's third *Critique,* they were not nearly formalistic enough.

Kant and Schiller

I'll have some change in pace today, because this time I have not written out a lecture; it was not necessary in this case because I'm dealing with a much easier text. I wouldn't dare to improvise about Kant, but about Schiller it's a little easier to know what is going on, and so there is no need for such detailed textual analysis. So what I'll be doing will be more in the nature of an exposition than a really tight argument, more in the nature of a class than a lecture. Therefore it is better to speak it—it's a little easier to listen to when it's spoken than when it's read.

Yet the point that I try to make, or the question to which I try to address myself by thus juxtaposing Schiller, and trying to take a closer look at just exactly what happened between Kant and Schiller—what happens when Schiller comments very specifically on Kant?—that event, that encounter, and the structure of that encounter, which is, as I say, not too difficult to explain, is in itself complex, and, I suppose, to some extent, important. It has to do with two matters, one of very general historical importance, the second of very much more direct import for these lectures.

The first has to do with the general problem of the reception of Kant, the *Critique*, and specifically the reception of the *Critique of Judgment*, an immensely important book that remains exceedingly important throughout the nineteenth and twentieth centuries and that is still steadily invoked, either directly or indirectly.

"Kant and Schiller" was transcribed by William Jewett and Thomas Pepper—and revised by the editor—from the audiotape of the fifth Messenger lecture de Man delivered at Cornell (3 March 1983). Notes were supplied by the transcribers and the editor.

You'll notice recently that when Walter Jackson Bate had something articulate to say about the humanities, the authority to which he referred first of all was Kant. And you may have noticed that when Frank Lentricchia was trying to get certain types of contemporary criticism which will remain unnamed, to give them their comeuppance, his reference again was to Kant, he went back to Kant.[1] So this is almost a joke, this "back to Kant."

But the presence of the third *Critique* within critical discourse—also in this country, and in a different way, of course, in Germany and in France, though frequently mediated by all kinds of other names, so that it is no longer Kant one gets but a whole series of names in between—that reception of Kant is very complex (the reception of the third *Critique*) and not well known. There are allusions to it right and left, but it isn't really explored. There's René Wellek's book *Kant in England*,[2] which I looked at recently and which is a remarkably tough-minded little book, from which it results that actually the English Romantics didn't get Kant right at all. But he uses the *Critique of Pure Reason* rather than the *Critique of Judgment*. In that whole field, indeed, a lot remains, of course, to be done, as usual. It's complex. But it has a pattern which I would to some extent try to evoke here.

There seems to be always a regression from the incisiveness and from the impact, from the critical impact of the original. There is an attempt—if indeed there is any truth at all in the way in which I suggested that Kant can be read to you two days ago, then Kant's statement is a very threatening one, both for the sake of philosophy and for the relationship between art and philosophy in general. So something very directly threatening is present there which one feels the need to bridge—the difficulties, the obstacles which Kant has opened up. So there is a regression, an attempt to account for, to domesticate the critical incisiveness of the original. And that leads then to texts like those of Schiller, which undertake to do just that. Out of a text like Schiller's *Letters on Aesthetic Education*, or the other texts of Schiller that relate directly to Kant, a whole tradition in Germany—in Germany and elsewhere—has been born: a way of emphasizing, of revalorizing the aesthetic, a way of setting up the aesthetic as exemplary, as an exemplary category, as a unifying category, as a model for education, as a model even for the state. And a certain tone that's characteristic of Schiller is a tone which one keeps hearing throughout the nineteenth century in Germany, which you hear first

---

1. See Walter Jackson Bate, "The Crisis in English Studies," *Harvard Magazine* 85:1 (September–October 1982): 46–53, and Frank Lentricchia, *After the New Criticism* (Chicago: University of Chicago Press, 1980). Cf. de Man's remarks on Bate in "The Return to Philology," in *The Resistance to Theory* (Minneapolis: University of Minnesota Press, 1986), and on Lentricchia in "Kant's Materialism" in this volume.

2. René Wellek, *Immanuel Kant in England 1793–1838* (Princeton, N.J.: Princeton University Press, 1931).

in Schiller himself, but which you then hear in Schopenhauer, which you hear in early Nietzsche—*The Birth of Tragedy* is purely Schillerian in its tone, and so on—which you still hear in a certain way in Heidegger. That tone always— a certain valorization of art, a priori valorization of art, which is a frequent theme throughout that tradition—it always appears doubled, it always appears doubled with a critical approach which is closer to that of the original Kant and which goes together with this much more positively valorized approach to art. We saw what the juxtaposition between Schiller and Kleist does, and we saw the way in which Kleist takes you back in a way to certain of the more threatening Kantian insights in terms of Schiller.[3] Or you would find a play like that between Schopenhauer and Nietzsche, the way in which Nietzsche—not just the Nietzsche of *The Birth of Tragedy*, but the later Nietzsche as well—acts critically in relation to Schopenhauer and, I would say, "de-Schillerizes" and "re-Kantizes" what Schopenhauer has been saying. Or, I would even suggest, to take a name which isn't purely German, that something like that could be said to go on between Heidegger on the one hand and Derrida on the other; so that the reading that Derrida gives of Heidegger, in which Heidegger would play the role of Schiller, Derrida would then appear as being closer to Kant, in a kind of similar critical examination of a certain claim for the autonomy and the power of the aesthetic which is being asserted in the wake of Schiller, but not necessarily in the wake of Kant. This is a very complex problem to which I plan to make no contribution whatsoever, except for looking a little more closely at that original model, the relationship between Kant and Schiller. Because that sets a pattern which will recur and which would be a possible way in which to organize the question of the reception of Kant throughout the nineteenth century, at least in Germany, though you would find similar elements in England. Matthew Arnold, for instance, is very Schillerian. Who would be the equivalents, who would be the Kant of Matthew Arnold? Ruskin? I don't know. It's worth playing with—certainly not Pater—but you would find interesting elements of the same type in the other tradition as well.

Okay. The topic also has to do with the question which is closer to our concern here, to our discussion here; because it seems to be, as so often is the case, that . . . Since I have now had questions from you and since I've felt some resistances . . . You are so kind at the beginning and so hospitable and so benevolent that I have the feeling that . . . But I know this is not the case and there's always an interesting episode in a series of lectures like that, I know that from experience. One doesn't necessarily begin in as idyllic a mood as things were here. But it doesn't take you too long before you feel that you're getting under people's skin, and that there is a certain reaction which is bound to occur, certain questions that

---

3. See de Man's "Aesthetic Formalization: Kleist's *Über das Marionettentheater*," in *The Rhetoric of Romanticism* (New York: Columbia University Press, 1984), which he delivered as the second Messenger lecture.

are bound to be asked, which is the interesting moment, where certain issues are bound to come up.

Well, the topic that has emerged and which I didn't deliberately want to—or which I didn't even know about, in a sense—has been this problem of the question of reversibility, of the reversibility in the type of models which I have been developing on the basis of texts. And this is linked to the question of reversibility, linked to the question of historicity. I find this of considerable interest and that's for me the interesting, productive thing to have come out of those lectures (except for the fact that I had to write three lectures, which I now have written out). This was not a deliberate theme. It has emerged by itself, and it has been brought out by a question, and it is therefore more interesting than any other to me.

I won't say much about this, but something at least. When I speak of irreversibility, and insist on irreversibility, this is because in all those texts and those juxtapositions of texts, we have been aware of something which one could call a progression—though it shouldn't be—a movement, from cognition, from acts of knowledge, from states of cognition, to something which is no longer a cognition but which is to some extent an *occurrence*, which has the materiality of something that actually happens, that actually occurs. And there, the thought of material occurrence, something that occurs materially, that leaves a trace on the world, that does something to the world as such—that notion of occurrence is not opposed in any sense to the notion of writing. But it is opposed to some extent to the notion of cognition. I'm reminded of a quotation in Hölderlin—if you don't quote Pascal you can always quote Hölderlin, that's about equally useful—which says: "Lang ist die Zeit, es ereignet sich aber das Wahre." Long is time, but—not truth, not *Wahrheit*, but *das Wahre*, that which is true, will occur, will take place, will eventually take place, will eventually occur.[4] And the characteristic of truth is the fact that it occurs, not the truth, but that which is true. The occurrence is true because it occurs; by the fact that it occurs it has truth, truth value, it is true.

The model for that, the linguistic model for the process I am describing, and which is irreversible, is the model of the *passage* from trope, which is a cognitive model, to the performative, for example. Not the performative in itself—because the performative in itself exists independently of tropes and exists independently of a critical examination or of an epistemological examination of tropes—but the transition, the passage from a conception of language as a system, perhaps a closed system, of tropes, that totalizes itself as a series of transformations which can be reduced to tropological systems, and then the fact that you *pass* from that conception of language to *another* conception of language in which language is no longer cognitive but in which language is performative.

---

4. See de Man's comments on this line (from the first version of Hölderlin's "Mnemosyne") in his Foreword to Carol Jacobs, *The Dissimulating Harmony: The Image of Interpretation in Nietzsche, Proust, Rilke and Benjamin* (Baltimore: Johns Hopkins University Press, 1978), p. xi.

And this passage, if it is thus conceived, that is, the passage from trope to per-formative—and I insist on the necessity of this, so the model is not the performa-tive, the model is the passage from trope to performative—this passage occurs always, and can only occur, by ways of an epistemological critique of trope. The trope, the epistemology of tropes, allows for a critical discourse, a transcendental critical discourse, to emerge, which will push the notion of trope to the extreme, trying to saturate your whole field of language. But then certain linguistic ele-ments will remain which the concept of trope cannot reach, and which then can be, for example—though there are other possibilities—performative. That pro-cess, which we have encountered a certain number of times, is irreversible. That goes in that direction and you cannot get back from the one to the one before. But that does not mean—because on the other hand, then, there the model of the per-formative, the transition from the trope to the performative, is useful again—it doesn't mean that the performative function of language will then as such be accepted and admitted. It will always be reinscribed within a cognitive system, it will always be *recuperated*, it will relapse, so to speak, by a kind of reinscription of the performative in a tropological system of cognition again. That relapse, however, is not the same as a reversal. Because this is in its turn open to a critical discourse similar to the one that has taken one from the notion of trope to that of the performative. So it is not a return to the notion of trope and to the notion of cognition; it is equally balanced between both, and equally poised between both, and as such is not a reversal, it's a relapse. And a relapse in that sense is not the same; it has to be distinguished in a way which I am only indicating here but which would require much more refined formulation—the recuperation, the re-lapse, has to be distinguished from a reversal.

Now, *history* is thought of here—and when it was asked the other day whether I thought of history as a priori in any sense, I had to say yes to that. Then, not knowing quite into which trap I'd fallen, or what or whether I had fallen into a trap, or what's still behind it—I still do not know. History, the sense of the notion of history as the historicity a priori of this type of textual model which I have been suggesting here, there history is not thought of as a progression or a regression, but is thought of as an event, as an occurrence. There is history from the moment that words such as "power" and "battle" and so on emerge on the scene. At that moment things *happen*, there is *occurrence*, there is *event*. History is therefore not a temporal notion, it has nothing to do with temporality, but it is the emergence of a language of power out of a language of cognition. An emergence which is, how-ever, not itself either a dialectical movement or any kind of continuum, any kind of continuum that would be accessible to a cognition, however much it may be conceived of, as would be the case in a Hegelian dialectic, as a negation. The per-formative is not a negation of the tropological. Between the tropological and the performative there is a separation which allows for no mediation whatsoever. But there is a single-directed movement that goes from the one to the other and which is not susceptible of being represented as a temporal process. That is historical, and it doesn't allow for any reinscription of history into any kind of cognition. The apparent regression which we talked about, the apparent regression of which we will see an example today, the regression from the event, from the materiality of the inscribed signifier in Kant, or from any of those several other disruptions which we have more or less precisely identified within the cognitive discourse of trope—this regression is no longer historical, because that regression takes place in a temporal mode and it is as such not history. One could say, for example, that in the reception of Kant, in the way Kant has been read, since the third *Critique*—and that was an occurrence, something happened there, something occurred—that in the whole reception of Kant from then until now, nothing has happened, only regression, nothing has happened at all. Which is another way of saying there is no history, which is another way of saying—which would delight my friend Jauss—that reception is not historical, that between reception and history there is an absolute separation, and that to take reception as a model for historical event is in error, is a mistake.[5] I should not use those terms interchangeably—let's call it . . . an error. I wouldn't think of Jauss as ever being in anything mistaken. One thing, however, is certain. The event, the occurrence, is resisted by reinscribing it in the cognition of tropes, and that is itself a tropological, cognitive, and not a historical move.

Now, we see one instance of this by looking at the way in which Schiller reinscribes Kant in the tropological system of aesthetics, which, as we saw, Kant had in a sense disarticulated, Kant had taken apart. I don't know what expression to use—you cannot say "go beyond"—he had interrupted, disrupted, disarticulated the project of articulation which the aesthetic—which he had undertaken and which he found himself by the rigor of his own discourse to break down under the power of his own critical epistemological discourse. A terrifying moment, in a sense—terrifying for Kant, since the entire enterprise of philosophy is involved in it, and was in that way threatened. Kant didn't notice at that moment . . . I don't think that Kant, when he wrote about the heavens and the sea there, that he was shuddering in mind. Any literalism there would not be called for. It is terrifying in a way which we don't know. What do we know about the nightmares of Immanuel Kant? I'm sure they were . . . very interesting . . . Königsberg there in the winter—I shudder to think.

Now, Schiller takes that on, takes on the concept of the sublime, specifically, in a relatively early essay which is called "Vom Erhabenen" (which is to be distinguished from a later essay which is called "Über das Erhabene"), "Of the Sublime," to which he gives as a subtitle "weitere Ausführung einiger Kantischen

---

5. See de Man's Introduction to Hans Robert Jauss, *Toward an Aesthetic of Reception,* trans. Timothy Bahti (Minneapolis: University of Minnesota Press, 1982), now reprinted as "Reading and History," in de Man, *The Resistance to Theory.*

Ideen," "further development of a few Kantian ideas."[6] And it is one of the few Schiller texts where he is really closely reading Kant and quoting Kant. And what he quotes and what he reads is paragraph 29 of the third *Critique*, the passage on the sublime which we talked about two days ago.[7]

Now, a first observation in terms of tropological system, is that, unlike Kant's style, Schiller's style is tropological—it's trope throughout, from beginning to end, and one specific trope, and a very important one, a very characteristic one, namely, chiasmus. There is not a single sentence in—Schiller invites parody, he invites schematization, and invites parody, because he cannot write two sentences which are not symmetrically bound around a chiasmic crossing. We'll see that any sentence I'm going to quote—I will certainly not be pointing it out to you all the time—would be thus organized, thus structured. What do I mean when I say these are chiastically structured? It is quite simple. For example, Schiller works emphatically, as you will have noticed if you have read only one paragraph, and I assigned a little bit at random whatever I assigned and asked you to read. Wherever you read Schiller, it's pretty much the same. At least as far as the particular stylistic and tropological structure is concerned—that will always be the same. You get a polarity, you get a variety of polarities, sharply marked, strictly opposed to each other; for example, a polarity like Nature and Reason. In the section on the sublime, it has to do with Terror, with being scared, with the agitation of Terror—and with the opposite of Terror, which is Tranquillity. The correct term in Schiller is *Gemütsfreiheit*, the word for free mind, so that you are "free," and tranquil therefore. Now in those scenes in the sublime, Nature is shown as dangerous, it is threatening, with its mountains and so on. So Nature is associated with Terror, whereas Reason, on the other hand, which is the free exercise of *Vernunft*, is associated with a specific kind of tranquillity. So you have always—and you can schematize this throughout—you have a polarity, and then another set of polarities there, opposing what I quoted, which is paired with the first as an attribute of the first:

Nature ——————————Terror
Reason ——————————Tranquillity

It is an attribute of Nature that it can be terrifying; it's an attribute of Reason that it is tranquil. Nature isn't always terrifying, but of sublime nature it's an attribute, a

---

6. References to Schiller's "Vom Erhabenen" and, later in the lecture, to his "Über die notwendigen Grenzen beim Gebrauch schöner Formen," are to the *Nationalausgabe* of Schiller's *Werke* (Weimar: Hermann Bohlaus Nachfolger, 1963) and are given by volume and page number. "Vom Erhabenen" is translated into English as "On the Sublime (Toward the Further Development of Some Kantian Ideas)" by Daniel O. Dahlstrom in Friedrich Schiller, *Essays*, ed. Walter Hinderer (New York: Continuum, 1993), pp. 22–44.

7. A reference to "Phenomenality and Materiality in Kant" (included in this volume), which de Man delivered as the fourth Messenger lecture at Cornell.

necessary attribute, we'll say. And Schiller makes a point of it, an argument, that sublime nature has to be terrifying. It has to be an element of the sublime nature of Nature, as it were. Whereas reason, sublime Reason, Reason on the level of the sublime, has to maintain a certain freedom of contemplation, which he calls *Gemütsfreiheit*, and which is tranquil. Normally, Nature he calls Terror and Reason he calls Tranquil, and that's the system from which you start out.

Schiller then starts to argue, to say that the sublime is not Nature acting on Terror, which means something quite simple, namely, the following: that, faced with the terrifying nature, faced with an abyss, for example, a sharp abyss, you can do something about it. You can remedy it by natural means; you can put up a fence, and then you will no longer be terrified. That, he says, is Nature working on Terror—because it's still working with a natural thing. A fence is a natural thing, even if you make it yourself it is still within the realm of the natural—natural objects, natural entities, wood, tools, and so on and so forth. That, says Schiller, is not sublime. There is nothing sublime about this. You may admire the cleverness of man who is able to do this, but it is not a sublime thing, not a sublime move at all. What will be sublime, what will be called sublime, is the action of Reason on Terror. Reason can act on Terror, not by preventing it, by making whatever is happening less dangerous, but by creating a detachment, by creating a liberty of the mind, which in certain conditions is possible. And where the mind will see that whereas by separating mind from body—for example, will see that whereas the body is threatened, the mind remains extremely free—which is fortunately true in the case. If one is ill, for example, one finds that one's mind gets terribly free and terribly active. In that case, Reason is acting on Terror, and you get the change in the pairs. There is a substitution of the attribute, because Terror, which is normally associated with Nature, will now be associated with Reason. And when that happens—those systems are always totalizing—there will be a symmetrical reversal—that's a reversibility for you. And the chiasmus is a reversible structure, a symmetrical and reversible structure. If Reason can act on Terror, if Reason can take on the attribute of Terror, then Nature will be able to take on the attribute of tranquillity, and you will be able to enjoy tranquilly, with a certain tranquillity, the sublime violence of Nature. The sublime is enjoyed to the extent that Nature can be enjoyed with a certain tranquillity.

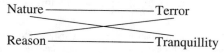

You see, I just want to put this pattern before you, not for its intrinsic merit—whether this is true or false I have not the slightest idea and not the slightest interest. It's true enough on some level of psychological verisimilitude. But it has a very specific structure, and it will be developed, it will be established by means of that structure. And that structure can be schematized in that trope of chiasmus, which is obsessionally recurrent throughout Schiller's discourse. You'll get it everywhere.

How does it work in relationship to Kant's theory of the sublime, which, as I remind you, was based in Kant on a passage, on a transition from something called the mathematical to the dynamic sublime? Schiller is going to change that explicitly and deliberately, and with good reasons of his own. He first of all is going to polarize Kant, because, as we saw in Kant, the difference, or the distinction, or the transition from the mathematical to the dynamic sublime is by no means a polarity. The dynamic sublime is not symmetrically opposed to the mathematical sublime. The relationship is not antithetical, it is something much more complex. We saw—as a matter of fact, we had a great deal of trouble—we did not succeed in identifying the nature of that relationship. Why does Kant need the dynamic sublime at all? There are various explanations that one can give. Finally, we had to resort to a linguistic model, a linguistic model of precisely the passage from trope to performative, in order, not to account for, but to explain why this juxtaposition, why this succession, this apparent sequence occurs in Kant. It is certainly not an opposition. One thinks of the dynamic sublime as a kind of residue after the tropological discourse has tried to saturate the field. One thinks of it as a passage from trope to performative, as a passage from cognition to power. But none of those—trope and performative are not antithetical to each other, they are . . . different, and that's it. In the same way that cognition and power are not antithetical with each other. There is a power of cognition, cognition has a power of its own. There are powers which are not dictated by cognition, and so on, so they are not antitheses; one does not exclude the other at all. Their relationship is a much more complex one, a much finer one—as Wordsworth, somewhere in the "Essay upon Epitaphs," speaks of a much finer relationship between entities than one of sheer opposition, and this is the case. Well, and the relationship between them, between the mathematical and the dynamic, is a discontinuity. It is not a dialectic, it is not a progression or a regression, but it is a transformation of trope into power, which is not itself a tropological movement, and which cannot be accounted for by means of a tropological model. You cannot account for the change from trope into performative, you cannot account for the change from the mathematical to the dynamic sublime in Kant—I argued at least—you cannot account for it according to a tropological model.

Now, in Schiller, we start instead from a sharp polarity, from a sharp, antithetical opposition between what he calls two "drives," *Triebe*. That word recurs constantly in Schiller—*Triebe*, a word that you know from Freud—a word that is not frequent in Kant, who speaks of laws, of *Gesetze*, but very rarely of the *Triebe*. The two drives which Schiller opposes to each other are the drive to know, the drive to represent (and, he says, the drive to change the world, to change nature), and another, a drive to maintain, to preserve, and to leave things unaltered by change. The example of the second, the drive to maintain, would be the desire for self-preservation. One doesn't want to die—one protects oneself by self-preservation, one wants things to remain as they are. On the other hand, the drive to know is a drive that is involved with change.

Nature can be an obstacle to either of those drives, but Schiller distinguishes between them and proposes a terminology which he says is preferable to Kant's terminology. Whereas Kant spoke of the mathematical and the dynamic sublime, he, Schiller, will oppose to each other what he calls the theoretical and the practical sublime. And let me quote to you, in an improvised and inadequate translation, the passage which I have in mind. And you will see—as I say, I will not keep pointing this out—how all those passages are set up as antithetical, chiastic, symmetrical sentences which correspond to each other syntactically entirely except for some substitutions of words which correspond to each other because they are antithetical. Here is the quotation: "In the theoretical sublime, Nature, as an object of cognition, stands in opposition with the desire to acquire representations, with the desire to know [*Vorstellungstrieb*]." That's what happens in the theoretical sublime. "In the practical sublime, nature, as an object of emotion, stands in opposition to our desire for self-preservation" (*Werke*, 20:174–75). See, the two sentences are the same, right? In the theoretical/in the practical sublime, nature/nature, object of cognition/object of emotion, stand in opposition to desires. On the one hand, desire to acquire representation; on the other hand, desire for self-preservation. Perfect symmetry: the one sentence has exactly the same syntactical structure as the other, and the changes that are made between them are always polar opposites: theoretical/practical, cognition/emotion, representation and desire for self-preservation, those are the polarities. "In the first case," that is, the theoretical sublime, "nature is considered only as an entity that should extend, that should expand our knowledge. In the second, it is represented as a power [*Macht*] that can determine our own predicament, our own situation." "Kant," says Schiller, "therefore calls the practical sublime the sublime of power or the dynamic sublime, in opposition to the mathematical sublime. Because it is impossible," says Schiller, "to decide whether the field of the sublime is fully covered by the concepts of mathematical and the dynamic sublime, I prefer,"—I, Schiller—"prefer to substitute the subdivision practical/theoretical sublime to that of mathematical/dynamic sublime."

It's a curious argument, though it does make sense, in a sense. He says—he feels, he doesn't make it explicit—that to the extent that mathematical and dynamic are not polar opposites, to the extent that they encroach upon each other, that it is difficult to distinguish between them, you cannot say that they cover the full field of the sublime. Whereas if you have really polar opposites, black and white, you can cover the entire field and establish your totalization much more easily. It is also curious that he would say, "Kant therefore calls the practical sublime the sublime of power." That's not what happens, it's he who calls the dynamic sublime the practical. The word "practical" does not occur at that point in

Kant, nor should it at that moment. So the mathematical sublime, or the theoretical sublime, is characterized in Schiller by a failure of representation—and that is correct in Kantian terms since we saw that the mathematical sublime is the inability to grasp magnitude by means of models of extension, by means of spatial models, so it is a correct interpretation. For Kant, the mathematical sublime is characterized by the failure of representation, whereas what Schiller calls the practical sublime is characterized by the physical inferiority of the body when it is in danger. Since the purpose of the practical sublime is self-preservation, it is characterized by the fact that Nature can threaten us because it is practically, empirically, stronger, can be stronger than we are, in a storm or in a fire or whatever you want to call it.

Now this notion of physical danger, of a threatening physical Nature, in an empirical sense—highly empirical, we are threatened concretely by fire, or by a tempest—you will find no trace of that whatsoever in Kant. There would be no mention of that in Kant's treatment of the sublime. The notion of danger occurs in Kant, and there is the example of a violent nature at times brought in as an example for a different reason. But the notion of danger occurs in Kant not as the direct threat of a natural force to our physical well-being, but, first of all, as you remember, in the shock of surprise, of *Verwunderung*, which we experience when confronted with something of extreme magnitude. We feel that our faculties, including the imagination, are unable to grasp the totality of what they encounter. It occurs, the danger occurs in Kant as a failure of representation, and it has to do, and will be explained, accounted for—it has to do with the structure of the imagination. Therefore it is of interest to Kant because it tells us something about the structure of the imagination. It tells us nothing about self-preservation. It tells us nothing about how to achieve self-preservation, about how to protect ourselves from tempests, or how to protect ourselves, so to speak, psychologically, from danger. Not by putting up a fence but by developing a kind of mental activity which allows us to separate ourselves from the danger. Here is Schiller, I quote Schiller: "The practical sublime is distinguished from the theoretical sublime in that it stands in opposition to the demands of our existence, whereas the theoretical stands in opposition only to the demands of our knowledge." Existence opposed to knowledge. "An entity or an object is theoretically sublime if it implies the representation of the infinite, which the imagination feels itself unable to grasp. An entity is practically sublime if it implies the representation of a danger which one's physical strength feels unable to overpower. We are defeated by the attempt to represent in the first form of the sublime; we are defeated by the attempt to oppose in the second case. An example of the first is that of the ocean at peace, an example of the second is that of the ocean in a tempest."

You see there is some distant echo here. Certainly he remembers to some extent the passage in Kant, where Kant was speaking of the sea and of the heavens, and where Kant spoke of a tranquil sea and of an ocean in movement. There is a distant memory of that, but it is entirely different in its function. It bears no relationship whatsoever to the function of those two stages, those two states, as they were described and used by Kant. The entire passage, again with his stress on practicality, on the pragmatic—rather than on the philosophical problem which concerned Kant, namely, the structure of the imagination—the whole impact of the passage is entirely different. The passage is exceedingly clear. We understand this perfectly well. Perhaps the translation is a little awkward, or I haven't read it right, but if you read it you will understand it. Anybody will understand it right away in this opposition.

Schiller goes on to valorize. And he will valorize the practical over the theoretical. The practical sublime, which is the only one he will keep talking about in the rest of the essay, is valorized completely at the expense of the theoretical sublime, where he got Kant right. So he adds something to Kant which is not in Kant, and then he valorizes what he has added as being more important than what really was in Kant. This valorization occurs in several stages. I quote him for you: "The theoretical sublime contradicts the desire for representation, for knowledge, the practical sublime contradicts the desire for self-preservation. In the first case, one single manifestation of our cognitive powers is being contested. In the second, however, it's the ultimate ground of all its manifestations, namely, existence itself, that is under attack." So the practical sublime has much more at stake, since our entire existence is being threatened, whereas the only thing that was threatened by the theoretical sublime was just our ability to represent, our ability to know. Who cares about knowing when the tempest is beating at his door? That's not the moment that you want to know; you want to be self-preserved, and you want to survive, psychologically, the assault to which you are subjected. Much more is at stake, your whole existence; whereas a little loss of knowledge can always be made up the next day, hmm? It is much more extensive and therefore it causes real terror, whereas the loss of knowledge, or a certain threat to knowledge, causes at most a displeasure.

Schiller continues in this valorization: "Our sensibility is therefore much more directly involved with the terrifying than with the infinite entity"—infinite was the theoretical sublime—"for the desire for self-preservation speaks with a louder voice than the drive for knowledge. For this very reason, because the object of terror aggresses our sensory existence with much more violence than the object of infinity, the distance between the sensory and the supersensory power in us is experienced much more vividly, and the superiority of reason and of inner freedom becomes all the more manifest. And since the essence of the sublime rests in the consciousness of this rational freedom, and since all pleasure associated with the sublime is founded on this consciousness, so it follows, and this is also confirmed by experience, that terror must move us more vividly and more pleasantly in an aesthetic representation than the infinite, and that therefore the practical sublime has a considerable advantage over the theoretical sublime in terms of emotional power" (*Werke*, 20: 174–75).

What is striking in those passages, which are quite convincing and which are psychologically and empirically entirely reasonable—they are also reasonable if you think of them in terms of Schiller's own concerns as a playwright, if you don't ask the philosophical question, "What is the structure of the faculty of the imagination?" but if you ask the practical question, "How am I going to write successful plays?" which was partly and legitimately Schiller's concern—you will provoke a lot more effect on an audience by using terror or using scenes of terror, also using scenes in which Nature is directly threatening, than by using abstractions, such as infinity, which are not easily represented on the stage. So there is a total lack, an amazing, naive, childish lack of transcendental concern in Schiller, an amazing lack of philosophical concern. He has no interest in it whatsoever. It doesn't bother him in the least that knowledge would be impossible, as long as he can fill his theater. I don't want to put it in contemptuous terms, but that's practical and that's necessary, whereas the other can wait. In Kant, however, the entire terror which is there, the unrest, arises from the incapacity of the faculties of reason and of imagination, and this is the only, and his only, and deeply philosophical, concern. Schiller seems much more practically concerned, he seems concerned—well, I put it derisively, with his own success as a playwright—but he's also more concerned, more legitimately, with the psychology of terror: How am I going to fight off terror, how am I going to resist terror?—by means of a psychological device, which emphasizes reason and the ability to maintain reason in the face of terror. That's a way to live through terror, even if you're physically annihilated by it. Curiously, this emphasis on the practical, this emphasis on the psychological, on the empirical, leads to a greater stress on the abstract powers, as is clear from the quotation where it is said that the distance between reason and nature is augmented by this, and the abstraction of those powers, in their abstraction, separates them more than before from the natural, the concrete, despite and because of the emphasis on the practical and on the pragmatic. The stress on the dichotomy between the practical and the theoretical results, as we will see soon enough, in the idealization of the practical, on the one hand—that we'll see—and, on the other hand, in a certain banalization, a certain psychologization of the theoretical. Whereas the theoretical, the issue of the theoretical, in general, in the mathematical and in the dynamic sublime, was Kant's overriding and only concern, and although this led to very difficult writing and to passages in Kant which are very difficult to interpret and to understand, we find nothing of this difficulty in Schiller, because here we are speaking of a psychological verisimilitude which all of us can understand, and in which all of us can participate, precisely to the extent that they are pragmatic, everyday, banal experiences. We all know that, confronted with danger, it's sort of nice to think of something else, and to be concerned with the movement of your own mind and with your reason. This is the way we cope with danger, this is the way we cope with pain, and so on and so forth, constantly, by this becoming conscious of it and therefore indulging in the play of the mind rather than in the actual physical threat. You can even do that, if you get skilled at it, in the very process of being in danger. You know that from your own experience if you have ever been in immediate danger. There is a kind of exhilaration of the mind—if you are given the time—at watching yourself being in that state of danger, and you find great solace in that possibility. It maintains the autonomy, the integrity of the mind—this is a correct psychological observation that Schiller is making. But it is not a philosophical observation, and it is certainly not the problem that concerns Kant. The important thing is that this apparent realism, this apparent practicality, this concern with the practical, will result in a total loss of contact with reality, in a total idealism.

Before you either contest this, or before you not contest but agree with it and hold it against Schiller, or think that it is something we are now far beyond and that we would never in our enlightened days do—you would never make this naive confusion between the practical and the pragmatic on the one hand and the philosophical Kantian enterprise on the other—before you decide that, don't decide too soon that you are beyond Schiller in any sense. I don't think any of us can lay this claim. Whatever writing we do, whatever way we have of talking about art, whatever way we have of teaching, whatever justification we give ourselves for teaching, whatever the standards are and the values by means of which we teach, they are more than ever and profoundly Schillerian. They come from Schiller, and not from Kant. And if you ever try to do something in the other direction and you touch on it you'll see what will happen to you. Better be very sure, wherever you are, that your tenure is very well established, and that the institution for which you work has a very well-established reputation. Then you can take some risks without really taking many risks.

In Kant this led—we say the main concern was a theory of the imagination. Schiller also comes to a theory of the imagination—the point hardly needs to be labored, but I still want to document it—which will be essentially and entirely different from Kant's. The imagination enters Schiller's vocabulary in relation to those considerations on terror. Terror, he says, has to be genuinely terrifying. It has to be, as we already said, beyond the reach of domestication by technological means. But, he adds, it should not be immediately threatening. Because if it is immediately threatening, you really don't have time to get your faculties going. You could imagine that you would, but it certainly, it would be better if you are not immediately threatened. It's better not to be on the boat that's being tossed up and down, it's better to stand on the shore and see the boat being tossed up and down, if you want to have a sublime experience. And that seems sensible enough, and we can agree with that. "We are dealing," he says, "we are dealing only with the case where the object of terror actually displays its power, but without aiming it in our direction, where we know ourselves, in a condition where we know ourselves to be in safety." And Kant had insisted on that too, in a certain way, and you can quote Kant to that effect. Though the status of safety in Kant, which has to do with tranquillity, with the affect of tranquillity, is entirely different from the status that we have here, because here Schiller is talking about a very practical, concrete thing, which is not at all what Kant was doing. Well, where we know ourselves to be in safety. "We only imagine this"—imagination—"we only imagine that we would be in the situation in which this power could reach us, and in which any resistance would be in vain." So we are exquisitely imagining how terrifying it would be to be on the boat, where we could not resist the onslaught of the waves. "Terror exists, then, only in the imagination, as the representation of a danger. But even the imaginary representation of danger, if it is at all vivid, suffices to awaken our sense of self-preservation, and it produces something analogous to what the real experience would produce." Analogous is an important word. "We start to shudder; a feeling of fear invades us; our senses are up in arms. Without this first onset of genuine suffering, without this actual"—the German word is *ernstlich*, serious, taken seriously—"without this actual attack on our existence, we would only be playing with the object of terror. It must be a serious threat [*es muß Ernst seyn*], or at least be sensed to be one, if reason is to find solace in the idea of its freedom. Moreover, the consciousness of our inner freedom can only have value and make a true claim if it is taken seriously. And it cannot be taken seriously if we only playfully engage with the representation of danger" (*Werke*, 20:181).

Now, if you compare this to the passage on the imagination in Kant, which we read last time—the sacrifice of the imagination, this devious economy between the imagination and reason, and so on and so forth—how intelligible and how convincing does this seem compared with the bizarre argument about reason and imagination, sacrifice, and so on which we found in Kant! This is obviously right, and highly intelligible. The reason for the oddity in the case of Kant's passage is that Kant was dealing with a strictly philosophical concern, with a strictly philosophical, epistemological problem, which he chose to state for reasons of his own in interpersonal, dramatic terms, thus telling dramatically and interpersonally something which was purely epistemological and which had nothing to do with the pragmata of the relationship between human beings. Here, in Schiller's case, the explanation is entirely empirical, psychological, without any concern for epistemological implications. And for that reason, Schiller can then claim that in this negotiation, in this arrangement, where the analogy of danger is substituted for the real danger, where the imagination of danger is substituted for the experience of danger, that by this substitution, this tropological substitution, that the sublime succeeds, that the sublime works out, that the sublime achieves itself, and brings together a new kind of synthesis. We would have a similar model to what we had here [indicating diagram we had earlier], with different elements. What now stand in relationship to each other are knowledge, *Erkenntnis*, which is like representation, which is like imagination; whereas self-preservation would be like reality.

And knowledge opposes self-preservation—as we've seen, *Erkenntnis*, theoretical knowledge, opposes to the practicality of the self-preservation—in the same way, in the same relationship, as that in which representation opposes reality. Knowledge is representation, fantasy, an imaginary thing, whereas self-preservation is a concrete physical thing and therefore of the order of the real. And that is the starting position in the polar opposition, in the play of antithesis here. Well, what happens in the development, in the so-called argument—though it's really purely structural, a structural model, a purely structural code of tropological exchange, symmetrical, like all tropes, and as such masterable—is that this self-preservation, as we saw in the analysis which he gives, acts by ways of the representation. We achieve self-preservation by substituting for the reality the imagined situation. So self-preservation becomes imagined instead of being really real, and therefore self-preservation now relates to representation. As a result the chiasmus is fulfilled, and knowledge will now relate to reality, which is another way of saying, as he says, that now our knowledge is real, it is *Ernst*, it is not purely imaginary, but is a real experience, genuine, some genuine terror in there, not pure play.

Knowledge ——————— Representation
Self-Preservation ————— Reality

He set up the simple polarity of *Ernst* and *Spiel*, that which is serious as opposed to that which is playful, and you'll remember what Kleist, in the story of the bear, did with that opposition and with that simple polarity, which he didn't allow to remain unchallenged. Because the notions of seriousness and of playfulness are now no longer pure—it is serious but only by analogy, it is not an actual fear but it is the trope of fear—one plays at danger as in a fiction or as in a play, but one is sheltered by the figurative status of the danger. It is the fact that the danger is made into a figure that shelters you from the immediacy of the danger. The tropological figuration here, this passage to the imagination, is what allows you to cope with the danger. Again, the figuration appears as a defense by means of which we cope with danger, by replacing the danger by the figure, by the analogon, by the metaphor, if you want, of danger. Again, the empirical moment of coping with danger, this empirical moment is nowhere present in Kant. And the appearance of figural language in Kant, in those passages of the third *Critique*, has to do, as we saw, with completely different scenes, the scenes of understanding and the juxtaposition of apprehension and comprehension, or the scene of the imagination sacrificing itself to reason and then recovering in the process, and so on and so forth. In no moment was there as psychologically simple a process going on as what we had there, and therefore whatever was told in Kant was not psychologically understandable or comprehensible. One could not understand Kant by transposing it to some kind of pragmatic, psychological, empirical experience. It's the difference between a philosopher and Schiller, who is not a philosopher. The type of understanding needed for Schiller is common understanding. The kind of understanding you need for philosophers is common understanding too, perhaps, but it is of a different nature. It is not of a personal and psychological nature.

The same theory of the imagination then moves on to what one could call— and it is an example in Schiller of a consistent dialectical development, and it is rare—a dialectics of danger and safety, in which danger then more explicitly names itself as death, and within which there is the notion of the moral, so important in Kant and so important in Schiller too. And Schiller takes on Kant, the notion that morality is freedom, but then the way in which he conceives morality and the way in which he conceives freedom are entirely un-Kantian. At any rate, here we go at it from a distinction between physical and moral safety. And Schiller suggests that there is such a thing as moral safety, which comes into being when, and only when, the danger is physically overwhelming. As long as it can be opposed physically it isn't serious, but when it is really physically overwhelming something else can come into play called "moral safety." He says the following: "We consider terror without fear, because we feel we can overcome the power it has over us as natural beings, either by the awareness of our innocence, or by the invulnerability, the immortality of our being. It follows that the feeling of moral security implies religious ideas. For only religion and not morality establishes safety, grounds for our sensory being" (*Werke*, 20:181). In relation to the specific threat now named in its generality of death, the moral safety which one can achieve in front of death would be, first, the idea of immortality, the religious idea of immortality. But Schiller, to his credit, doesn't pause there, doesn't remain, he complicates it dialectically. Because to the extent that the notion of immortality would always be interpreted by us in a physical, besides an intellectual, sense— sort of the notion, as in Rilke, that even after death you would still be able to eat grapes.[8] That has always struck me as a very reassuring thought about immortality, but it is not a very serious religious conviction, I am afraid. But to the extent therefore that it has, besides intellectual, physical implications, Schiller says also that the thought of immortality in itself is not sublime. More sublime, more capable of the sublime, is the notion of innocence, which is based on a notion of divine justice and personal innocence. As long as we are innocent and as long as God is just, nothing can really happen to us. Thus postulating a kind of interrelationship between the divine and the human, precisely the kind of relationship between the sacred and the human, between the sacred and the discourse of humanity, which was contested in Hegel. Here this exchange takes place, and perhaps curiously, it leads to a sharp separation between our material and our intellectual being. "For," says Schiller, "for the representation of the sacred to be practically sublime, our feeling of security must not relate to our existence, but to our principles,

---

8. Cf. de Man's citation of Rilke's "Quai du rosaire" in *Allegories of Reading* (New Haven: Yale University Press, 1979), p. 42.

Grundsätze, to the principles of our being. We must be indifferent to our fate as natural creatures, as long as we feel intellectually dependent on the effects of its power" (*Werke*, 20:182). This independence of the intellect—in order for it to be truly free—must consist, it turns out, of a similarity or even an identity between the divine will and the laws of our own reason, so that the link between the divine and reason is constantly maintained. It leads, more clearly now, to the complete severance of our intellectual and moral being on the one hand, from our natural existence on the other. "We call," says Schiller, "practically sublime any entity which makes us aware of our weakness as a natural creature, but which at the same time awakens an entirely different kind of resistance in us, resistance to the terror. This counterforce in no way rescues us from the physical existence of the danger, but, what is infinitely more, it isolates our physical existence from our personality. It is therefore not a particular and individual material security, but an ideal security, which extends to all possible and imaginable situations, and of which we have to become conscious in the aesthetic contemplation of the sublime. It learns to consider the sensory part of our being, the only part of us that can be in danger, as an exterior natural object that is of no concern to our person, to our moral self" (*Werke*, 20:185).

That is idealism. If you want to know what the model of an idealistic statement is—not in the sense that we speak of German Idealist philosophy but in the sense that we speak of idealism as an ideology—this is a specifically ideological idealist statement. Because it posits pure intellect: it goes much too far in the direction of establishing its belief in the intellect, because it posits the possibility of a pure intellect entirely separated from the material world, entirely separated from the sensory experience, which was precisely what was unreachable for Kant. You'll remember the Kant passage where Kant accounts for the necessity of the imagination because, he says, we are not pure intellect and can never be it. As fallen beings—and it is a theological concept—we are incapable of pure intellect. Here is held up the possibility of pure intellect. So it posits pure intellect, which was unreachable in Kant, because in Kant the imagination was the very symptom of this incapacity, of the incapacity of achieving pure intellect rather than its cause—or than the agent of its remedy—in Schiller, pure intellect comes in, as imagination comes in, to remedy our incapacity, whereas in Kant it is the failure of the imagination that leads to aesthetic contemplation. The two discourses are completely disjoint from each other at this point, and this idealization is precisely what does not take place in Kant. In Schiller, the aesthetic, at this point—and he changed on that to some extent, as we shall see—in Schiller the aesthetic is transcended by a pure intellect, which in Kant is theologically and philosophically inconceivable. This transcendence of the aesthetic in Schiller differs entirely from the disruption of the aesthetic as return to the materiality of the inscription, to the letter, that we found in Kant.

So, that's the apparent paradox which I want you to develop. This stress on the practical, this stress on the psychological, on the verisimilitude, all that makes Schiller intelligible, all that awakens our assent and that is persuasive, leads to a radical separation between mind and body, to an idealism which is untenable in Schiller's own terms. So that both the starting point in this essay—the starting point in the pragmatic opposition between practical and theoretical sublime which substitute for Kant's categories of the mathematical and the dynamic sublime, the starting point—and also the end point, namely, the idealistic transcendence of the aesthetic by pure intellect, because at this point we grow beyond the aesthetic to a level of pure intellect—what we have in Schiller there is entirely, at the beginning and at the end, entirely un-Kantian. The idealism of Schiller contrasts with the transcendental-critical language of Kant. Schiller appears as the ideology of Kant's critical philosophy.

The tropological system in Kant, the system of trope in Kant, when it occurs, is a purely formal principle, a purely linguistic structure which was shown to function as such, whereas in Schiller it is the *use* made of tropes, of chiasmus as the *teleology*, as the aim of an ideological desire, namely, the desire to overcome terror—it is in such a way that tropology is made to serve a *Trieb*, to serve as device. It is no longer a structure, it is enlisted in the services of a specific desire. It acquires therefore an empirical and a pragmatic content, which it didn't have in Kant, at the very moment that it asserts its separation from all reality. There is therefore a curious mixture in this early essay of Schiller between a claim of practical, empirical, psychological effectiveness, combined with, on the other hand, a total ideality.

Now this is early Schiller, and although I will go a little fast in this, Schiller modified to some extent some of those notions, especially the superiority of the mind over body, so to speak. He refined and modified some of those notions in what appears to be a self-critique of his early idealism and its replacement by a more balanced principle. And the main text in which this occurs is the later *Letters on Aesthetic Education*, about which I will say only a few things and then leave the floor free for some questions.

In the *Letters on Aesthetic Education*, we also start out from a polarity, but that polarity is much more complex and much richer, especially in its temporal aspects, than the simple opposition between practical and theoretical. It is still a polarity which is stated in terms of *Triebe*, in terms of pulsions, in terms of drives. But the two drives which Schiller here names are, on the one hand, what he calls the *sinnlicher Trieb*, sensory desire, and, on the other hand, what he calls *Formtrieb*, desire for form. That seems banal enough, but the way in which those two are characterized, developed, is of interest. Because he mostly does it in terms of an opposition between two temporal modes, which is suggestive. The sensory drive, which is the giving in to an immediate appeal of the moment, therefore has the singularity of the moment that excludes everything else from it; whereas the desire for form, the drive for form, which aspires to a generality or to an absolute, to a law, has a temporal structure which wants to encompass as large an area as possible.

Therefore those two drives would appear to be totally incompatible. The one wants everything at one moment, the other wants to spread out things over as long—the one is totally particular and individual, the other is totally general and absolute. The subtlety, the refinement here—Schiller admits this, he says they would be totally incompatible and that man would therefore be hopelessly divided, if it weren't for the fact that they do not encounter each other, that the two elements in the opposition do not meet. They would be incompatible, he says, and they must therefore be prevented from entering into a dialectical relationship in which one would negate the other. This is not a quotation, this is my paraphrase; but it is a paraphrase of a quotation which is quite clear. What one should observe is that those two incompatible tendencies do not occur in the same object, and that what does not meet each other, what doesn't encounter each other, can also not oppose each other: "Was nicht aufeinander trifft, kann nicht gegeneinander stoßen" (Letter XIII, pp. 84–85).[9] So there can be no struggle between them as long as you keep them from encountering each other. As long as the *Formtrieb*, the desire for form, and the *sinnlicher Trieb*, the desire for immediate gratification—pleasure now—do not meet, they will leave us relatively in peace. They would be incompatible, he says, and they must therefore—no he doesn't say it, I say it—and they must therefore be prevented from entering into a dialectical relationship in which the one would negate the other.

The way to do this—in order to keep them from thus entering into a dialectical relationship with each other—is by preserving perfect reversibility between them. This is where the notion of reversibility comes in. If between form and what he calls sensory *Trieb*—if they are perfectly reversible, if they are absolutely symmetrical, then they will never encounter each other. This is an example of the use of reversibility as a way to avoid the dialectic, let alone the more radical disruption of the inscription or of the letter or any other form of such a disruption which we have encountered in various forms. Here is the quote from Schiller, and it also, curiously, lines him up, or he lines himself up, with certain philosophical names at that moment. The quotation is from a footnote but it's a crucial passage in the *Letters*: "As soon as one assumes an originary and therefore necessary antagonism of the two drives, no other way exists by which to maintain the unity of humanity than to submit the sensory to the intellectual. This, however"—which is more or less what he did, himself, in the first essay—"this, however, can only produce

---

9. References are to Schiller's *On the Aesthetic Education of Man*, ed. and trans. Elizabeth M. Wilkinson and L. A. Willoughby (Oxford: Oxford University Press, 1967), and are given by letter number and page number. As de Man notes later in the lecture, the text to which he actually refers is a German edition of this book, and his translations of Schiller thus do not correspond exactly to those of the editors in their English version.

monotony, *Einförmigkeit*, and not harmony, and humanity would remain forever divided. The hierarchy, the pattern of domination and submission, has to take place, but it must be alternating instead of being simultaneous. For although it is true that limits can never determine the absolute, and that freedom can never be dependent on time, it is equally true that the absolute does not have the power to determine limits, that the situation in time cannot be made to depend on freedom."

That's again an example. Those sentences are absolute; I can keep going that way, I can write fifty more sentences which keep going that way, it will always make sense. The situation in time cannot be made dependent on freedom. "Both principles are therefore mutually dependent on each other, yet mutually coordinate. They stand to each other in a relation of reversible reciprocity," the German word is *Wechselwirkung*, exchange. "There is no matter without form, and there is no form without matter." At that point, Schiller attributes the possibility of such exchanges to Fichte. There's a gesture toward Fichte in opposition to Kant. And the name of Fichte is exceedingly important in this entire development. I'm not going to go into that. Suffice it to say that, as far as I can see, this is a gross misrepresentation of what in Fichte is a real dialectical movement. Fichte is, as much as Hegel, a real dialectical mind, and to substitute simple reversibility for dialectical negation in Fichte is to misrepresent Fichte. "In a transcendental philosophy," Schiller continues, "where everything aspires to free form from content, and to cleanse necessity from all chance and random elements, one gets quickly accustomed to considering anything material as an obstacle, and to represent the sensory, which functions in this case as an impediment, in a necessary contradiction with reason. Such an approach is certainly not in the spirit of the Kantian system, but it could well be attributed to the letter of this system."

This is a remarkable misinterpretation of Kant as a dualism. It takes off not from Kant but from Schiller's own misreading in "Of the Sublime," in which a dualism between sensory and ideal is postulated as being in Kant, which then is said not to occur in Fichte, and as such it seems to me entirely to misrepresent the Kant-Fichte relationship as well. Suffice it to say, since I don't want to go into the details of that, that no such polarities, that no such sharp antinomies and such sharp polarities exist in Kant. They never do, in those terms. If there are triadic movements in Kant, they are not very strong, simple polarities. Whereas in Fichte, where there are such oppositions, they always enter into dialectical substitutions which involve a considerable power of negation. In Schiller we have no dialectics, no exchange on the level of the drives. But, he says, an exchange takes place, because we cannot just stay there with those two drives existing next to each other and not engaging each other. In order to get out of that, he says the exchange takes place not on the level of existence, but on the level of principles and of ideas. There the exchange between form and sensory experience, formal and sensory experience, can occur. "From the alternation of two opposed drives, and out of the synthesis, the *Verbindung*, of two opposed principles, we have seen how the beautiful originates, whose highest ideal therefore consists in the most perfect conceivable equilibrium between reality and form."

How this synthesis is made possible, on the level of principles, is of interest. The plea for the possibility and the necessity of this synthesis is made in the name of an empirical concept, which is that of humanity, of the human, which is used then as a principle of closure. The human, the needs of the human, the necessities of the human are absolute and are not open to critical attack. Because the category of the human is absolute, and because the human would be divided, or would be reduced to nothing if this encounter between the two drives that make it up is not allowed to take place, for that reason a synthesis has to be found. It is dictated, it is forced upon us, by the concept of the human itself. We are back to a pragmatic, empirical concept. And humanity functions in the *Letters on Aesthetic Education* in the same way that self-preservation functions in the case of the early essay. Both are pragmatic principles of closure which are not open to any critical discourse.

Humanity, which then has to be itself the composite of those two drives, is then equated with a balanced relationship between necessity and freedom, which Schiller calls free play, *Spieltrieb*, and which then becomes the determining principle of the human. The human is determined by this possibility of free play—"I play, therefore I am," or something of the sort (see Letter XV, pp. 106–7). Hence the need, which follows, for a free and humanistic—because the notion of free and humanity go together—education, which is called an aesthetic education, and which is still the basis of our liberal system of humanistic education. Also the basis of concepts such as "culture," and the thought that it is possible to move from individual works of art to a collective, massive notion of art, which would be, for example, one of national characteristics, and which would be like the culture of a nation, of a general, social dimension called "cultural." And hence, as a logical conclusion of that, the concept in Schiller of an aesthetic state, which is the political order that would follow, as a result of that education, and which would be the political institution resulting from such a conception.

Schiller has been much praised for this enlightened humanism. And often he has been praised for it in opposition to Kant. For example, here is a passage from his excellent translators and editors, Wilkinson and Willoughby: "Whereas Kant leaves us with the impression that an order decreed from above acts upon us, an order which suddenly appears in full regalia, capable of at once issuing stern orders which it receives from a reason originating in a noumenal realm, Schiller expressly asserts that he is concerned with the gradual development of an order that originates from below, that is to say, from the phenomenological assumptions of the mind and the will."[10]

---

10. Wilkinson and Willoughby, "Introduction," *On the Aesthetic Education of Man*, p. xcii.

That sounds a little odd, and it's because it's not a quotation of the original English. I translate this from a German translation of Wilkinson and Willoughby, which is the only thing I had available, I'm sorry. But it is clear enough what is being said. In opposition to Kant, who is tyrannical, because he works transcendentally from above, Schiller is human and psychologically valid, and what's called "phenomenological" here really means empirical and psychological. The use of "phenomenological" here is striking as highly dubious, because Schiller is not phenomenological, he is empirical; he is psychological in an empirical sense. Schiller is praised for this, and rightly so. The concept of play is a highly civilized concept, and the civilizing cultural impact of Schiller is associated with the notion of play.

Something remains to be said about this notion of play and its various meanings in the *Letters on Aesthetic Education* in Schiller, and that will be the end. Play means, first of all, *Spielraum*, the play, the space that you need in order to prevent the dialectical encounter from taking place. You need a little play between those two things. You need a little distance between them to keep them from colliding with each other. And as such, play has that pleasant and reassuring and suggestive function.

Play also means in Schiller equilibrium, harmony, on the level of principles, between, on the one hand, necessity, rule, *Gesetz*, and, on the other hand, chance, what is arbitrary. Play, games are a good example of that. They have laws—you have to play soccer according to very specific laws—at least they try, though at Cornell we dismally fail—on the one hand, and, on the other hand, there is something deeply arbitrary about those laws, because who says that the penalty has to be shot from ten yards or something—why not eleven yards and why not nine yards? It's an absolutely arbitrary decision, but which taken within itself is the principle of law, and which functions as a law. That is how the human is defined also. The human is defined as a certain principle of closure which is no longer accessible to rational critical analysis. And we know from Kleist how this notion of balance between the human and what is not human can get out of hand. And how, for example, the appearance of a transcendental principle of signification in language comes to upset the human. To say that the human is a principle of closure, and that the ultimate word, the last word, belongs to man, to the human, is to assume a continuity between language and man, is to assume a control of man over language, which in all kinds of ways is exceedingly problematic. We'll see an example of somebody who states this problematic nature of language tomorrow, by talking about Benjamin.[11] No suggestion is made, there is entirely ignored the possibility of a language that would not be definable in human terms, and that would not be accessible to the human will at all—none—of a language that would

11. See "Conclusions: Walter Benjamin's 'The Task of the Translator,'" in de Man, *The Resistance to Theory*, which was delivered as the sixth Messenger lecture.

to some extent not be—in a very radical sense, not be human. So that we would at least have a complication, an initial complication, in which the principle of closure is not the human—because language can always undo that principle of closure—and is not language either, because language is not a firm concept, is not a concept of an entity which allows itself to be conceptualized and reified in any way.

Play in the third place is defined—first as *Spielraum*, [second] as equilibrium—is then also defined as *Schein*, as in *Trauerspiel* or in *Lustspiel*, where play indicates theatrical representation, appearance, theatricality. And Schiller gives us a very eloquent praise of *Schein*, of the ability to dwell with the appearance—which, he says, in sort of a sketch of an anthropology, characterizes primitive societies as well as advanced societies. Societies come into being when there is an interest for, he says, *Putz und Schein*, for ornament and for appearance. At that moment the aesthetic is present and it works as a powerful, defining, social force. Art is praised, like *Schein*, as a principle of irreality, because a strict opposition is maintained between reality and appearance, with art being entirely on the side of appearance. Only people who are very stupid, says Schiller, or people who are extraordinarily smart, too smart, have no use for *Schein*, have no use for appearance. Those who are entirely stupid don't need appearance, they are unable to conceive it; those who are entirely rational don't have to resort to it (Letter XXVI, pp. 190–93). In that you could substitute—one who would be entirely stupid in those terms would be Kant, for example, when he describes the world as being completely devoid of teleological impact, as having no appearance but only reality. And one of those who are much too smart, who are smart through and through and can saturate the entire world with intellect, would be, for example, Hegel, who would not, according to this assumption, need *Schein* anymore.

Well, when Kant and Hegel use *Schein*, they mean something very different. In Kant, we spoke of *Augenschein* and saw what that was, which was certainly not in opposition to reality, but which was precisely what we see, and as such more real than anything else, though it is a reality which exists on the level of vision. And when Hegel speaks of *das sinnliche Scheinen der Idee*, and defines beauty as the sensory appearance of the idea, then he has at the very least—and perhaps more than that—but he has at the very least in mind *Erscheinung* as phenomenalization, as the appearance of the object in the light of its own phenomenality. And in both cases, in the case of both Kant and of Hegel, as we saw, there is a road that goes from this notion of *Schein* to the notion of materiality. Such a road cannot be found in Schiller, and that is why for Schiller the concept of art, which at that moment is mentioned and is stressed, will always and without any reservation be a concept of art as imitation, as *nachahmende Kunst*. And praise of imitation, the joy of imitation, which is very real, is accounted for entirely in the fact that art is appearance of the reality as such, an imitation of reality: "gleich sowie der Spieltrieb sich regt, der abscheidige Pfaden findet, wird ihm auch der nachahmende Bildungstrieb folgen." "Precisely as the play comes into being, because it takes pleasure in appearance, the imitation, the mimesis, the desire for imitation will occur in art." So that is play as *Schein*.

Finally, not so much in the *Letters on Aesthetic Education* but in a little essay that is complementary to it and which is called "On the Necessary Borderlines in the Use of Beautiful Forms" ("Über die notwendigen Grenzen beim Gebrauch schöner Formen"), it becomes clear that play also functions in Schiller as a concept of figure, as a concept of figuration. One form in which play is achieved is as figure. It is done again by a polarity. "Discourse," he says, "must have an organic, sensory element, which is chaotic but which is concrete"—which is like the sensory drive which we spoke of, which is of the moment but which is immediately seductive but which is not organized, which is not strictly organized, on the one hand—"on the other hand, a discourse must have a unified meaning"—this sensory, this what he calls organic, sensory element, doesn't really have meaning, they're just discrete moments, and no continuity—"But on the other hand, discourse must have a unified meaning, a totality, an abstract but unified total meaning which stands in opposition to those concrete moments." You see that it is another version of the opposition between *Formtrieb* and *Erkenntnistrieb*. "Intelligence," he says, "is pleased by order, *Gesetzmäßigkeit*, but fantasy, imagination is flattered by this anarchy" (*Werke*, 21:9). There will then be, as you can expect, a chiasmic exchange of attributes between both, by means of *Spiel*, and intellect will acquire certain of the attributes of freedom and arbitrariness, whereas, on the other hand, the imagination, fantasy, will acquire some of the elements of order and of system that are necessary for a definition of language as meaning.

Here, the comparison to make with Kant is with Kant's statements about figuration, about what he calls hypotyposis, which is the difficulty of rendering, by means of sensory elements, purely intellectual concepts. And the particular necessity which philosophy has, to take its terminology not from purely intellectual concepts but from material, sensory elements, which it then uses metaphorically and frequently forgets that it does so. So that when philosophy speaks of the *ground* of being, or says that something *follows*, or that something *depends* on something else, it is really using physical terms, it is really using metaphors, and it forgets that it does so.[12] Since the "Mythologie blanche," we have all become aware of that and we would never do this nasty thing again! At any rate, hypotyposis for Kant is certainly a problem for understanding, and a very difficult problem that again threatens philosophical discourse; whereas here it is offered by Schiller as a solution, again in the form of a chiasmus, for a similar opposition. The sensory, then, unlike the hypotyposis in Kant, becomes a metaphor for reason. This extends to humanity, which, it turns out, is not entirely a principle of

---

12. Cf. "The Epistemology of Metaphor" in this volume.

closure, because humanity is not single—but it has a polarity, it has the polarity of male and female that inhabits it, and this is how Schiller copes with that problem. "The other sex," he says, the female sex, "can and should not share scientific knowledge with man, but by ways of its figural representation, it can share the truth with him. Men tend to sacrifice form to content. But woman cannot tolerate a neglected form, not even in the presence of the richest content. And the entire internal configuration of her being entitles her to make this stern demand. It is true, however, that in this function, she can only acquire the material of truth, and not truth itself. Therefore, the task which Nature disallows women, the other sex, this task must be doubly undertaken by man if he wishes to be the equal of woman in this important aspect, in this important aspect of his existence. He will therefore try to transpose as much as possible out of the realm of the abstract, in which he governs and is master, into the realm of the imagination and of sensibility. Taste includes or hides the natural intellectual difference between the two sexes. It nourishes and embellishes the feminine mind with the products of the masculine mind, and allows the beautiful sex to feel what it has not thought, and to enjoy what it has not produced by its labor" (*Werke*, 21:16–17). That much for women. Perhaps Schiller's humanism is showing some of its limits here. At any rate, the theoretical conclusion of this passage would be that just as the sensory becomes without tension a metaphor for reason, in Schiller, women become without oppression a metaphor for man. Because the relation of woman to man is that of the metaphor to what it indicates, or that of the sensory representation to reason.

In the same way, Schiller's considerations on education lead to a concept of art as the metaphor, as the popularization of philosophy. Philosophy, as you saw, is the domain of men, art is—basically, the beautiful is—the domain of women. The relationship is that of metaphor. And that relation is similar to a kind of knowledge which is less rigorous, less scientific, and which is more popular. So in that same way, education leads to a concept of art as the popularization of philosophy. Philosophy isn't taught in an aesthetic education, Kant is not taught. Schiller would be taught, because it is a popularization, a metaphorization of philosophy. As such, the aesthetic belongs to the masses. It belongs, as we all know—and this is a correct description of the way in which we organize those things—it belongs to culture, and as such it belongs to the state, to the aesthetic state, and it justifies the state, as in the following quotation, which is not by Schiller:

Art is the expression of feeling. The artist is distinguished from the non-artist by the fact that he can also *express* what he feels. He can do so in a variety of forms. Some by images; others by sound; still others by marble—or also in historical forms. The statesman is an artist, too. The people are for him what stone is for the sculptor. Leader and masses are as little of a problem to each other as color is a problem for the painter. Politics are the plastic arts of the state as painting is the plastic art of color. Therefore politics without the people or against the people are nonsense. To transform a mass into a people and a people into a state—that has always been the deepest sense of a genuine political task.[13]

It is not entirely irrelevant, not entirely indifferent, that the author of this passage is—from a novel of—Joseph Goebbels. Wilkinson and Willoughby, who quote the passage, are certainly right in pointing out that it is a grievous misreading of Schiller's aesthetic state. But the principle of this misreading does not essentially differ from the misreading which Schiller inflicted on his own predecessor—namely, Kant.

Thank you.

Discussion

M. H. ABRAMS: I didn't see anybody else raise his hand. What I want to say now is not at all in opposition to your illuminating analyses of Schiller, not even a supplement. I'd like to put it in a different perspective, which is my favorite one, namely, historical, not the perspective you call historicity, but a succession of intellectual events. What both Kant and Schiller inherited was a long tradition, of course, as you pointed out, of discussions of the sublime—I think, primarily in the English tradition, though there were Boileau and others. But primarily the English tradition. And the English tradition, in the British empirical way, was psychological, in the mode of Locke and his followers, Addison, and so on. Now, these people—there is no single instance of the sublime, or example of the sublime, or analysis of any aspect of the sublime which you can think of as psychological, either in Kant or in Schiller, which didn't exist before. This is in no way to denigrate them. Now, as I see it, what Kant did, just as he did in the aesthetic of beauty, was to take the psychological events that constitute a sublime experience, the phenomenon, the sublime as experience, and simply accept them. That is it. Just as he did with the experience of the beautiful. Now, his enterprise is to explain how such an experience is possible. And how it's possible is to be explained in terms of the faculties that the mind necessarily brings to all its experiences. Well, Kant was in a rather difficult bind there, because he hadn't begun his critiques with the intention of writing a critique of aesthetic judgment. And the faculties he posits were faculties which were posited largely to explain the possibility of judgments of truth and goodness—moral and rational judgments. Now, when he came to the third *Critique*, these were the faculties he had to work with. And I think that establishes both the limits of what he says, and also the kind of

---

13. Joseph Goebbels, *Michael, Ein deutsches Schicksal in Tagebuchblättern* (Munich: F. Eber, 1933), p. 21; quoted by Wilkinson and Willoughby, "Introduction," p. cxlii. The novel is translated into English by Joachim Neugroschel as *Michael* (New York: Amok Press, 1987), p. 14.

extraordinary suggestiveness there is. Because working with faculties of understanding, reason, judgment, and imagination, and being pretty well tied to what he said about the limits or the mode of operation those faculties employed, he was really in a very difficult, limited—he had a limited philosophical idiom with which to explain the possibility of the various modes of judgments of the beautiful and the experience of the sublime.

Now, Schiller was under no such limitations. He bought wholesale, as you've pointed out very well, the psychological and empirical description of the sublime. It suited his practical purposes, as a writer and a playwright, as you've said, and he was able—I think nothing he said psychologically was not precedented in the English. For example, what you dealt with at the end in describing and analyzing that early essay of his is what the British were trying to do in other terms when they pointed out that the return into ourselves from the horrible dangers of the sublime . . . exposure to this, and by establishing what later British psychologists called aesthetic distance, putting aesthetic distance between us and it. But now, the interesting thing in Schiller is his tendency to put these psychological concepts in this chiasmic relationship. I think I have learned a lot from the way you did this. This is exactly what he does.

Now there is a curious irony, because while you point out that this is not genuinely dialectical, I do think that his representing or dealing with his basically psychological, empirical materials in these terms, especially as we find it in the *Aesthetic Letters*, moves over Kant and really establishes, more than any other predecessor, more than any other precursor, for Hegel, his dialectical processes. Because this crossing over, as you call it, in his chiasmus, is very largely Kant's passing over, *übergehen*, from the concept to its apparent opposite, and then the recovery of itself in itself. And even in the *Aesthetic Education*, the term *Aufhebung*, in the critical Kantian sense, does occur. So what we get is the psychological materials, given a kind of pseudo-, quasi-dialectical shape, if you like, which Hegel was able to buy and refine, to a point that some of us might think is reductio ad absurdum, or some might think to the ultimate sublime, of that process. So you get another kind of crossing over between Kant and Schiller here. And provided the crossing over—I can't help saying that taking this kind of historical approach, I think that there's a risk of deconstructing these people, far be it from any tendency to do so you have exhibited, though you may go on to make that kind of approach a little more overt. I agree that the risk in the historical approach is always deconstructive, in some very important sense. As a defense against that, I would say that no matter what history is, the ultimate question for us, as *users* of these theories, is their profitability when applied. No matter how these people, no matter how Kant may have gotten into the bind in which he found himself by the history of his thinking, ultimately the aesthetic judgment is enormously useful for us in dealing with aesthetic experience. And, I think, Schiller, in his own way, too, is enormously useful for us in dealing with aesthetic experience.

DE MAN: I would find little to dispute in what you have said. Your end conclusion is pragmatic. It is the use of those categories rather than their philosophical truth or falsehood value which is the bottom line, which has the final say, which is very much what Schiller said. And in that you are a true and correct reader of Schiller. But just to make one point there, where I would not agree with you. I agree with the historical perspective entirely. The place to locate that best would be, perhaps, in the way all those three texts return to Burke and define themselves in relation to Burke's essay on the sublime, about which Kant makes an implicit complaint that it is too empirical. And that is the great change in Kant, that the English empiricism is maintained, but understood. It is the moment—this is relevant to your comment—where a theory of the faculties, which is still fundamentally a psychology, would be a prolegomena, a preparation for a philosophical question, rather than being a preparation for an empirical use, whereas the faculties are, the theories of the faculties are used for psychological effectiveness, or for psychological, pragmatic ends. In Kant, where we also have a theory of the faculties, as you say very correctly, and as such a psychology. But that psychology is not for the use or for the benefit of mankind. It is used to explore certain philosophical principles, philosophical questions, philosophical tensions which are at stake.

Where I think I differ at least on one point from you is in the notion that chiasmus is dialectical, and that it is pre-Hegelian. I think the point to examine this—and I alluded to it in passing—has to do with Fichte. And at the moment Schiller says, What I am doing is like Fichte, and unlike Kant in being like Fichte. I think, at that moment, he places himself within a filiation, because there is a filiation that goes from Kant to Fichte to Hegel—that is undeniable. There is a genuine dialectical element in Kant, there is a genuine dialectical element in Fichte, and of course in Hegel it's too genuine to be true. But there is a dialectic, there is only dialectical force when there is encountered a negation; that is, the labor of the negative is absolutely essential to the concept of the dialectical. It is there in Kant, it is there in Fichte in a complicated way, it is there certainly in Hegel. It is not there in Schiller, to the extent that the harmony is not to be disturbed, to the extent that the opposites are not to meet, to the extent that the opposites are to compose with each other in a way which is not a mediation, which is not certainly a negation of the one by the other. From the moment that moment is missing, we have fallen back simply into the pragmatic, I think, simply into the empirical, in a way which even English empiricism, neither Locke nor Hume, really ever did, in that sense. So that I would agree . . . but I don't think that Schiller, in the essays, one would have to distinguish . . . and there are dialectical moments in Schiller's plays and so on. But I don't think, in the essays, in the philosophical essays, that the dialectic occurs. They are not, in that sense, pre-Hegelian. They have the appearance of the pre-Hegelian, they have the appearance of the crossing over. But in Hegel the dialectic is not just chiasmic. Because the dialectic is not symmetrical, is not a reversibility, and it is not reducible to a formal principle of language which would be like that of a trope. There is no trope of the dialectical as such, which could cover the dialectical. That is a big difference, because at that moment the linguistic implication, the linguistic model, is different. Therefore I think that the continuity you point out is certainly there. But we do feel, also feel in historical terms, in intellectual-historical terms, throughout the nineteenth and twentieth century, a tension between, on the one hand, the Schillerian and, on the other hand, a Kantian reading of the aesthetic. I think I started out by pointing to that, and I don't think you can account for that in straightforward, positivistic, intellectual-historical terms. If you want to see a continuity from Kant to Schiller to Fichte to Hegel, and you call that continuity the dialectic, I think there is a difference there, and this difference is important, I think.

ABRAMS: I don't think we disagree there. One way of putting it is to say that for Hegel and these others, death matters. Death is always involved. When there's a passing over, something dies. There's a resurrection—there's a resurrection and Schiller makes light of that, as in those passages you dealt with. So for that very essential part of the dialectic there's no fuel in Schiller. Schiller's soft there, very soft. But there, if you point to another aspect of Schiller, then I think what Schiller does in the *Aesthetic Letters* is closer to Hegel than either Fichte or Kant. And it depends on the aspect you're emphasizing.

DE MAN: Sure.

ABRAMS: The seriousness of death, I agree, is terribly important, and I don't want to minimize that aspect in Hegel. But when you look at the aspect of movement, constant motion—nothing stands still—I don't find that in Fichte. I mean there's opposition, there's thesis, antithesis, synthesis, but it's a conceptual . . .

DE MAN: It's conceptual, but it's a movement . . .

ABRAMS: . . . kind of movement, a self-movement of the Spirit in Hegel where nothing stands still, everything moves . . .

DE MAN: . . . a self-reflection . . .

ABRAMS: . . . are where you start from simplicity, simplex unity, and somehow from within itself it moves. Well, I find that motion in Schiller. So when they emphasize the mobility of the Hegelian system, and that's, he keeps insisting, his big thing—everything is a moment, nothing stands still. And by moment he means instant as well as aspect. There I think the *Aesthetic Letters* are closer than either of the others. And Kant's antinomies, of course, are immobile; they're always there.

DE MAN: Well, I think that's a wide area of agreement. The other thing that stands between us is death.

ABRAMS: I think death is important.

DE MAN: Okay.

DOMINICK LA CAPRA: Would you apply your argument, the argument that despite appearances, Kant's transcendental philosophy, that has the most powerful inscription and is in some sense the condition of possibility of history, and which then undergoes a kind of relapse into a compromise—would you apply that argument to the relation between philosophy and nonphilosophy, or philosophy and empiricism in Kant himself? Or is that problem somewhat different? There is a problem in Kant about the relationship between philosophy and nonphilosophy. For example, in section 28 of the third *Critique*, he comes across a point where he says: my argument may perhaps seem somewhat strange or far-fetched, but in reality, if you appeal to the common man, it somehow informs the understanding of the common man, perhaps unbeknownst to him. And that's the way philosophy's leaning on empirical . . .

DE MAN: That is not a Schillerian moment in Kant, in my terms. That is not a falling back or a relapse into a loss of the . . . no. It remains the burden of the Kantian enterprise to put the common, the practical, the commonplace together with, to articulate it with the most refined critical attempts of reason. And the references in Kant to the commonplace, which take place frequently, and which take place in the curious use of very *terre à terre* examples, or in a certain kind of diction which is semipopular—you will get similar things in Hegel—there is a kind of common language in the tensions between the use of the Latin terms which he uses and the German terms which he makes up for them. All that is not at all to be interpreted, I think, as a relapse of the crucial moment in Kant. I am not at all suggesting that in Kant there is an isolation of the philosophical enterprise. To the contrary, if the notion of materiality means anything, it means that there is a necessity for such a relationship which is coercive, which is compelling. Which doesn't mean that the relationship is achieved by means of the particular mediation of the aesthetic, which is where he puts the burden of achieving this relationship. That's another matter. But the failure here, if failure there is—failure is hardly a word to do justice to what is happening at that moment, which is something much more complicated than simply a failure, and which certainly doesn't get thematized or explicitly stated as a failure. But the failure, let's say, if failure there is, is not the failure of a relapse or of a misreading of Kant, of some aspect by Kant of another aspect of it. It is the problem itself. The materiality of the problem is contained in that the difficulty of that noncompatibility, necessary compatibility and equally necessary disruption of the two—that is a very historical moment. That is a moment of a very concrete occurrence, of a very concrete event in his own language, in his own diction, in his own letter, in his own language. So, that would not be, there are no moments in Kant after the third *Critique* of—there is no relapse in Kant that I can see. There is a relapse in the tradition of the way in which Kant has been read, yes, and Schiller is the first and prime example of that, or one of the first. Does this answer somewhat?

LA CAPRA: He also says it also problematizes the distinction between philosophy and nonphilosophy as well.

DE MAN: It certainly problematizes it, but it doesn't problematize it by putting them on two different sides. Perhaps better to speak, in this case, since nonphilosophy does not really explicitly appear in the third *Critique*, since the problem of practical reasons, which are nonphilosophy, in a sense, which have to do with the practical, and as such would appear to be nonphilosophical in a way, are not directly treated. But if you take the difference between—which is here more germane—between philosophy and art, it is not the case that in Kant philosophy and art are separated as they are separated in Schiller. Art has a very specific philosophical function, which can be considered as inscribed within the philosophical enterprise. And it is as such that art occurs for Kant. Kant is not, like Schiller, concerned to write well, or to write a novel. He is concerned with art as a philosophical problem. So the philosophization of art, the fact that art can be inscribed in the discourse of philosophy, is essential to the Kantian enterprise. That's what the third *Critique* is about. As such, art and philosophy do not separate, they are not the same thing, but they are not separate, they are not polar opposites, they are not in contradiction with each other, they have a complex and supplementary relationship to each other which is not simply dialectical, certainly not that of an antinomy or of a negation. Much more complex. A fortiori this would be true of the practical, which is even more of the nonphilosophical, of the common knowledge.

DAVID MARTYN: My question returns to irreversibility. Fichte, if I remember correctly, in the *Wissenschaftslehre*, goes to great lengths to avoid the kind of reversible relationship that you talked about—look what happens to self and nonself—and finds they are reversible in some way, and by means of the verb *meiden*, will set up a dialectic. And I can see there a distinction between irreversibility and reversibility. I wonder if the relationship which you were pointing out in Kant, or the passage which is not reversible, is in some way analogous to this, to what Fichte does?

DE MAN: Yes, it is similar. It happens in Fichte in a very different vocabulary, and in a very different mode. But the pattern of the destruction is—in Fichte this goes through the problem of self-reflection, right, which is already, which is really pre-Hegelian, but which has this similar characteristic, and where the notion of freedom occurs, again in the Kantian sense. This is a large question. But the relationship Kant-Fichte-Hegel stands in urgent need of exploration. All we have is Hegel's own critical texts on the philosophy of Fichte. And if one does undertake that relationship, the study of that relationship, one important rule is, forget about Schelling—he messes up the works a great deal. But that's a perverse piece of advice.

You said yesterday you had a burning question . . . but it's burned out?

CHRISTOPHER FYNSK: In the context of what you said today, I'm curious about your remark concerning the Schillerian tendencies in Heidegger.

DE MAN: Oh dear . . .

FYNSK: You mentioned that Derrida is to Heidegger as Heidegger is to Kant. And I agree, I think, about the Schillerian tendencies in "The Origin of the Work of Art." You have these assertions about the autonomy of the work, its unity, and so forth. Nevertheless, with the idea of the articulation of world and earth, which is the subversion of the articulation of transcendental metaphysics, there is an effort to think a kind of appearance or *Erscheinung* which is not phenomenal in the Hegelian sense, and I wonder if it's not some kind of phenomenal materiality in the Kantian sense, because when there is this . . . traced in the figure, the only thing that can be said is *that it is*, that the word is.

DE MAN: That's a big argument, and there's a lot to be said on both sides of this, and this requires a comprehensive reading of Heidegger that is hard, you know, to do quickly. But there is certainly, there is an invitation on Heidegger's part to read him as you do. But there is a certain deviousness there.

You know, a piece in Heidegger that is exceedingly useful on this particular thing, and on the word *Schein* and on the phenomenalism of *Schein*, is an exchange with Staiger about the interpretation of a poem by Mörike, which ends with[14]—the poem is called "Auf eine Lampe." It has to do with light, *Schein*. Fine poem. In the exchange, the debate between Staiger and Heidegger, Heidegger insists on a less naive notion of appearing. He is very eloquent there in talking of *Lichtung*, and understands phenomenality in a way which would not have been accessible to Husserl, I would say. There is an extension of the notion of phenomenality, an ontologization of the notion of phenomenality which is highly suggestive, and which has held me enthralled for many years—just as an example of its power. But I think it is not material, and that if you read Heidegger with Nietzsche, or if you read Heidegger with Derrida,

---

14. See Martin Heidegger and Emil Staiger, "Zu einem Vers von Mörike," first published in *Trivium* 9 (1951): 1–16, and reprinted as "Ein Briefwechstel mit Martin Heidegger," in Emil Staiger, *Die Kunst der Interpretation* (Zurich: Atlantis Verlag, 1963), pp. 34–49. It is translated by Berel Lang and Christine Ebel in "A 1951 Dialogue on Interpretation: Emil Staiger, Martin Heidegger, Leo Spitzer," *PMLA* 105:3 (May 1990): 409–35.

with certain aspects of Derrida, or with Kant, for that matter—and the place to go would be the book on Kant—that one would see that the concept of the imagination there, that what happens in Heidegger's interpretation of imagination in Kant is not all that different from Schiller's pattern of the imagination. Though of course the justification is not pragmatic, but ontological—but that doesn't make it necessarily unpragmatic. There is the claim to materiality in Heidegger, but—well, I am not sure. I certainly cannot rapidly say. The question is exceedingly relevant and exceedingly important, a central question.

Thank you very much.

The Concept of Irony

The title of this lecture is "The Concept of Irony," which is a title taken from Kierkegaard, who wrote the best book on irony that's available, called *The Concept of Irony*. It's an ironic title, because irony is not a concept—and that's partly the thesis which I'm going to develop. I should preface this with a passage from Friedrich Schlegel, who will be the main author I'll have to talk about, who says the following, talking about irony: "Wer sie nicht hat, dem bleibt sie auch nach dem offensten Geständnis ein Rätsel."[1] "The one who doesn't have it (irony), to

"The Concept of Irony" was transcribed and edited by Tom Keenan—and revised by the editor—from the audiotape of a lecture given at Ohio State University, Columbus, Ohio, 4 April 1977. De Man's lecture was based on two (perhaps even three) sets of notes (some pages of which go back to his seminar at Yale on "Theory of Irony" in spring 1976): one set includes an outline titled *"Irony*—the story of irony—"; a second set is the continuation of an unfinished essay titled "Ironies of Allegory." Some material from these notes (cited as *N1* and *N2*) has been included in the footnotes here, and some was used to reconstruct a gap between the two sides of the audiotape. Significant insertions or additions are in square brackets. De Man's own parenthetical remarks are in parentheses (in brackets within quotes). Translations are de Man's unless otherwise indicated. All notes were supplied by Tom Keenan.

1. Friedrich Schlegel, *Lyceum* Fragment 108, in *Charakteristiken und Kritiken I (1796–1801)*, ed. Hans Eichner, in *Kritische Friedrich Schlegel Ausgabe* (Paderborn-Vienna-Munich: Verlag Ferdinand Schöningh, 1967), 2:160. In English, see Friedrich Schlegel, *Dialogue on Poetry and Literary Aphorisms*, trans. Ernst Behler and Roman Struc (University Park and London: Pennsylvania State University Press, 1968); and *Friedrich Schlegel's "Lucinde" and the Fragments*, trans. Peter Firchow (Minneapolis: University of Minnesota Press, 1971). De Man generally refers to the Behler and Struc translation or provides his own. The editions will be cited as *K.A.* 2; Behler and Struc; and Firchow.

him it remains, even after the most open disquisition, an enigma." You will never understand—so we can stop right here, and all go home.

There is indeed a fundamental problem: the fact that if irony were indeed a concept it should be possible to give a definition of irony. If one looks into the historic aspects of that problem, it seems to be uncannily difficult to give a definition of irony—although later, in the course of this discourse, I will attempt a definition, but you won't be much the wiser for it. It seems to be impossible to get hold of a definition, and this is itself inscribed to some extent in the tradition of the writing on the texts. If I take the period I will be mostly referring to, namely, the writings on irony, the theorization of irony in German Romanticism in the early part of the nineteenth century (the period when the most astute reflection on the problem of irony is going on), even in that time it seems to be very difficult to get hold of a definition. The German aesthetician Friedrich Solger, who writes perceptively about irony, complains at length that August Wilhelm Schlegel—who is the Schlegel we will be talking about the least (Friedrich is the one we want)—although he had written on irony, really cannot define it, cannot say what it is. A little later, when Hegel, who has a lot to say about irony, talks about irony, he complains about Solger, who writes about irony, he says, but who doesn't seem to know what it is he is writing about. And then a little later, when Kierkegaard writes on irony, he refers to Hegel, whose influence he is at that moment trying to get out of, and he more ironically complains about the fact that Hegel doesn't really seem to know what irony is. He says what and where Hegel talks about it, but then he complains and says he really doesn't have much to say about it, and what he says about it whenever he talks about it is just about always the same, and it isn't very much.[2]

So there seems to be something inherently difficult in the definition of the term, because it seems to encompass all tropes, on the one hand, but it is, on the other hand, very difficult to define it as a trope. Is irony a trope? Traditionally, of course, it is, but: is it a trope? When we examine the tropological implications of irony, and we will be doing this today, do we cover the field, do we saturate the semantic area that is covered by this particular trope? Northrop Frye seems to think it's a trope. He says it is "a pattern of words that *turns* away from direct statement or its own obvious meaning," and he adds, "(I am not using the word in any unfamiliar sense . . .)."[3] "A pattern of words that turns away"—that turning away is the trope, the movement of the trope. Trope means "to turn," and it's that turning away, that deviation between literal and figural meaning, this turning

2. Søren Kierkegaard, *The Concept of Irony*, trans. Lee M. Capel (Bloomington: Indiana University Press, 1968), pp. 260–61. In *NI* de Man refers to pp. 247–48 of Kierkegaard, *Über den Begriff der Ironie*, trans. Emanuel Hirsch (Düsseldorf and Cologne: Eugen Diederichs Verlag, 1961).

3. Northrop Frye, *Anatomy of Criticism* (Princeton, N.J.: Princeton University Press, 1957), p. 40. De Man's emphasis in *NI*.

away of the meaning, which is certainly involved in all traditional definitions of irony, such as "meaning one thing and saying something else," or "praise by blame," or whatever it may be—though one feels that this turning away in irony involves a little more, a more radical negation than one would have in an ordinary trope such as synecdoche or metaphor or metonymy. Irony seems to be the trope of tropes, the one that names the term as the "turning away," but that notion is so all-encompassing that it would include all tropes. And to say that irony includes all tropes, or is the trope of tropes, is to say something, but it is not anything that's equivalent to a definition. Because: what is a trope, and so on? We certainly don't know that. What is then the trope of tropes? We know that even less. Definitional language seems to be in trouble when irony is concerned.

Irony also very clearly has a performative function. Irony consoles and it promises and it excuses. It allows us to perform all kinds of performative linguistic functions which seem to fall out of the tropological field, but also to be very closely connected with it. In short, it is very difficult, impossible indeed, to get to a conceptualization by means of definition.

It helps a little to think of it in terms of the ironic man, in terms of the traditional opposition between *eiron* and *alazon*, as they appear in Greek or Hellenic comedy, the smart guy and the dumb guy. Most discourses about irony are set up that way, and this one will also be set up that way. You must then keep in mind that the smart guy, who is by necessity the speaker, always turns out to be the dumb guy, and that he's always being set up by the person he thinks of as being the dumb guy, the *alazon*. In this case the *alazon* (and I recognize that this makes me the real *alazon* of this discourse) is American criticism of irony,[4] and the smart guy is going to be German criticism of irony, which I of course understand. I have in mind, on the American side, an authoritative and excellent book on the problem of irony, Wayne Booth's *A Rhetoric of Irony*.[5] Booth's approach to irony is eminently sensible: he starts out from a question in practical criticism, doesn't get involved in definitions or in the theory of tropes.[6] He starts from a very reasonable question, namely: is it ironic? How do I know that the text with which I am confronted is going to be ironic or is not going to be ironic? It's very important to know that: lots of discussions turn around this and one always feels terrible when one has read a text and one is told later on that it's ironic. It is a very genuine question—whatever you have to do, it would indeed be very helpful and very desirable to know: by what markers, by what devices, by what indications or signals in the text we can decide that a text is ironic or is not?

This supposes, of course, that such a thing can be decided, that the decision we make in saying that a text is ironic can be made, and that there are textual elements

---

4. *N1*: "alazon is Am. criticism (not Burke)."

5. Wayne Booth, *A Rhetoric of Irony* (Chicago: University of Chicago Press, 1974).

6. *N1*: "empirical approach—but can one avoid theorization of irony?"

which allow you to make that decision, independently of problems of intention which might be hidden or might not be apparent. Wayne Booth is aware of the fact, although he puts it in a footnote, that there is a philosophical problem involved in this decision, to decide that a text is ironic or not, and that you can always put in question whatever decision you make once you think you have arrived at that decision. His footnote will be, in a way, my starting point. You remember that in his book he makes a big point of distinguishing what he calls stable or definite irony from another kind of irony which would not be stable and with which he deals much less. He says the following: "But no interpreter of stable irony ever needs to go that far, even though some ironies, as we see in part III, do lead to the infinite" [p. 59]. There's going to be more talk of this infinite in a moment. But then he has a footnote where he raises the question. "In this way," he says, "we rediscover, in our practical task of reading ironies (which is the task he's set for himself), why Kierkegaard, in his theoretical task of understanding the concept of irony, should have defined it finally as 'absolute infinite negativity.' Irony in itself opens up doubts as soon as its possibility enters our heads, and there is no inherent reason for discontinuing the process of doubt at any point short of infinity. 'How do you know that Fielding was not being ironic in his ostensibly ironic attack on Mrs. Partridge?' If I am answered this with a citation or other 'hard' data in the work, I can of course claim that Fielding was ironic in his use of *them* (instead). But how do I know that he was not really pretending to be ironic in *their* use, not in fact ironically attacking those who take such data without irony? And so on. The spirit of irony, if there is such a thing, cannot in itself answer such questions: pursued to the end, an ironic temper can dissolve everything, in an infinite chain of solvents. It is not irony but the desire to understand irony that brings such a chain to a stop. And that is why a rhetoric of irony is required if we are not to be caught, as many men of our time have claimed to be caught, in an infinite regress of negations. And it is why I devote the following chapters to 'learning where to stop'" [p. 59 n. 14; Booth's emphases].

This is a very reasonable, very sensible, and very perceptive note. The way to stop irony is by understanding, by the understanding of irony, by the understanding of the ironic process. Understanding would allow us to control irony. But what if irony is always of understanding, if irony is always the irony of understanding, if what is at stake in irony is always the question of whether it is possible to understand or not to understand? The main theoretical text on irony next to Kierkegaard, to which I will refer later but without reading it exhaustively, is a text by Friedrich Schlegel which happens to be called "Über die Unverständlichkeit"—"On the impossibility of understanding," "On incomprehensibility," "On the problem of the impossibility of understanding."[7] If indeed irony is tied

---

7. Friedrich Schlegel, "Über die Unverständlichkeit," in *K.A.* 2:363–72; "On Incomprehensibility," in Firchow, pp. 257–71.

with the impossibility of understanding, then Wayne Booth's project of understanding irony is doomed from the start because, if irony is of understanding, no understanding of irony will ever be able to control irony and to stop it, as he proposes to do, and if this is indeed the case that what is at stake in irony is the possibility of understanding, the possibility of reading, the readability of texts, the possibility of deciding on *a* meaning or on a multiple set of meanings or on a controlled polysemy of meanings, then we can see that irony would indeed be very dangerous. There would be in irony something very threatening, against which interpreters of literature, who have a stake in the understandability of literature, would want to put themselves on their guard—very legitimate to want, as Booth wants, to stop, to stabilize, to control the trope.

It would have been difficult, though not impossible, but more difficult, for Wayne Booth to write this way, and to write the sentence I've just quoted, if he had been more cognizant of the German tradition which has dealt with the problem, rather than centering his argument as he does on the practice of eighteenth-century English fiction. Booth knows about the Germanic tradition, but he wants to have nothing to do with it. This is what he says: "But, fellow romantics, do not push irony too far, or you will pass from the joyful laughter of *Tristram Shandy* into Teutonic gloom. Read Schlegel," he says [p. 211]. Clearly we shouldn't do this, if we want to keep at least reasonably happy. I'm afraid I'm going to read Schlegel, a little bit, though I don't think of Schlegel as particularly gloomy. But then I'm not entirely sure that the laughter in *Tristram Shandy* is entirely joyful either, so I'm not sure how safe we are with *Tristram Shandy*. But at any rate, it's a different kind of texture. Schlegel's own German contemporaries and critics, and there were many, didn't think he was gloomy at all. They actually rather held it against him that he was not nearly serious, and not nearly gloomy, enough. But (I will say this as a simple and not particularly original historical statement), if you are interested in the problem and the theory of irony, you have to take it in the German tradition. That's where the problem is worked out. You have to take it in Friedrich Schlegel (much more than in August Wilhelm Schlegel), and also in Tieck, Novalis, Solger, Adam Müller, Kleist, Jean Paul, Hegel, Kierkegaard, and all the way up to Nietzsche. An enumeration from which I more or less pointedly omit Thomas Mann, who is generally considered to be the main German ironist. He is, but he is less important than any of the others I mentioned. But Friedrich Schlegel is the most important, where the problem really gets worked out.

Schlegel is an enigmatic figure, a curious work and a curious person. It's an enigmatic career, and a work which is by no means impressive—very fragmentary, unconvincing, with no really finished works, only books of aphorisms and unfinished fragments—a fragmentary work entirely. It's a bewildering personal career, also politically bewildering. He has just one finished work, a little anecdotal roman à clef called *Lucinde*, which is not a novel that most people nowadays still read a great deal (they're making a mistake, but that's the way it is).

Still, that little novel, which isn't very long and which seems to be anecdotally related to his love relationship with Dorothea Veit before he married her, has provoked a totally unpredictable amount of irritation in the people who commented on it later on. Though it seems slight enough and not very serious, whoever wrote about it later—and some very big names wrote about it—got extraordinarily irritated whenever this novel came up. This is the case most notoriously with Hegel, who refers to Schlegel and *Lucinde* and loses his cool, which doesn't happen so easily to Hegel. Whenever this comes up he gets very upset and becomes insulting—he says Schlegel is a bad philosopher, he doesn't know or he hasn't read enough, he should not speak, and so on. And Kierkegaard, although he is trying to get away from Hegel, echoes Hegel in the discussion of *Lucinde* which intervenes in his book on irony. He calls it an obscene book and gets very upset too, so much so that he has to invent (we'll come back to that in a moment) a whole theory of history to justify the fact that one should get rid of Friedrich Schlegel, that he's not a real ironist. And this is significant, in a sense. What is it in this little book that got people so upset? Hegel and Kierkegaard—that's not *n'importe qui*.[8]

This continues in *Germanistik*, in the academic study of German literature, where Friedrich Schlegel plays an important part but where there is considerable resistance to him. It would hardly be hyperbolic to say (and I could defend the affirmation) that the whole discipline of *Germanistik* has developed for the single reason of dodging Friedrich Schlegel, of getting around the challenge that Schlegel and that *Lucinde* offer to the whole notion of an academic discipline which would deal with German literature—seriously. The same thing happens with Friedrich Schlegel's defenders, where there is a counterattempt to say that he is not really frivolous but in fact a serious writer. When that happens, in a curious way, the issue which is raised by Friedrich Schlegel, and by *Lucinde* in particular, is also being dodged. This is the case with critics who fall out of the academic tradition, critics such as Lukács, Walter Benjamin, and more recently Peter Szondi and others, to whom we will return briefly at the end of this lecture.

What is it, then, in *Lucinde* that gets people so upset? It's a slightly scandalous story, where people aren't really married, but that's not sufficient reason to get so upset—after all, *on en avait vu d'autres*. There is in the middle of *Lucinde* a short chapter called "Eine Reflexion" (A reflection), which reads like a philosophical treatise or argument (using philosophical language which can be identified as that of Fichte), but it doesn't take a very perverse mind, only a slightly perverse one, to see that what is actually being described is not a philosophical argument at all but is—well, how shall I put it?—a reflection on the very physical questions involved in sexual intercourse. Discourse which seems to be purely philosophical can be read in a double code, and what it really is describing is something which we do

---

8. *N2* refers to: Hegel, *Vorlesungen über die Ästhetik I*, Theorie Werkausgabe (Frankfurt am Main: Suhrkamp, 1970), vol. 13, pp. 97–98; and Kierkegaard, *Über den Begriff der Ironie*, p. 292.

not generally consider worthy of philosophical discourse, at least not in those terms—sexuality is worthy of it, but what is being described is not sexuality, it's something much more specific than that.

Now, if this sends you all to *Lucinde* you will probably be disappointed (not if you really know what's going on). I'm not going to refer to this, but there is a particular scandal here, one which got Hegel and Kierkegaard and philosophers in general, and other people too, very upset. It threatens in a fundamental way something which goes much deeper than this apparent joke. (It is a joke, but we know that jokes are not innocent, and this is certainly not an innocent passage.) There seems to be a particular threat emanating from this double relationship in the writing, which is not just a double code. It's not just that there is a philosophical code and then another code describing sexual activities. These two codes are radically incompatible with each other. They interrupt, they disrupt, each other in such a fundamental way that this very possibility of disruption represents a threat to all assumptions one has about what a text should be. This is a genuine enough threat to have generated in its turn a powerful critical and philosophical argument, which set up a whole tradition of studies that have dealt with Friedrich Schlegel—or with equivalent things in German Romanticism, but they are never as acute as they are in the case of Schlegel.

The way in which Schlegel is being defused, the way in which irony is being defused (and we will see in a moment to some extent why irony is involved in this, which is not the case at first sight), follows a somewhat systematic path. Schlegel is being defused by reducing irony to three things, by coping with irony in terms of three strategies which are related to, not independent of, each other. First, one reduces irony to an aesthetic practice or artistic device, a *Kunstmittel*. Irony is an artistic effect, something a text does for aesthetic reasons, to heighten or to diversify the aesthetic appeal of this text. This is traditionally how authoritative books about irony deal with the problem. For example, the authoritative study on irony by a German author, Ingrid Strohschneider-Kohrs, *Die Romantische Ironie in Theorie und Gestaltung* [Tübingen: Max Niemeyer Verlag, 1960], deals with irony in those terms, using Schiller and the notion of the aesthetic as play, as free play. Thus irony allows one to say dreadful things because it says them by means of aesthetic devices, achieving a distance, a playful aesthetic distance, in relation to what is being said. Irony in that case is a *Kunstmittel*, an aesthetic, and can be absorbed into a general theory of aesthetics, which may be a very advanced, Kantian or post-Kantian, at least Schillerian, theory of aesthetics.

Another way in which irony can be dealt with, and can be in a sense defused, is by reducing it to a dialectic of the self as a reflexive structure. The chapter in Schlegel in question is called "Eine Reflexion" and has to do with reflexive patterns of consciousness. Irony clearly is the same distance within a self, duplications of a self, specular structures within the self, within which the self looks at itself from a certain distance. It sets up reflexive structures, and irony can be described as a moment in a dialectic of the self. It is in that way, to the extent that I have written about the subject, that I have dealt with it myself, so what I have to say today is in the nature of an *autocritique*, since I want to put in question this possibility.[9] At any rate, that's the second way of dealing with irony, by reducing it to a dialectic of the self.

The third way of dealing with irony (and this is very much part of the same system) is to insert ironic moments or ironic structures into a dialectic of history. Hegel and Kierkegaard, in a sense, were concerned with dialectical patterns of history, and, somewhat symmetrically to the way it can be absorbed in a dialectic of the self, irony gets interpreted and absorbed within a dialectical pattern of history, a dialectics of history.

The reading which I propose (basically the reading of two fragments in Schlegel) will to some extent put in question those three possibilities—that's what I will try to do with you today. The fragments which I'm using are very well known, and there's nothing original in their selection. I'll start from a fragment, *Lyceum* Fragment 37, where indeed Schlegel seems to be speaking of irony within an aesthetic problematic. The problem is how to write well: how shall we write well? (The translation which you have [Behler and Struc] is an excellent translation. The only reproach that I could make to this translation is that it is too elegant. Schlegel is elegant, in his own way, but in order to be at all elegant in English you have to do away with anything that smacks of philosophical terminology. That has been done to some extent in this translation, thus hiding the use of philosophical vocabulary, in this case, I'm afraid, not to describe sexual intercourse, but to describe whatever Friedrich Schlegel is describing. There is a presence of philosophical terminology here, which is, as we shall see in a moment, very important.) Here's what Schlegel says:

> In order to be able to write well upon a subject, one must have ceased to be interested in it; the thought which is to be soberly expressed must already be entirely past and no longer be one's actual concern. As long as the artist invents and is inspired, he remains in a constrained [*illiberal*, coerced] state of mind, at least for the purpose of communication. He then wants to say everything, which is the wrong tendency of young geniuses or the right prejudice of old bunglers. Thus he fails to recognize the value and dignity of self-restraint [*Selbstbeschränkung*, self-limitation], which is indeed for both the artist and the man the first and the last, the most necessary and the highest goal. The most necessary: for wherever we do not restrain ourselves, the world will restrain us; and thus we will become its slave. The highest: for we can restrain ourselves only in those points and aspects (along those

---

9. See "The Rhetoric of Temporality" (1969), reprinted in the second edition of Paul de Man, *Blindness and Insight: Essays in the Rhetoric of Contemporary Criticism* (Minneapolis: University of Minnesota Press, 1983), pp. 187–228.

lines) where we have infinite power in self-creation and self-destruction [*Selbstschöpfung und Selbstvernichtung*]. Even a friendly conversation which cannot at any given moment be broken off voluntarily with complete arbitrariness has something illiberal about it. An artist, however, who is able and wants to express himself completely, who keeps nothing to himself and would wish to say everything he knows, is very much to be pitied. There are only three mistakes one has to be on guard against. What appears to be and ought to appear as unlimited arbitrariness and consequently unreason or superreason, must in reality be absolutely necessary and reasonable; otherwise caprice (becomes willful, becomes illiberal, and self-restraint)[10] will turn into self-destruction [*Selbstvernichtung*]. Secondly: one should not hasten too much towards self-restraint, but allow self-creation, that is, invention and enthusiasm, to develop until it has matured. Thirdly: self-restraint must not be exaggerated."[11]

That seems to be a reasonable enough, a very aesthetic, passage. It has to do with a kind of economy of enthusiasm and control in the act of writing, which one might call a mixture of classical restraint with romantic abandon. It is very possible to read the passage this way, placing it as such in the history of the relationship between German classical and German romantic literature at that time, a mixture which would lead in Schlegel's program to a *progressive Universalpoesie*,[12] a progressive literature in which those two elements would be harmoniously mixed. But more is involved, more is at stake. The use of the terms which I stressed— *Selbstschöpfung*, *Selbstvernichtung*, *Selbstbestimmung* or *Selbstbeschränkung*,

---

10. This passage is omitted in the Behler and Struc translation from which de Man quotes.

11. Behler and Struc, pp. 124–25; *K.A.* 2:151; cf. Firchow, p. 147. A loose page of *N1* bears a draft translation of *Lyceum* Fragment 37:

"To write well about something, one must no longer be interested in it: the idea one wishes to express with composure [*Besonnenheit*] must already have passed by entirely, should no longer be of primal concern to us. As long as the artist is in a state of passion and enthusiasm, he is, at least as far as expression is concerned, in a state of coercion [*illiberal*]. He will want to say everything—and this is the misguided tendency of a young genius, or the proper caution of old dullards. In so doing, he ignores the value and the dignity of *self-limitation* [*Selbstbeschränkung*], although it is the most necessary and the highest of obligations for the artist as for man in general. It is the most necessary: for wherever one does not restrict [*beschränkt*] oneself, one is restricted by the world. It is the highest: for one can restrict oneself only in the points and along the lines where one has *infinite* power, in *self-creation* and in *self-destruction*. Even an amicable conversation that cannot be gratuitously broken off at any moment [*aus unbedingter Willkür*] has something coercive. A writer, however, who wants to say everything, who holds nothing back, and wants to say all that he knows, is to be felt sorry for. One has to beware of only three dangers. Pure gratuitousness, what appears and should appear as irrational or superrational, must become downright necessary and reasonable (economy); otherwise the mood becomes one of willfulness, and again coercive (obsessional), and self-limitation turns into self-destruction. Second: one should not hurry too much with self-limitation, and first leave ample room for self-creation, for passion and enthusiasm to come fully into being. Third: one should not overdo the self-limitation."

12. See *Athenäum* Fragment 116, *K.A.* 2:182–83.

self-limitation or self-definition—are philosophical terms which, as is well known, Schlegel borrowed from the contemporary philosopher Johann Gottlieb Fichte. Schlegel himself, in the essay called "Über die Unverständlichkeit," designated what were for him the three main events of the century: the French Revolution, the publication of *Wilhelm Meister*, and the publication of Fichte's *Grundlage der gesamten Wissenschaftslehre*, which therefore is for him as important an event as the French Revolution [*K.A.* 2:366; cf. Firchow, p. 262]. That's not quite the way we look upon it now—I don't assume Fichte is something you read every night before going to bed, but maybe you should. At any rate, if you want to get into Schlegel, it is necessary to have some contact with Fichte, and I will have to talk for a moment (I'm sorry) about Fichte and do some exposition on that.

Those three moments—self-creation, self-destruction, and what he calls self-limitation or self-definition—are the three moments in Fichte's dialectic. Fichte is the theoretician of the dialectic before Hegel. Hegel is inconceivable without Fichte. In Fichte, the dialectic is stressed, and is developed in a highly systematized way, and it is the object of the particular book from which Schlegel borrows it (the *Grundlage der Gesamten Wissenschaftslehre*).[13] The generally received idea about Fichte—what one knows about Fichte, if anything—is that Fichte is the philosopher of the self, the man who set up the category of the self as an absolute. We think of Fichte, therefore, as being in the tradition of what we would call nowadays phenomenology of the self, and so on and so forth. That is a mistake. Fichte is not essentially to be thought of as the philosopher of the self, if we think of the self (as we necessarily have to) in terms of a dialectic of subject and object, in terms of a polarity of self and other. Fichte's notion of the self is not itself a dialectical notion, but is the necessity or the condition of any dialectical development at all. The self, in Fichte, is a logical category. And Fichte talks about the self not in terms of anything experiential, not of anything we think of when we say 'self': ourselves, or somebody else, or even a transcendental self in any form. Fichte talks about the self as such as a property of language, as something which is essentially and inherently linguistic. The self is, says Fichte, posited originally by language. Language posits radically and absolutely the self, the subject, as such. *"Das Ich setzt ursprünglich schlechthin sein eignes Sein,"* *"the I posits originally its own being"* [p. 18, *S.W.* 1:98; emphasis in original], and the self does this—can only do this—by means of an act of language. Therefore

---

13. Johann Gottlieb Fichte, *Grundlage der gesamten Wissenschaftslehre* (1794), ed. Fritz Medicus (Hamburg: Felix Meiner Verlag, 1979); *Science of Knowledge (Wissenschaftslehre) with First and Second Introductions*, trans. Peter Heath and John Lachs (New York: Appleton-Century-Crofts/ Meredith Corporation, 1970; reprinted Cambridge: Cambridge University Press, 1982). Following de Man, page references are to the German edition. Both the English and German texts carry marginal references to the pagination of Fichte's *Sämtliche Werke*, cited here additionally as *S.W.* 1. All translations are de Man's.

the self is, for Fichte, the beginning of a logical development, the development of a logic, and as such has nothing to do with the experiential or the phenomenological self in any form, or at least not originally, not first of all. It is the ability of language to posit, the ability of language to *setzen*, in German. It is the catachresis, the ability of language catachretically to name anything, by false usage, but to name and thus to posit anything language is willing to posit.

From the moment language can thus posit the self, it can also, and it has to, posit the opposite, the negation of the self—which is not the result of a negation of, but which is itself an act of positing equivalent to, the act of the positing of the self.[14] To the extent, the same way, that the self is being posited, the nonself (*das nicht-Ich*) is implied in the very positing of the self, and is as such equally posited. "Entgegensetzen ist schlechthin durch das Ich gesetzt," says Fichte, "to posit-against (the negation of the positing) is also posited by the I," at the same time. The I, language, posits A and posits minus-A at the same time, and this is not a thesis and antithesis, because the negation is not an antithetic negation, as it would be in Hegel. It is different. It is itself posited and it has nothing to do, for example, with a consciousness. About this self, which is thus posited and negated at the same time, nothing can be said. It's a purely empty, positional act, and no acts of judgment can be made about it, no statements of judgment of any kind can be made about it.

There is a third stage in which the two contradictory elements which have been posited engage each other, so to speak, come in contact with each other and delimit each other, by isolating in those entities which have been posited parts which Fichte will call "properties (*Merkmale*)" [p. 31, *S.W.* 1:111]. The self that's posited by language has no properties—it is an empty, nothing can be said about it. But because it posits its opposite, the plus and the minus can get to some extent in contact with each other, and they do this by delimiting and defining each other: *Selbstbeschränkung, Selbstbestimmung—Selbstbeschränkung*, which is involved [p. 28, *S.W.* 1:108]. Fichte says: "*Einschränken* heißt: die Realität desselben durch Negation nicht *gänzlich*, sondern zum *Teil* aufheben." "*To limit, to determine*, is to suspend (*aufheben*, Hegel's term) in part the reality (of the self and the nonself) by negation, but not *entirely*, but to some *extent* (*zum Teil*, to a degree)" [p. 29, sec. 8, *S.W.* 1:108; emphasis in original]. And the parts thus isolated in the self become properties of the self (*Merkmale*). From that moment, it is possible to start making acts of judgment involving the self. It becomes possible to say things about entities, and the entity being as such a posited self, it becomes possible to make comparisons between them and to start to emit acts of judgment. What was originally a mere catachresis now becomes an entity as we know it, a collection of properties, and it becomes possible to compare them with each other and to find

---

14. *N1*: "negation is radical, in the sense that it is not derived from or in any way subsidiary in relation to an act of position but entirely co-extensive with it."

between different entities resemblances and differences. These are, according to Fichte, acts of judgment—an act of judgment is to see what entities have in common, or to see in what they differ.

I have to push the development a little further for reasons which I hope will become clear in a moment. Judgments or acts of judgment, which now allow for language, for a logic, to develop, proceed according to two patterns—either as synthetic judgments or as analytical judgments. Synthetic judgments are judgments in which you say that some thing is like another. Following Fichte [p. 33, *S.W.* 1:113], whenever you do that, every entity which is like another must be unlike it in at least one property. You must be able to distinguish between them in at least one property: if I say that A is like B, it supposes an X in which A and B are distinct or different. If I say that a bird is an animal, this supposes a distinction between animals, that there are differences between animals which allow me to make this comparison statement, between animals in general and birds in particular [p. 36, *S.W.* 1:116]. That's a synthetic judgment, which thus postulates differences, assumes differences, when a similarity is being stated. Or, if I make an analytic judgment, a negative judgment, if I say that A is not B, then it supposes a property X in which A and B are alike. If I say, for example, that a plant is not an animal, it supposes a property that plants and animals have in common, which in this case would be the principle of organization itself, which plant and animal have to have in common for me to be able to say, to make the analytic judgment, that something is not like something else [p. 36, *S.W.* 1:116]. You see that, in this system, every synthetic judgment always supposes an analytical judgment. If I say that something is like something, I have to imply a difference, and if I say that something differs from something, I have to imply a similarity.

There is a very specific structure here, by means of which the properties which are isolated in the entities circulate between those several elements, and that the circulation of those properties becomes itself the basis of any act of judgment. Now this structure (and this may not be convincing, I don't know, but I'll just announce it as a statement), this particular structure which is here being described— the isolation and the circulation of properties, the way in which properties can be exchanged between entities when they are being compared with each other in an act of judgment—is the structure of metaphor, the structure of tropes. This very movement which is being described here is the circulation of properties, the circulation of tropes, within a system of knowledge. This is the epistemology of tropes. This system is structured like metaphors—like figures in general, metaphors in particular.

Now, there is a third stage in this, and then the worst is over. Every judgment, says Fichte [pp. 35–38, *S.W.* 1:115–18], implies also a thetic judgment; it is analytical, synthetic, but it is also thetic. This is a judgment in which the entity now doesn't compare itself to something else but in which the entity relates to itself, a reflexive judgment. The prototype, the paradigm, of the thetic judgment is the judgment, indeed, "I am," in which I assert the existence of myself, in which the existence of the subject—which was originally, as you know, just posited by language—is now being stated as existent, where predication takes place. It is an empty predication, infinitely empty, and the statement "I am" is as such to some extent an empty statement [p. 37, *S.W.* 1:116]. But this statement doesn't have to be made necessarily in the first person—it can be done in the form of stating properties of the self, for example (it's Fichte's example), [:"man is free." If "man is free" is considered a synthetic judgment (positive, comparison)—that is, man belongs to the class of free beings—then this supposes that there must be men that are not free, which is impossible. And if it is considered an analytic judgment (negative, distinction)—that is, man is in opposition to all species that stand under the coercion of nature—then there must be another species that shares the property of freedom with man, and there is none. "Man is free" is not simply synthetic or analytic; in the thetic judgment "man is free," freedom is structured as an *asymptote* (as is, Fichte adds, aesthetic judgment). "Man should come infinitely close to an unreachable freedom," "Der Mensch soll sich der an sich unerreichbaren Freiheit ins Unendliche immer mehr nähern" (p. 37, *S.W.* 1:116–17). Man's freedom can thus][15] be stated as an infinite point toward which he is under way, as a kind of asymptote toward which he comes closer and closer, as a kind of infinite movement of ascent (or descent, it doesn't matter), toward which man is under way. As such, the notion of the infinite, which is essential in this whole problematic, is at play.

You can translate this abstraction (this excessive abstraction, if you want) into a slightly more concrete experience, though that is illegitimate, because it is at the beginning, I remind you, not an experience—it is a linguistic act. From the moment that there are comparative judgments, it becomes possible to speak of properties of the self and it may appear as an experience; it becomes possible to talk about it in terms of an experience. With that necessary caveat, you can, to some extent, translate this into experiential categories, and you can think of this self as some kind of super-, transcendental self which man approaches, as something that's infinitely agile, infinitely elastic (and those are Friedrich Schlegel's words), as a self that stands above any of its particular experiences and toward which any particular self is always under way. (This is something, if you want, like Keats talking about Shakespeare's "negative capability," about Shakespeare as the man who can take on all selves and stand above all of them without being anything specific himself, a self that is infinitely elastic, infinitely mobile, an infinitely active and agile subject that stands above any of its experiences. The reference to

---

15. The section inserted within square brackets is not transcribed from the tape. It fills the gap between the two sides of the only tape recording of this lecture, and is taken almost verbatim from *N2* (with help from *N1*'s version of the same moment in de Man's exposition) and Fichte's text.

Keats, and more specifically the reference to Shakespeare, would not be amiss in this case.)[16]

Now, this whole system, as I have begun to sketch it out here, is first of all a theory of trope, a theory of metaphor, because (that's why I had to go through those steps) the circulation of the property (*Merkmal*) described in the act of judgment here is structured like a metaphor or a trope, is based on the substitution of properties. It's structured like a synecdoche, a relationship between part and whole, or structured like a metaphor, a substitution on the basis of resemblance and of differentiation between two entities. The structure of the system is tropological. It is the tropological system in its most systematic and general form.

But it is not just that, because it is also a performative system, to the extent that it is based on an original act of positing that exists in a linguistic mode in the form of the catachresis, of the power of *setzen*, which is the beginning of the system and which itself is a performative rather than a cognitive. There is first a performative, the act of positing, the original catachresis, which then moves to a system of tropes; a kind of anamorphosis of tropes takes place, in which all the tropological systems are engendered, as a result of this original act of positing.

Fichte describes this (I haven't done justice to it) in a highly systematic way. He describes it as what one can only call an allegory—it is a narrative, a story that he tells, hardly an exciting story as I told it, but in Fichte it's very exciting indeed. It is an allegory, the narrative of the interaction between trope on the one hand and performance as positing on the other hand. It is therefore like a theory of narrative, and it sets up a coherent system, fully systematic, in which there exists a unity between the system on the one hand, and the form of the system on the other. And it sets this up as a narrative line: the story of the comparison and the distinction, the story of the exchange of the properties, the turn where the relation is to the self, and then the project of the infinite self. This all makes a coherent narrative, one in which there are radically negative moments. It's a complexly negative narrative: the self is never capable of knowing what it is, can never be identified as such, and the judgments emitted by the self about itself, reflexive judgments, are not stable judgments. There's a great deal of negativity, a powerful negativity within it, but the fundamental intelligibility of the system is not in question because it can always be reduced to a system of tropes, which is described as such, and which as such has an inherent coherence. It is genuinely systematic. Schlegel has said somewhere: one must always have a system. He also said: one must never have a system.[17] At

---

16. Keats, letter to George and Tom Keats, 21, 27(?) December 1817, in *The Selected Poetry of John Keats*, ed. Paul de Man (New York: Signet/NAL, 1966), pp. 328–329; cf. de Man's Introduction, p. xxv.

17. A reference to *Athenäum* Fragment 53: "Es ist gleich tödlich für den Geist, ein System zu haben, und keins zu haben. Es wird sich also wohl entschließen müssen, beide zu verbinden" (*K.A.* 2:173; Behler and Struc, p. 136).

any rate, before you can say that you must never have a system, you have to have a system, and Fichte had a system. Here the system is the tropology, the tropological system, and a narrative line which that system is bound to engender—the arabesque, as Schlegel will say, of the tropological narrative. And what the arabesque narrates, what it tells, is the anamorphosis of the tropes, the transformations of the tropes, into the system of tropes, to which the corresponding experience is that of the self standing above its own experiences.

That seems to be what Schlegel is saying in *Lyceum* Fragment 42 (the other fragment that I want to read), in which he is describing this detached self, the self that speaks in philosophy, he says, and that speaks in poetry. He describes it as follows (he's talking about philosophy and distinguishing between philosophy and what he calls rhetoric—this is not rhetoric the way I use it, but the rhetoric of persuasion—which he considers a minor form as compared to philosophy):

> Philosophy is the true home of irony, which might be defined as logical
> beauty: for wherever men are philosophizing in spoken or written dia-
> logues (he's thinking of Socrates, of course), and provided they are not
> entirely systematic, irony ought to be produced and postulated; even the
> Stoics regarded urbanity as a virtue. It is true, there is also a rhetorical
> irony which, if sparingly used, performs a very excellent function, espe-
> cially in polemics, but compared to the lofty urbanity of the Socratic muse,
> rhetorical irony is like the splendor of the most brilliant oratory compared
> to ancient high tragedy (namely, very inferior to it). In this respect, poetry
> alone can rise to the height of philosophy, since it is not, as oratory, based
> upon ironic passages [*Stellen*]. (The irony is everywhere, it's not just in
> specific passages.) There are ancient and modern poems which breathe in
> their entirety, and in every detail, the divine breath of irony. In such poems,
> there lives a real transcendental buffoonery. Their interior is permeated by
> the mood [*Stimmung*] which surveys everything and rises infinitely above
> everything limited, even above the poet's own art, virtue, and genius;
> and their exterior form by the histrionic style of an ordinary good Italian
> *buffo*.[18]

Now this buffo has given the critics a lot of trouble, and that's what it's all about. Because what we get in the passage (that's why we spent so much time on Fichte) is the full assimilation and understanding of the systematic Fichtean system, in all its implications. We get a remarkably concise summary of the Fichtean system here, where the negativity of that self is stressed—because it is the detachment in relation to everything, and also in relation to the self and to the writer's own work, the radical distance (the radical negation of himself) in relation to his own work. This particular mood (*Stimmung*) is interiorly what we find in poetry. But what we find exteriorly in poetry, or in the actual, exterior, outward meaning,

---

18. Behler and Struc, p. 126; *K.A.* 2:152.

is the buffo. The buffo here has a very specific meaning, which has been identified in scholarship very convincingly. The buffo, what Schlegel refers to in commedia dell'arte, is the disruption of narrative illusion, the *aparté*, the aside to the audience, by means of which the illusion of the fiction is broken (what we call in German *aus der Rolle fallen*, to drop out of your role). This concern with the interruption has been there from the beginning—you remember that, in the first thing we read, Schlegel said you have to be able to interrupt the friendly conversation at all moments, freely, arbitrarily.

The technical term for this in rhetoric, the term that Schlegel uses, is *parabasis*. Parabasis is the interruption of a discourse by a shift in the rhetorical register. It's what you would get in Sterne, precisely, the constant interruption of the narrative illusion by intrusion, or you get it in *Jacques le Fataliste*, which are indeed Schlegel's models. Or you get it in Stendhal, still later on, or (which is specifically where Schlegel refers to) extensively in the plays of his friend Tieck, where the parabasis is constantly being used. There's another word for this, too, which is equally valid in rhetoric—the word *anacoluthon*. Anacoluthon or *anacoluthe* is more often used in terms of syntactical patterns of tropes, or periodic sentences, where the syntax of a sentence which raises certain expectations is suddenly interrupted and, instead of getting what you would expect to get in terms of the syntax that has been set up, you get something completely different, a break in the syntactical expectations of the pattern.

The best place to go if you want to find out about *anacoluthe* is in Marcel Proust, who in the third volume of the *Recherche*, in the section called "La Prisonnière," discusses the lies of Albertine. You remember that Albertine lies. She tells him terrible things, or at least he imagines she tells him terrible things. She is always lying, and he analyzes the structure of her lies. He says she begins a sentence in the first person, and so you expect that what she's telling you—they're dreadful things—she's telling you about herself, but by some device in the middle of the sentence, without your knowing it, suddenly she's not talking about herself anymore but about that other person. "Elle n'était pas, elle-même, le sujet de l'action," and, he says, she does this by means of the device "que les rhétoriciens appellent anacoluthe."[19] It is a striking passage, a profound understanding of the structure of anacoluthon: this syntactical disruption which, exactly in the same way as a parabasis, interrupts the narrative line. So the buffo is a parabasis or an anacoluthon, an interruption of the narrative line, of the elaborate arabesque or line which Fichte had set up. But parabasis is not enough, for Schlegel. Irony is not just an interruption; it is (and this is the definition which he gave of irony), he

---

19. Marcel Proust, *À la recherche du temps perdu* (Paris: Gallimard, Bibliothèque de la Pléiade, 1954), 3:153. Proust's text reads: "Ce n'était pas elle qui était le sujet de l'action," and has "grammairiens" for "rhétoriciens." Cf. Paul de Man, *Allegories of Reading* (New Haven: Yale University Press, 1979), pp. 289–90 and 300–301, esp. n. 12, and n. 21.

says, the "permanent parabasis,"[20] parabasis not just at one point but at all points, which is how he defines poetry: irony is everywhere, at all points the narrative can be interrupted. The critics who have written about this have pointed out, rightly, that there is a radical contradiction here, because a parabasis can only happen at one specific point, and to say that there would be permanent parabasis is saying something violently paradoxical. But that's what Schlegel had in mind. You have to imagine the parabasis as being able to take place at all times. At all moments the interruption can happen, as, for example, in the chapter of *Lucinde* from which I started; the philosophical argument at all times is brutally interrupted when you see that it corresponds to something completely different, to an event which has nothing to do with the philosophical argument. This interrupts, disrupts, profoundly the inner mood (the *Stimmung*), in the same way that in this passage the inner mood being described is completely disrupted by the exterior form, which is that of the buffo, that of the parabasis, that of the interruption, that of the undoing of the narrative line. And we now know that this narrative line is not just any narrative line: it is the narrative structure resulting from the tropological system, as it is being defined systematically by Fichte. So that we can complete, if you want, Schlegel's definition: if Schlegel said irony is permanent parabasis, we would say that irony is the permanent parabasis of the allegory of tropes. (That's the definition which I promised you—I also told you you would not be much more advanced when you got it, but there it is: irony is the permanent parabasis of the allegory of tropes.) The allegory of tropes has its own narrative coherence, its own systematicity, and it is that coherence, that systematicity, which irony interrupts, disrupts.[21] So one could say that any theory of irony is the undoing, the necessary undoing, of any theory of narrative, and it is ironic, as we say, that irony always comes up in relation to theories of narrative, when irony is precisely what makes it impossible ever to achieve a theory of narrative that would be consistent. Which doesn't mean that we don't have to keep working on it, because that's all we can do, but it will always be interrupted, always be disrupted, always be undone by the ironic dimension which it will necessarily contain.

Now, in what linguistic element does this parabasis occur? In what element of the text does the parabasis as such take place?[22] Let me approach this obliquely by referring to Schlegel's theory, or implicit theory, of an authentic language (*reelle Sprache*). This comes up frequently in the discussion of Friedrich Schlegel, where

---

20. "Die Ironie ist eine permanente Parekbase.—"; Schlegel, "Zur Philosophie" (1797), Fragment 668, in *Philosophische Lehrjahre I (1796–1806)*, ed. Ernst Behler, in *K.A.* (Paderborn-Vienna-Munich: Verlag Ferdinand Schöningh, 1963), 18:85. Cf. *Allegories of Reading*, p. 300 n. 21, and "The Rhetoric of Temporality," pp. 218ff.

21. *N1*: "irony is (permanent) parabasis of allegory—intelligibility of (representational) narrative disrupted at all times."

22. *N1*: "(from anacoluthon to play of signifier in Rousseau's *Confessions*)." See "Excuses (*Confessions*)" in *Allegories of Reading*, pp. 278–301.

the claim is generally made, especially by aesthetic critics like Strohschneider-Kohrs and others, that Schlegel had an intuition of an authentic language (*reelle Sprache*) and that he saw it to be present in myths, for example. But, unlike Novalis (who is always held up as the example of the successful poet, the poet who produced real work, as compared to Schlegel who produced nothing but fragments), who also saw authentic language in myth, Schlegel somehow drew back from it, didn't have the power, or the confidence, or the love, to abandon himself to it, and he retreated from it. To the contrary, it is said, Novalis could acquiesce to myth, and therefore became the great poet which we all know him to be, whereas Schlegel only wrote *Lucinde*.

Schlegel treats authentic language in the "Rede über die Mythologie,"[23] and he does so in the passage where he discusses the similarity between the wit which is characteristic of romantic poetry (by which he means the poetry of Cervantes and of Shakespeare—not Romanticism, in a sense, but literary imagination, where wit includes both the Coleridgean fancy and the imagination) and mythology. In mythology, he says, "I find great similarity with the marvelous wit of romantic poetry." He discusses this particular distinctive feature of romantic poetry which he says is like mythology: wit is present in mythology the way it is present in romantic poetry. He describes it by a series of attributes, which is all well known in the theory of Romanticism, very much corresponding to the received ideas about Romanticism. He says it's an "artificially ordered confusion," the "seductive symmetry of contradictions," the "marvelous and the perennial alternation of enthusiasm and irony." It lives, he says, "even in the smallest part of the whole" and it is all an "indirect form of mythology." "The structure of wit and mythology is the same," he says. "The arabesque is the oldest and the most original form of the human imagination. But they [wit and mythology] could not exist without something primal and original (that seems to be the authentic language) that cannot be imitated, that lets the original nature and the original force [*Kraft*] shine through, despite the transformations which it undergoes, and that allows," he says, "with naive profundity, the glow (of this original language) to shine through." In the first version he wrote of this, he had written that what shines through as *reelle Sprache* was "the strange (*das Sonderbare*), even the absurd [*das Widersinnige*], as well as a childlike yet sophisticated naïveté [*geistreiche* naïveté]." And this version—the strange and the absurd and the sophisticated or sentimental naive—together corresponds very much to our notion of Romanticism as a playful irrationality, as a playful fantasy. When Schlegel rewrote this, he took those terms out (*Sonderbare*, *Widersinnige*, *geistreiche* naïveté), and instead of them he put three other terms. What *reelle Sprache* allows to light, to shine through, is "error, mad-

---

23. *K.A.* 2:311–22 at pp. 318–19; cf. Behler and Struc, "Talk on Mythology," pp. 81–88 at p. 86 (translates second version only). *NI* adds reference to: "*reelle Sprache* in 'Über die Unverständlichkeit,' p. 364."

ness, and simpleminded stupidity" [*K.A.* 2:319 n. 4]. And then he says: "This is the origin of all poetry, to suspend the notions and the laws of rational thought and to replace us within a beautiful confusion of fantasy in the original chaos of human nature (for which mythology is the best name)."

This chaos is not what traditional interpretation of this passage has considered a somehow beautiful, irrational but beautiful, symmetry. But it is, in Schlegel's own words and marked by the fact that it is the replacement of what he had first said, "error, madness, and stupidity." The authentic language is the language of madness, the language of error, and the language of stupidity. (*Bouvard et Pécuchet*, if you want—that's the authentic language, what he really means by *reelle Sprache*.) It is such because this authentic language is a mere semiotic entity, open to the radical arbitrariness of any sign system and as such capable of circulation, but which as such is profoundly unreliable. In the essay "Über die Unverständlichkeit," he works this out by literalizing the metaphor of gold, *reelle Sprache* as gold, what is really of value. But *reelle Sprache* turns out to be not just gold but much more like money (or, more specifically, like the money he doesn't have at that time to publish the *Athenäum*)—namely, it is circulation which is out of hand, not like nature but like money, which is a sheer circulation, the sheer circulation or play of the signifier, and which is, as you know, the root of error, madness, stupidity, and all other evil. You have to think of this money like money in Balzac's *La Peau de chagrin*, the wear and tear of *usure*, of usury.

And it is a free play of the signifier: "Über die Unverständlichkeit" is full of puns, etymological puns in the manner of Nietzsche, in which a great deal is made of plays on *stehen* and *verstehen*, *stellen* and *verstellen*, of *verrücken* (insanity), and so on. He quotes Goethe: "die Worte verstehen sich selbst oft besser, als diejenigen, von denen sie gebraucht werden" ("words understand each other often better than those who make use of them" [*K.A.* 2:364]). Words have a way of saying things which are not at all what you want them to say. You are writing a splendid and coherent philosophical argument but, lo and behold, you are describing sexual intercourse. Or you are writing a fine compliment for somebody and without your knowledge, just because words have a way of doing things, it's sheer insult and obscenity that you are really saying. There is a machine there, a text machine, an implacable determination and a total arbitrariness, *unbedingter Willkür*, he says [*Lyceum* Fragment 42, *K.A.* 2:151], which inhabits words on the level of the play of the signifier, which undoes any narrative consistency of lines, and which undoes the reflexive and the dialectical model, both of which are, as you know, the basis of any narration. There is no narration without reflection, no narrative without dialectic, and what irony disrupts (according to Friedrich Schlegel) is precisely that dialectic and that reflexivity, the tropes. The reflexive and the dialectical are the tropological system, the Fichtean system, and that is what irony undoes.

It is not surprising, therefore, that the very distinguished criticism from which

Schlegel has benefited has always maintained the opposite, especially in its attempt to shelter him against the suspicion of frivolity. The best critics who have written on Schlegel, who have recognized his importance, have wanted to shelter him from the accusation of frivolity, which was generally made, but in the process they always have to recover the categories of the self, of history, and of dialectic, which are precisely the categories which in Schlegel are disrupted in a radical way.

To give just two examples—and that will be the end—Peter Szondi, who wrote very well on Schlegel, discussing the reflexive structure, says the following: "in Tieck, the part (the theatrical part, the role) speaks about itself as role (reflexively). It has insight into the dramatic determination of its own existence and in so doing it is not reduced; but, to the contrary, it rises to a new power. . . . The comedy of Tieck's plays is due to the pleasure of the reflection: it is the distance that reflection gains with regard to its own structure that is appreciated by means of laughter."[24] Here is the aesthetic *Aufhebung* of irony by means of the notion of distance. That could indeed be said of the comic, and in a sense Szondi is not discussing irony but confusing the two. He's thinking more about Jean Paul, and giving a theory of the comic. Irony is not comedy, and theory of irony is not a theory of comedy. This could be said about a theory of comedy, but it is precisely what a theory of irony is not. It is disruption, disillusion.

Benjamin, in *Der Begriff der Kunstkritik in der deutschen Romantik*,[25] following Lukács to some extent, sees the impact of the parabasis much better. He sees the destructive power, the negative power, of the parabasis, fully. He sees that "the ironization of form consists in a deliberate destruction of the form" [p. 84]—not at all an aesthetic recuperation but, to the contrary, a radical, complete destruction of the form, which he calls "the critical act," which undoes the form by analysis, which by demystification destroys the form. Benjamin describes the critical act as such in a remarkable passage. He says: "far from being a subjective whim of the author, this destruction of the form is the task of the objective moment in art, (the moment) of criticism. . . . This type of irony (which originates in

24. Peter Szondi, "Friedrich Schlegel und die romantische Ironie. Mit einer Beilage über Tiecks Komödien" (1954), reprinted in *Schriften* (Frankfurt am Main: Suhrkamp, 1978), 2:11–31. De Man (in *NI*) cites the Szondi essay from its reprinting in Hans-Egon Hass and Gustav-Adolf Mohrlüder, eds., *Ironie als literarisches Phänomen* (Cologne: Kiepenheuer and Witsch, 1973), pp. 149–62 at pp. 159 and 161. The essay is available in English, translated by Harvey Mendelsohn, as "Friedrich Schlegel and Romantic Irony, with Some Remarks on Tieck's Comedies," in Peter Szondi, *On Textual Understanding and Other Essays* (Minneapolis: University of Minnesota Press, 1986), pp. 57–73 at pp. 71, 73. De Man quotes from the same essay in "The Rhetoric of Temporality," pp. 219–20.

25. Walter Benjamin, *Der Begriff der Kunstkritik in der deutschen Romantik*, Werkausgabe vol. 1, *Gesammelte Schriften* (Frankfurt am Main: Suhrkamp, 1980). References are to this edition. As in the case of the Szondi essay cited in note 24, de Man (in *NI*) cites the Benjamin text from the excerpt printed in Hass and Mohrlüder, pp. 145–48. The hyphens in "de-constructing" and in "Ab-bruch" are de Man's in *NI*.

the relationship of the particular work to the indefinite project) has nothing to do with subjectivism or with play, but it has to do with the approximation of the particular and hence limited work to the absolute, with its complete objectivation at a cost of its destruction" [p. 85]. At the moment when all seems lost, when the work is totally undone, it gets recuperated, because that radical destruction is a moment in the dialectic, which is seen as a historical dialectic in the progression toward the absolute, in a Hegelian scheme. He says, and he uses this Hegelian language here (it's very clear, very moving, very effective): "the ironization of form is like the storm which lifts up [aufheben] the curtain of the transcendental order of art and reveals it for what it is, in this order as well as in the unmediated existence of the work" [p. 86]. "Formal irony . . . represents the paradoxical attempt still to construct the edifice by de-constructing it [am Gebilde noch durch Ab-bruch zu bauen], and so to demonstrate the relationship of the work to the idea within the work itself" [p. 87]. The idea is the infinite project (as we had it in Fichte), the infinite absolute toward which the work is under way. The irony is the radical negation, which, however, reveals as such, by the undoing of the work, the absolute toward which the work is under way.

Kierkegaard will interpret irony in the same way (very Kierkegaardian passage in Benjamin . . .). He will also submit the evaluation of a certain ironic moment in history to its place in history. Socratic irony is valid irony because Socrates, like Saint John, heralds the arrival of Christ, and as such he came at the right moment. Whereas Friedrich Schlegel, or the German ironists his contemporaries, were not at the right moment. The only reason that they are to be discarded is that they were out of joint with the historical movement of history, which for Kierkegaard remains the final instance to which one has to resort in order to evaluate. So irony is secondary to a historical system.

I'll just oppose one quotation of Schlegel to this and to Szondi's assertion. In "Über die Unverständlichkeit," Schlegel says the following: "But is nonunderstanding, then, something so evil and objectionable?—It seems to me that the welfare of families and of nations is grounded in it; if I am not mistaken about nations and systems, about the artworks of mankind, often so artful that one cannot enough admire the wisdom of the inventors. An incredibly small portion (of nonunderstanding) suffices, provided it is preserved with unbreakable trust and purity, and no restless intelligence dares to come close to its holy borderline. Yes, even the most precious possession of mankind, inner satisfaction, is suspended, as we all know, on some such point. It must remain in the dark if the entire edifice is to remain erect and stable (that's the edifice which, according to Benjamin, we built by taking it apart); it would lose its stability at once if this power were to be dissolved by means of understanding. Truly, you would be quite horrified if your request were answered, and the world would all of a sudden become, in all seriousness, comprehensible. Is not this entire infinite world built out of nonunderstanding, out of chaos, by means of understanding? [Und ist sie selbst diese *unendliche Welt, nicht durch den Verstand aus der Unverständlichkeit oder dem Chaos gebildet?*]"[26]

That sounds very nice, but you should remember that the chaos is error, madness, and stupidity, in all its forms. Any expectation that one may have that deconstruction might be able to construct is suspended by such a passage, which is very strictly a pre-Nietzschean passage, heralding exactly "Über Wahrheit und Lüge." Any attempt to construct—that is, to narrate—on no matter how advanced a level, is suspended, interrupted, disrupted, by a passage like this. As a result, it also makes it very difficult to conceive of a historiography, a system of history, that would be sheltered from irony. Friedrich Schlegel's interpreters have all felt this, which is why all of them, including Kierkegaard, have to invoke history as hypostasis as a means of defense against this irony. Irony and history seem to be curiously linked to each other. This would be the topic to which this would lead, but this can only be tackled when the complexities of what we could call performative rhetoric have been more thoroughly mastered.

Thank you very much.

---

26. *K.A.* 2:370; cf. Firchow, p. 268. As with the texts of Szondi and Benjamin, de Man (in *NI*) cites this text from the Hass and Mohrlüder collection, pp. 295–303 at pp. 300–301.

Reply to Raymond Geuss

The tenuous relationships between the disciplines of philosophy and literary theory have recently been strengthened by a development which, at least in this country and over the last fifty years, is somewhat unusual. Literary theorists never dispensed with a certain amount of philosophical readings and references, but this does not mean that there always was an active engagement between the two institutionalized academic fields. Students of philosophy, on the other hand, can legitimately and easily do without the critical investigation of literary theorists, past or present: it is certainly more important for a literary theorist to read Wittgenstein than for a philosopher to read I. A. Richards, say, or Kenneth Burke. But the situation has become somewhat more mobile. Several members of the philosophical profession have prominently taken part in literary conferences, including the yearly meetings of the Modern Language Association, and some literary theorists have been present in person or have been represented by their writings at gatherings organized by philosophers. It would certainly be an exaggeration to speak of an active, lively dialogue between them; yet symptoms of a renewed interest are discernible on both sides. Since many problems, technical as well as substantial, are shared by both fields, such a trend can only be salutary. It may not only prevent duplications but also renew the approach

Raymond Geuss's "A Response to Paul de Man" (i.e., to de Man's "Sign and Symbol in Hegel's *Aesthetics*") and de Man's "Reply to Raymond Geuss" both appeared in *Critical Inquiry* 10:2 (December 1983). All page references to Geuss's "Response" are to this issue of the journal. All notes are de Man's.

to recurrent questions by the shock of unfamiliar, perhaps even incongruous, perspectives.

From the narrow point of view of the literary theorist, the interchange offers at least one immediate advantage: the benefit of truly attentive and close readings. The exchanges within the precincts of the literary establishment have not lacked in animation, but they tend to remain personal, moralistic, and ideological in a manner that is not exactly conducive to precision. Most of the recent polemics aimed at literary theory bear no relationship whatever to the texts they claim to attack. Philosophical readers, more accustomed to the rigors of argument, are less prone to be obviously ad hominem: they have a tighter sense of the nuances and the specificities of discursive texts. Of course, they do not have a monopoly on the subtleties of close reading, and it is only on a first level of approximation that they can thus be set apart from their counterparts in departments of literature. The real problem starts a little further on, in an attempt to state the difference (if it exists) between a close "philosophical" and a close "literary" reading of a text. It is clear, for example, that most of Raymond Geuss's objections to my paper "Sign and Symbol in Hegel's *Aesthetics*" have to do with the manner of reading philosophical writings prior to the substance that such a reading reveals. In the remarks that follow, I will try not to lose sight of this pragmatic aspect of the encounter.

Geuss's stance, throughout his commentary, is to shelter the canonical reading of what Hegel actually thought and proclaimed from readings which allow themselves, for whatever reason, to tamper with the canon. Such an attitude, I hasten to add, is not only legitimate but admirable: when it is pursued—as is here the case—with genuine authority, it is in no way reductive. There is no merit whatever in upsetting a canonical interpretation merely for the sake of destroying something that may have been built with considerable care. This is all the more so in the case of a truly systematic, consistent, and self-critical philosopher, who certainly would not have taken lightly to such epithets as "vacillating" or "duplicitous" applied to his writings. The commentator should persist as long as possible in the canonical reading and should begin to swerve away from it only when he encounters difficulties which the methodological and substantial assertions of the system are no longer able to master. Whether or not such a point has been reached should be left open as part of an ongoing critical investigation. But it would be naive to believe that such an investigation could be avoided, even for the best of reasons. The necessity to revise the canon arises from resistances encountered in the text itself (extensively conceived) and not from preconceptions imported from elsewhere.

My misgivings about a nonproblematic reading of Hegel's *Aesthetics* and about the acceptance at face value of Hegel's main pronouncements about art do not stem from some previously arrived at conviction about the nature of the aesthetic, of symbolic language, or of any other key concept. Nor does it stem, as Geuss suggests, from an allegiance to Nietzsche's notions of interpretation. It starts out from a difficulty, a recurrent uncertainty in the *reception* of the *Aesthetics*, a difficulty perhaps more acute in the case of this particular Hegel text than of any other. The *Aesthetics* always was and still is a crux in the interpretation of Hegel. It was so for Kierkegaard, who extended the problematic in the direction of religion, and for Marx, who extended it in the direction of the philosophy of law. The same configuration is repeated today in the decisive importance given to the *Aesthetics* in the two main twentieth-century attempts to reinterpret Hegel: in Heidegger and in Adorno (who started out from Kierkegaard).[1] For obvious reasons of economy, I could only allude to this complex matter by referring not to a philosopher but to a literary historian, Peter Szondi. Szondi's poetic sensitivity as by instinct locates the question of the aesthetic where it belongs—in the area of symbolic language.

It is on this same point, the symbolic nature of language and art, that Geuss's canonical defense appears for the first time open to the reproach of literalism. The term "symbolic" appears conspicuously in the *Aesthetics*, though it is not always used in the same sense. In part 2 of the treatise, the history of art, as is well known, is divided in three parts: symbolic, classical, and romantic art. "Symbolic" here functions as a historical term in a system of periodization. Geuss is certainly right in saying that the symbolic art form Hegel associates with India and Persia is only preartistic and preparatory to the high period of art which Hegel, following Winckelmann and Schiller, locates in Hellenic classicism. As such, "classical" art is not "symbolic" art. Hegel says as much, albeit with more qualifications than Geuss: "It follows that a classical style [*Darstellungsweise*] can in *essence* no longer be *symbolic* in the more precise sense of the term, although some symbolic ingredients remain intermittently present in it."[2] This "more precise sense of the term" is the historical sense, the only one that Geuss acknowledges. But, in the same section of the *Aesthetics*, Hegel also glosses "symbolic" in purely linguistic terms, by setting up a distinction between sign and symbol (see *Ästh. II*, p. 327). This differentiation belongs to all language in general, regardless of period or nationality. It accounts, among other things, for the fact that Hegel extends his discussion of symbolic art forms way beyond primitive art into the present, whereas, in the case of classical art, the end is put where it chronologically belongs, in Roman satire.[3] The term "symbolic" thus functions in a linguistic as well

---

1. See Theodor W. Adorno, *Gesammelte Schriften* (Frankfurt am Main: Suhrkamp, 1979), vol. 2: *Kierkegaard: Konstruktion des Ästhetischen*, and *Drei Studien zu Hegel* (1970).

2. G. W. F. Hegel, *Werke in zwanzig Bänden* (Frankfurt am Main: Suhrkamp, 1970), vol. 14: *Vorlesungen über die Ästhetik II*, p. 20; all further references to this volume, abbreviated *Ästh. II*, to vol. 13 (*Vorlesungen über die Ästhetik I*), abbreviated *Ästh. I*, and to vols. 8 and 10 (*Enzyklopädie der philosophischen Wissenschaften I* and *III*), abbreviated *Enz. I* or *III*, will be included parenthetically in the text; my translations.

3. In the last section of the symbolical art forms, entitled "The Conscious Symbolism of the Comparative Art Form," Hegel deals with such "modern" genres as allegory, fable, enigma, parable, and so on, all of which are notoriously postclassical (see *Ästh I*, pp. 486–546).

as in a historical register. The two realms are not unrelated, but different properties prevail in each. In the linguistic perspective, for example, it cannot be said that classical art is not symbolic. On the contrary, it is the highest possible fulfillment of symbolic language, the very Hegelian dialectical moment in which the symbolic fulfills itself in its own sublation. For Hegel always considers the symbolic by way of an increasing proximity between sign and meaning, a proximity which, by principles of resemblance, analogy, filiation, interpenetration, and so forth, tightens the link between both to the ultimate point of identity. This identity reaches its climax (*Vollendung*) in classical art, though not without its own costs in negation, sacrifice, and restriction that do not have to concern us here. Far from being nonsymbolic, classical art is the moment at which the semiotic function of language, which is, in principle, arbitrary and detached from meaning, is entirely transformed into a symbolic function.

The quotation which asserts Hegel's explicit commitment to a symbolic concept of art is therefore entirely devoid of ambiguity. Later complications make sense only against the background of this categorical assertion: "In the case of *art*, we cannot consider, in the symbol, the *arbitrariness* between meaning and signification [Gleichgültigkeit *von Bedeutung und Bezeichnung derselben*], since art itself consists precisely in the connection, the affinity, and the concrete interpenetration of meaning and of form" (*Ästh. I*, p. 395). Indeed, I cannot see how Geuss can deny (see p. 381 n. 3) that this sentence has to do with the distinction between sign and symbol, when it appears in the context of a discussion of this very distinction; the terminology (*Symbol* and *Zeichen*) in the immediately preceding sentence, as well as the examples (national banners), and the analytical inferences are all very close to the section in the *Encyclopedia* (paragraph 458) in which the differentiation between sign and symbol is worked out in greater detail. The burden of translation in this sentence is not, as Geuss maintains, the antecedent of *derselben* but the italicized term *Gleichgültigkeit* ("indifference," in the sense of not caring for or not relating to something or someone). *Derselben* simply refers to *Bedeutung* and distinguishes between the substance of a meaning (*Bedeutung*) and the mode of signification by which the meaning is reached (*Bezeichnung derselben*). In the case of the sign, as Hegel has just stated, the sign and the meaning do not share a common property and are therefore estranged ("indifferent," *gleichgültig*) from each other. Whereas, in the case of the symbol and of art, the opposite is the case, and the estrangement has become a close affinity (*Verwandtschaft*). The sentence says exactly what it means to say: the aesthetic sign is symbolic. It is *the* canonical sentence of Hegel's *Aesthetics*, and any attempt to make it say something else is either false or, as I suspect is the case here, says the same thing but in less precise terms.

The reference to the discussion of sign and symbol in paragraph 458 of the *Encyclopedia* leads to the other main disagreement between Geuss and myself, namely, his contention that "the philosophy of subjective spirit does not seem a promising place to start [a discussion of the *Aesthetics*]" (p. 381). The canonical bent of his reading here extends to my own text and schematizes it beyond recognition. It is, for example, not the case that, in my essay, "sign" and "symbol" stand in a constant "relation of opposition to each other" (p. 375). This reference is presumably to my statement that "the relationship between sign and symbol . . . is one of mutual obliteration." "Obliteration" is both more and less than "opposition," and the entire argument can be seen as a way to account for the change that leads from a "dichotomy" between sign and symbol to the metaphor of "obliteration." At the point in the exposition when I discuss Hegel's distinction between sign and symbol, the stress is not on the arbitrariness of the sign (which could possibly, though not necessarily, be put in polar opposition to the *motivation* of the symbol) but on the active power which permits the intellect to appropriate the properties of the outside world to its own ends. By this *activity* (Hegel refers to *Tätigkeit der Intelligenz* [*Enz. III*, paragraph 458, p. 270]) the intellect becomes the subject that subjects the natural object to its powers. Hegel's interest in the sign is entirely based on the similarity between the intellect as speaking and thinking subject and the sign as the product of this same intellect. There is a direct connection between Hegel's considerations on the sign, in paragraph 458 of the *Encyclopedia*, and his affirmation, in the same book, that "the simple expression of the existing subject, as thinking subject, is *I*" (*Enz. I*, paragraph 20, p. 72). The move from the theory of the sign to the theory of the subject has nothing to do with my being overconcerned with the Romantic tradition, or narcissistic, or ("c'est la même chose") too influenced by the French. It has, in fact, nothing to do with me at all but corresponds to an inexorable and altogether Hegelian move of the text. That this "thinking subject" is in no way subjective, in the ordinary sense of the term, nor even specular, in the Cartesian mode, is something that any careful reader of Hegel knows.

The same direct line travels from the assertion that the thinking subject somehow erases (the term in Hegel's lexicon is *tilgen*) the natural world to the disagreement on the use of the verb *meinen* in paragraph 20. Geuss contests my reading of *meinen* as having, next to others, the connotation of "opinion" in the sentences: "Was ich nur *meine*, ist *mein*" and "so kann ich nicht sagen, was ich nur *meine*" (*Enz. I*, paragraph 20, p. 74); see Geuss, p. 380). In my turn, I must accuse him of mishearing the German language when he interprets *meinen* only as *vouloir dire* (or, as in Stanley Cavell's title, *can* we mean what we say?), that is, as signifying intent, as "intend[ing] to refer to some particular individual thing" (p. 380). The "nur" in "was ich nur meine," which I in no way neglect (and bracket on one occasion— but for entirely different reasons than those attributed to me), is precisely what confirms the normal vernacular use of "eine Meinung haben." *Meinung*, or "opinion," is, from an epistemological point of view ("*nur* Meinung"), inferior to *Wissen*, for example, as *doxa* is "inferior" to *episteme*. The possessive article, indispensable when one speaks of opinion, disappears when one speaks of truth; one says "*meine*

Meinung" but "*die* Wahrheit." That the question of opinion has to come up at this point stems from the fact that Hegel also has defined "thinking" as being—like the sign—"appropriation," "making mine." The pun on *meinen* as "making mine" around which Hegel keeps circling, also at the beginning of the *Phenomenology*, is therefore entirely legitimate. But it underlies what turns out to be an ever present point of resistance in the Hegelian system: if truth is the appropriation in thought and, hence, in language, of the world by the I, then truth, which by definition is the absolutely general, also contains a constitutive element of particularization that is not compatible with its universality. The question always surfaces, in Hegel, when language surfaces, in paragraphs 20 and 458 of the *Encyclopedia*, in the section on sensory evidence in the *Phenomenology*, in the *Science of Logic*, and so on. The aporia is admirably condensed in the sentence which names the double function of the word "I" as being, at the same time, the most general and the most particular of terms: "Wenn ich sage: 'Ich,' *meine* ich mich *als diesen* alle anderen Ausschließenden: aber was ich sage, Ich, ist eben jeder" (*Enz. I*, paragraph 20, p. 74). By restricting his reading of *meinen* to the question of conceptualization (which derives from what is being said but does not reach nearly so far), Geuss needlessly cuts himself off from an entire cluster of problems (the deictic function of language, the proleptic structure of thought, the distinction between knowledge as *erkennen* and *wissen*, etc.), all of which run as the proverbial *roter Faden* through the entire corpus of Hegel's works. And he especially cuts himself off from the possibility of linking Hegel's epistemology and, by extension, his logic to a largely implicit theory of language, a theme that gives its importance to the sections in the *Aesthetics* where this link is most openly being established.

The same misplaced timidity distorts Geuss's discussion of the term "idea" in Hegel's definition of "the beautiful" as "the sensory manifestation of the idea" (p. 378). According to Geuss, "'the idea' in Hegel's technical sense, as a term in metaphysics, plays no role" in the consideration of the faculties of the mind (p. 379). Consequently he can reproach me for having confused, in Hegel's definition of "the beautiful," the metaphysical sense of the idea with that of the psychology of representation (*Vorstellung*).[4] Indeed, by linking this definition to the

---

4. I cannot agree with Raymond Geuss when he asserts that I interpret the idea, by analogy with the English Romantics, as interiorization (see pp. 378–79). At the point in the paper that refers to English Romanticism, I am not giving a reading of "the sensory appearance of the idea" which "assimilates Hegel to Wordsworth and the English Romantics" (pp. 379, 378). The passage is instead polemically directed against the interpretation of Romanticism as interiorization that is so prominent in authors such as M. H. Abrams, Geoffrey Hartman, Harold Bloom, and so on. The theme is taken up more extensively in a sequel to the paper, entitled "Hegel on the Sublime." What is being discussed in these sections is not Hegel's definition of "beauty" but what is called "the ideology of the symbol" as a defensive strategy aimed against the implications of Hegel's aesthetic theory. My own reading of "the sensory appearance of the idea" is given as concisely as possible when it is said that "it could . . . best be translated by the statement: the beautiful is symbolic."

question of language, one is directed to the section in the *Encyclopedia* that has to do with what is called, in the tradition of the eighteenth century, psychology: the study of the faculties of consciousness, including the faculty of representation. It is under the general heading "Psychologie," in subdivision "ß" ("Die Vorstellung") of subdivision "a" ("Der theoretische Geist") that the discussion of sign and symbol is located. We are at least two stages removed from the absolute Spirit where the discussion of Art as Idea should presumably take place. But the idea, which is the metaphysical ground of its own activity as spirit (*Geist*), is omnipresent throughout and at all stages of the system. When Hegel speaks—on the level of the subjective spirit—of perceiving, imagining, representing, and thinking, this always occurs from the perspective, so to speak, of the idea. Perception, representation, or thought is always perception, representation, or thought *of the idea* and not just of the natural or empirical world. This is precisely what sets Hegel apart from his eighteenth-century predecessors. In discussing language, which is an agent of representation, one discusses the idea. This is all the more obvious when what is under discussion is the aesthetic, not just as idea but as its sensory manifestation.

Hence, also, the transition to what is avowedly the most tentative and least developed assertion of Geuss's article: the link between language (as inscription) and the aesthetic (as sensory manifestation), through the mediation of memorization (*Gedächtnis*). Perception, imagination, representation, recollection, and such are all *manifestations* of the idea, but it is nevertheless the case that none of them necessarily entails its *sensory* manifestation. Only memorization (as opposed to recollection, *Gedächtnis* as opposed to *Erinnerung*), to the extent that it implies notation and inscription, is necessarily a sensory and phenomenal manifestation; hence the link with inscribed language and with the particular temporality which makes art both the most proleptic and the most retrospective of activities. Again, by reducing the "pastness" of art to a merely descriptive, historical observation that differentiates classical from modern art, Geuss's literalism loses contact with the generalizing dynamics of the dialectic.

What is always at stake, in each of these areas of disagreement, is an accusation, in the best of circumstances, of overreading or, more often, of plain misreading by misunderstanding or falsification of the German syntax: "even when it is not incorrect, the reading is forced, because it does not faithfully reproduce what Hegel said." It is true, to take the most vulnerable point, that Hegel nowhere says, in so many words, that the aesthetic is structured like a linguistic inscription in a memorization. It is also true that he does not exactly tell the story of a threatening paradox at the core of his system against which his thought has to develop a defense in whose service the aesthetic, among other activities, is being mobilized. No one could be expected to be *that* candid about his uncertainties: Hegel could hardly openly say something like this and still be Hegel. What is suggested by a reading such as the one I propose is that difficulties and discontinuities (rather than "vacillations," which is Geuss's term rather than mine) remain in even as masterful and tight a text as the *Aesthetics*. These difficulties have left their mark or have even shaped the history of the understanding of Hegel up to the present. They cannot be resolved by the canonical system explicitly established by Hegel himself, namely, the dialectic. This is why these difficulties have at all times been used as a point of entry into the critical examination of the dialectic as such. In order to account for them, it is indispensable that one not only listen to what Hegel openly, officially, literally, and canonically asserts but also to what is being said obliquely, figurally, and implicitly (though not less compellingly) in less conspicuous parts of the corpus. Such a way of reading is by no means willful; it has its own constraints, perhaps more demanding than those of canonization. If one wishes to call it literary rather than philosophical, I'd be the last to object—literary theory can use all the compliments it can manage to get these days. That the terms "literary" and "philosophical," then, do not correspond to "members of a department of literature" and "members of a department of philosophy" is clear from the virtues of Geuss's own text. Since my topic here has been Hegel and not Geuss, I did not have the opportunity to stress those virtues. I think, among others things, of the defensive energy that is manifest in the refusal to concede anything, in the *acharnement* of his critique. This reaction proves conclusively that he has heard, in my essay, uncertainties that go well beyond my canonical assertion of their existence and that his reading is therefore, in the best sense, "literary." Why should it otherwise have compelled me to repeat once again, with worse intolerance, what, in my own terms, should be beyond doubt and contestation?

Index

Compiled by Eileen Quam and Theresa Wolner

Theory and History of Literature

Paul de Man (1919-83) held appointments at Cornell University, Johns Hopkins University, the University of Zurich, and Yale University. At his death, he was Sterling Professor of Humanities, with an appointment in comparative literature and French, at Yale. His works include *Blindness and Insight: Essays in the Rhetoric of Contemporary Criticism* (Minnesota, 1983), *Allegories of Reading: Figural Language in Rousseau, Nietzsche, Rilke, and Proust* (1979), *The Rhetoric of Romanticism* (1984), *The Resistance to Theory* (Minnesota, 1986), *Critical Writings, 1953-1978* (Minnesota, 1989), and *Romanticism and Contemporary Criticism: The Gauss Seminar and Other Papers* (1993).

Andrzej Warminski is professor of comparative literature at the University of California, Irvine, and author of *Readings in Interpretation: Hölderlin, Hegel, Heidegger* (Minnesota, 1987) and *Material Inscriptions* (forthcoming).